COLOR HIM
ORANGE

THE
JIM BOEHEIM
STORY

COLOR HIM ORANGE

THE JIM BOEHEIM STORY

Scott Pitoniak

TRIUMPH
B O O K S

Library of Congress Cataloging-in-Publication Data
Pitoniak, Scott.
  Color him orange : the Jim Boeheim story / Scott Pitoniak.
      p. cm.
    ISBN 978-1-60078-517-7
  1. Boeheim, Jim. 2. Basketball coaches—United States—Biography.
3. Syracuse University—Basketball. 4. Syracuse Orange (Basketball team)
I. Title.
    GV884.B63P58 2011
    796.323092—dc23
    [B]

                                                        2011025570

This book is available in quantity at special discounts for your group or organization. For further information, contact:

Triumph Books LLC
542 South Dearborn Street
Suite 750
Chicago, Illinois 60605
(312) 939-3330
Fax (312) 663-3557
www.triumphbooks.com

Printed in U.S.A.

ISBN: 978-1-60078-517-7

Design by Sue Knopf

To Ed Shaw,
my college roommate and dear friend.
The Syracuse Orange has never had a truer fan.

Contents

Acknowledgments

ALTHOUGH I DIDN'T REALIZE IT AT THE TIME, my research for this book actually began back in the winter of 1965–66 when I started following Syracuse University basketball as a 10-year-old in Rome, New York, about a 45-minute drive east of Manley Field House. Dave Bing was my favorite Orange hoopster in those days. And if you had ever seen him play, you'd understand why. Bing was a graceful athlete who had an uncanny ability not only to rise above the rest but to remain airborne longer than everyone else. He would go on to become a consensus All-American, a seven-time NBA All-Star, and a member of the Naismith Memorial Basketball Hall of Fame. His backcourt mate back then was Jim Boeheim—a skinny, bespectacled guy with a funny-looking jump shot who was smart enough to realize that if he hung around Bing, good things would happen.

When I arrived on the Syracuse campus as a student eight years later, Bing was long gone, but Boeheim was still there. He remained skinny and bespectacled, but he had traded his player's garb for some god-awful plaid sport coats while working as an anonymous assistant to coach Roy Danforth. It wasn't until my senior year, 1976–77, that I and my fellow crazies who sat in the student section known as the Zoo became more familiar with Boeheim. He had replaced the personable and loquacious Danforth as head coach, and none of us knew what to expect.

The Boeheim Era tipped off auspiciously as two precocious freshmen, Roosevelt Bouie and Louis Orr, helped the Orangemen go 26–4. It was during that season that I interviewed the coach for the first time for my hometown newspaper. During the next three and a half decades, I would interview him scores of times and, like most reporters who covered the team, I occasionally would incur his wrath. There were instances when a story or a column struck a nerve and Boeheim would call my sports editor to complain, a practice he employed with other writers, as well.

Over time, our relationship improved as each of us became more understanding of this often awkward dance between coach and reporter. My questions began eliciting insight rather than sarcasm, and Jim went out of his way to provide me with background information for stories and columns I was researching. There were times when he was funny in a self-deprecating way, almost charming.

There's no doubt that his second wife, Juli, and the presence of his three young kids helped soften him. But I also believe that the national championship, the Hall of Fame induction, and the appreciation shown by the fans, the school administration, and even we ink-stained wretches also played roles in his transformation. (That's not, though, to say he mellowed completely—his tongue-lashing of local reporters following a victory at the Carrier Dome midway through the 2010–11 season conjured memories of the not-always–good old days when he and his media detractors were occasionally at odds.)

I had been attempting to convince Jim to collaborate on an autobiography for several years, but he wouldn't budge. He said he had no interest in writing a book—at least not while he was still coaching. Finally, Tom Bast at Triumph Books asked me if I would be interested in writing an unauthorized biography of Boeheim, and I said, "Yes."

Though Jim was a little miffed when I told him we were going ahead with the project, he wound up being cooperative, filling in blanks and expounding on things when necessary. For that I am grateful. And everyone associated with the program and whom I contacted from his past—including his younger sister, Barbara Boeheim, and many of his lifelong friends from his hometown of Lyons, New York—were extremely helpful in providing insights into what makes Jim tick.

I discovered that Jim, like most of us, is a complex individual with many sides—some good, some not so good. His Hall of Fame career was largely shaped by an ultracompetitive father, a nurturing but also competitive mother, his small-town roots, and his lifelong friends, especially Bing. My journey through his years uncovered a man who is extremely intelligent and opinionated, but also, at times, thin-skinned, whiny, and sarcastic. I learned just how deep his loyalty and devotion to his program and his college alma mater runs. And I also discovered a kindhearted side to the person who is as driven to raise funds for Coaches vs. Cancer as he is to accumulate victories on the court.

A biography should explain how and why a person became who he or she is. It is my hope that whether you like or dislike this incredibly accomplished basketball coach and philanthropist, you'll come away with a better understanding of him.

A book is always a team effort, and I had some great teammates assisting me with this project. This is my third book published by Triumph, and each experience has been a good one. Thanks to the aforementioned Tom Bast for believing in this subject and to developmental editor Noah Amstadter for seeing it to fruition.

The following, in alphabetical order, are many of the people whom I've either interviewed about Jim and Syracuse basketball through the years or whose work provided reference and perspective (I apologize in advance for any folks I may have omitted): Rafael Addison, Patricia Alena, Wendell Alexis, Lew Andreas, Carmelo Anthony, Carol Bailey,

Tom Batzold, Kim Baxter, Jay Bilas, Frank Bilovsky, Dave Bing, Dick Blackwell, Ryan Blackwell, Jim Blandino, Mark Blaudschun, Greg Boeck, Barbara Boeheim, Jim Boeheim, Juli Boeheim, Lee Boice, Rick Bonnell, Roosevelt Bouie, Rick Bozich, Steve Bradley, Erik Brady, Tony Bruin, Earl Buchanan, Barry Buchsbaum, Arnie Burdick, Marty Byrnes, Jim Calhoun, Jack Carey, Hal Cohen, Derrick Coleman, Larry Costello, Jay Cox, Jake Crouthamel, Roy Danforth, Ken Davis, Dorothy DeBout, Mike DeCola, Eric Devendorf, Donna Ditota, Sherman Douglas, Kueth Duany, Gene Duffey, Sue Edson, Dave Elfin, Donn Esmonde, Andrea Evangelist, Gary Fallesen, John Feinstein, Bernie Fine, Jonny Flynn, Craig Forth, Tom Foster, Dave Gavitt, Rev. Paul Gongloff, Tom Gould, Allen Griffin, Rudy Hackett, Vaughn Harper, Jason Hart, Isabelle Hartman, Marty Headd, Mark Heisler, George Hicker, Otis Hill, Geoff Hobson, Louise Hoffman, Mike Hopkins, Rick Jackson, Jennifer Jacobs, Marius Janulis, William Kates, Andy Katz, John Kekis, Sean Kerins, Armen Keteyian, Larry Kimball, Sean Kirst, Manny Klutchkowski, Bob Knight, Bill Koenig, Tony Kornheiser, Bob Krengel, Mike Krzyzewski, Dave and Leona Lauster, Tim Layden, Jimmy Lee, Fred Lewis, Todd Lighty, Brendan Malone, Jim Mandelaro, Brian Martin, Mike McAlary, Jack McCallum, Brian McLane, Pat McMullen, Donovan McNabb, Gerry McNamara, Jeremy McNeil, Ron Mergenthaler, Chuck Miller, Len and Edna Minnich, Greg Monroe, Pete Moore, Malcolm Moran, John Moriello, Lawrence Moten, Demetris Nichols, Ed Nicklas, Arinze Onuaku, Jill Ouikahilo, Billy Owens, Josh Pace, Arthur Pachter, Bob Parker, Joan Pecorello, Sam Penceal, Digger Phelps, Val Pinchbeck, Joel Pinckney, Leo Pinckney, Preston Pisellini, John Pitarresi, Rick Pitino, Bud Poliquin, Louie Orr, David Ramsey, Ethan Ramsey, Andy Rautins, Leo Rautins, Bill Reddy, Matt Reynolds, Chuck Richards, Lenn Robbins, Charley Ross, Bob Ryan, Jonathan D. Salant, Robert Sanzone, Tony Santelli, Jim Satalin, Danny Schayes, Dolph Schayes, Phil Schoff, Chris Sciria, Tony Scott,

Rony Seikaly, Jack Seitzinger, Steve Serby, Dale Shackleford, Ed Shaw, Preston Shumpert, Lazarus Sims, Joey Sindelar, Keith Smart, Dean Smith, Bob Snyder, Buzz Stoetzel, Theresa Streb, Bill Strickland, Kim Sholly, Pete Thamel, Etan Thomas, John Thompson, Stevie Thompson, Howard Triche, Rex Trobridge, Mike Vaccaro, Bill Vanderschmidt, Bud VanderVeer, Valerie Vecchio, Dick Vitale, Gene Waldron, John Wallace, Hakim Warrick, Dwayne "Pearl" Washington, Mike Waters, Dick Weiss, Tim Welsh, Adrian Wojnarowski, Alexander Wolff, John Wooden, and Jay Wright.

Periodicals that provided great background included: *The Basketball Times, Bergen County Record, The Boston Globe, Chicago Tribune, The Daily Orange, The Detroit News, Eastern Basketball, ESPN The Magazine, Finger Lakes Times, Hartford Courant, Knoxville News-Sentinel, Los Angeles Times, Louisville Courier-Journal, Lyons Republic,* The Lyons Tale high school yearbooks, *The National, New York Daily News, New York Post, The New York Times, Newsday, The Onondagan, Philadelphia Daily News, Philadelphia Inquirer, Rochester Democrat and Chronicle, Rochester Times-Union, Sports Illustrated, The Sporting News, Syracuse Herald-Journal, Syracuse Post-Standard, Syracuse University Magazine,* Syracuse University basketball media guides (1962-present), *USA TODAY, Wayne County Star,* and *The Washington Post.*

I also relied on nine books as sources, including *Playing Write Field: Selected Works by Scott Pitoniak,* which I wrote in 1997, and *Slices of Orange: Great Games and Performers in Syracuse University Sports History,* which I cowrote with former newspaper colleague Sal Maiorana in 2005. The other books that were extremely helpful were: *Legends of Syracuse Basketball* by Mike Waters; *Tales from the Syracuse Hardwood* by Bud Poliquin; *Syracuse Basketball: A Century of Memories* edited by Bob Snyder; *Syracuse Basketball: 1900–1975* by Rod Macdonald; *Raw Recruits* by Alexander Wolff and Armen

Keteyian; *"Grip's" Historical Souvenir of Lyons, N.Y.* by Edgar Luderne Welsh; and *A Look at Lyons: History and Images of Lyons, New York* by Andrea Evangelist.

Lastly, a doff of the cap to my wife, Beth; my children, Amy and Christopher; and our cat, Sassy, for their understanding. I couldn't have done this without their love and support.

Cheers,

Scott Pitoniak

April 1, 2011

Introduction

THE WITNESSES INSIST they haven't embellished the tale in order to make it even taller. They swear on a stack of Bibles the story is true.

The anecdote goes like this:

Jim Boeheim, Rick Pitino, and their wives are lying on a beach in Hawaii many years ago when the conversation turns to where they would live if they could choose any place on the planet.

"Park Avenue, New York City," says Pitino's wife, Joanne.

"Paris, France," replies Boeheim's first wife, Elaine.

"Honolulu, Hawaii," chimes in Pitino.

"Syracuse, New York," says Boeheim.

The Pitinos and Elaine do double takes when they hear the Syracuse University basketball coach's response. *Syracuse, New York? A place with less sun than Seattle and more snow than Buffalo?* They wonder if Boeheim has imbibed too many mai tais beneath the blistering Pacific sun.

"Syracuse is like Hawaii for eight months of the year," he explains to the incredulous trio. "The other four months, I don't care about the weather because we're playing basketball."

After Boeheim finishes his Chamber of Commerce pitch for his unusual concept of paradise, the Pitinos and Elaine gather up their towels and move several feet away. They joke to Jim that they don't want to keep the company of a man who's clearly delirious.

"Jim is what I call a nester," Pitino explains many years later. "He's the kind of guy who will find a good restaurant and be content to go there 100 straight times before checking out another restaurant. It's a good thing [his current wife] Juli came along, or Jim would still be eating at Denny's five days a week."

Boeheim was mocked royally by the national media when the story first came to light. And it still elicits roaring laughs whenever Pitino and his former boss are on the banquet circuit.

Still, there's something admirable about Boeheim's perception of paradise and sense of loyalty. Particularly in an era when no one seems to stay put anymore.

Given his enormous success as a basketball coach, Boeheim easily could have pulled up roots several times by now in search of greener (as in the color of money) pastures that other schools and the NBA offered. But the guy who grew up in Lyons, a tiny canal town 45 minutes east of Syracuse, never was drawn to the big-city lights. The mortician's son essentially arrived on the SU campus as a gangly, bespectacled walk-on basketball player in the summer of 1962 and was quite content to never leave.

"I guess I've always viewed things a little differently than most people," he said. "Most people believe the grass is greener on the other side. But I guess I was fortunate enough early on to appreciate the greenness of the grass on my side of the fence."

And by deciding to be a nester rather than a nomad for nearly half a century and stringing together more 20-victory seasons than any coach in college basketball history, Boeheim has become to Syracuse what John Wooden was to UCLA, Adolph Rupp was to Kentucky, Mike Krzyzewski is to Duke, and Joe Paterno is to Penn State—a legend in his adopted hometown, the face of a university. And it could be argued that Boeheim's ties to his school run even deeper than the aforementioned because he played there, too. Which means he's been a part of the Syracuse basketball program for 49 of its 112 years—a span of almost 1,600 games.

It hasn't always been a smooth ride, but what long journey ever is? At times, Boeheim has been his own worst enemy. His whiny demeanor led to an occasionally tempestuous relationship with the media, referees, and some of his players. His close relationship with a program booster and his contacts with a basketball street agent resulted in sanctions against the SU program in the early 1990s that briefly put his job in jeopardy. The albatross of not being able to win the big one burdened him until his Carmelo Anthony–led squad cut down the nets in New Orleans in 2003 on the very same Superdome court where Indiana's Keith Smart had broken his heart 16 years earlier. And he had to endure a bout with prostate cancer, bringing back painful memories of the disease that claimed his parents and a number of close friends, including former North Carolina State coach Jim Valvano.

But through it all, Boeheim's loyalty to his school never wavered. And as he grew older, he grew happier. In his mid-fifties, he met Juli Greene. She not only captured his heart but softened his soul, bringing out the kinder, gentler side of his personality. At Juli's urging, he has thrown himself full bore into philanthropic causes. And, now, his greatest legacy may not wind up being his plaque in the Naismith Memorial Basketball Hall of Fame in Springfield, Massachusetts, but rather the nearly $10 million he has raised in his work for Coaches vs. Cancer.

The where-you-want-to-live-if-you-could-live-anywhere anecdote about Boeheim still evokes looks of incredulity and roars of laughter all these years later. *Syracuse, New York? Paradise? Yeah, right.*

But as Jim Boeheim discovered long ago, paradise, like beauty, lies in the eye of the beholder. Sometimes you find it by staying put.

CHAPTER 1

Putting Down Roots in Upstate New York

IT DOESN'T MATTER FROM WHICH DIRECTION YOU JOURNEY. North or south through the rolling cornfields and apple orchards on Route 14, or east or west on Route 31, which runs parallel to the historic Erie Canal. The eye-grabbing orange signs are there to welcome you to Lyons, New York, and inform you immediately and proudly that this Wayne County town of roughly 6,000 inhabitants, equidistant from Syracuse and Rochester, is where it all began for its most famous son, Jim Boeheim, coach of Syracuse University's 2003 national championship basketball team.

"When he finally won it all after those painful close calls, nobody felt better for Jimmy than the people here," said Mike DeCola, a high school basketball and Little League baseball teammate of Boeheim's, who's been friends with the Hall of Fame coach since they were about six years old. "The town had a big celebration for Jimmy that summer. We had him and his family ride to the ceremonies on a fire truck and gave him one of the signs that we were going to put up. And he told us that that recognition from his hometown meant more to him than the visit to the White House to meet the President of the United States. And we believed him because no matter how much success Jimmy's had, he's never forgotten his roots. Lyons will always be a big part of who Jimmy Boeheim is, and he'll always be a big part of Lyons."

Actually, the Boeheim name became synonymous with this town south of Lake Ontario long before the legendary basketball coach was born. Jim's great-great-grandfather, Friedrich W. Boeheim, and his wife, Phillipina, arrived in this upstate New York settlement on a canal boat in 1853. A native of Wuettenberg, Germany, Boeheim, like many immigrants, had boarded the mule-towed vessel and headed west on the 363-mile long canal that connected the Hudson River with Lake Erie. He likely had been told that boom towns and villages had sprouted along the famous man-made waterway and that there were opportunities to make money and own land. It's not known how far west Friedrich and his wife had intended to travel. All we know is that a help wanted sign convinced them to get off the boat in Lyons. The sign had been held aloft by Hiram Hotchkiss, an enterprising entrepreneur who was on the verge of establishing himself as the "peppermint king of the world." Hotchkiss was looking to hire a cook, and although Boeheim possessed carpentry rather than culinary skills, he apparently was willing to give it a shot in hopes that he would be able to establish a cabinet-making business on the side. Plus, of all the places he had seen along the canal, this was the area that probably appealed most to him. The town seemed bustling and vibrant, the land fertile and scenic, and there were a number of German immigrants to make him and his young bride feel at home in a new land.

Boeheim would come to learn that the settlement originally had been known as "the forks" because, in the southern part of town, Ganargua Creek, or Mud Creek as it was called, and the Canandaigua Outlet joined to form the Clyde River. But it was renamed Lyons by early settler and land agent Charles Williamson, because the junction reminded him of the bucolic town of Lyon, France, where the Rhone and Saone rivers meet.

It's not clear how successful a cook Boeheim became, but the job Hotchkiss offered must have tided him over long enough for him to get his furniture business up and running roughly a year later. In 1854, the German-born carpenter opened a small cabinet shop on Jackson Street where he also made caskets. From today's perspective, this might seem a strange, almost humorous business combination, but it was quite common in the mid-nineteenth century for furniture makers to also construct caskets and even perform burials. Word of the high quality of Boeheim's cabinets, tables, chairs, dressers, and caskets spread quickly throughout the town, and it wasn't long before Friedrich moved into a building on Canal Street that was three times larger and where he began grooming his 14-year-old son, Frederick B., to follow in his footsteps. By 1880, the younger Boeheim had joined the firm, and several years later the business was moved again to more spacious surroundings, this time to a three-story brick building on Water Street. Because it bordered the canal path and featured a freight elevator, the location was better suited to gather supplies and ship products to other canal towns in either direction.

Two signs adorned the new building, which occupied nearly an entire block. The one painted above the second floor read: F.W. BOEHEIM & SONS, while a larger sign, above the first floor, read: FURNITURE AND UNDERTAKING. Following his father's death in 1905 at age 80, Frederick took over the business and expanded sales even further by doing more newspaper advertising. An ad in the October 10, 1906, edition of the *Wayne Democratic Press* urged readers to go to Frederick Boeheim's for furniture, undertaking, and picture frames. Talk about life-and-death, one-stop shopping.

Like his father before him, Frederick groomed his son to take over the business, and that occurred in 1926 when a third Frederick Boeheim—the coach's grandfather—became the new head of the firm. He had married Lettie Armeda Taylor in 1911, and they had five children. Their second child—the coach's father, James Arthur Boeheim—was born in 1917 in Lyons. He began working for his father when he was 12, helping pick up chairs and loading furniture into the delivery trucks. He attended Syracuse University before transferring to the Cincinnati College of Mortuary Science, where he received a degree in 1939. Upon graduating, he joined the family business full time, and following their father's death in 1951, he and his older brother, Frederick T., took over the firm—making them the fourth generation in a family that Lyons' residents fondly referred to as the "Burying Boeheims." But the brothers' partnership would last only three years. When Frederick left to become a traveling salesman for an embalming supply company in Westport, Connecticut, James Boeheim, known to everyone in town as Jim, became the sole owner and operator.

The first Jim Boeheim was a driven man in every endeavor he pursued, and some surmise that his fierce determination and competitiveness was not only inherited but also shaped by a life-changing event when he was a young boy. The story goes that he and one of his brothers discovered their father's revolver one day and began fooling around with it. The gun accidentally went off and a .22-caliber slug sliced through Jim Sr.'s lower back and came to rest near his spine. Though they knew there probably would be complications, doctors determined that the location of the bullet made it too risky to remove, so they decided to leave it be. As a result of the wound, one of Jim's legs wound up being two inches shorter than the other, and he spent the rest of his life walking with a limp and started using a cane in his early forties. "It could have been worse," Boeheim said years later. "I could be bones and dust over in a field in Africa or someplace like Guadalcanal. Maybe I was lucky." Lucky because his injury prevented him from being drafted into the service during World War II.

Despite the handicap, he still managed to play baseball and basketball with friends, but he mainly sated his competitive appetite with games that did not require running and jumping, such as golf, ping-pong, pool, and bridge. Those who knew him say he was a poor loser and told stories of him arguing and stomping away after defeats, no matter how insignificant the contest.

Boeheim viewed business as a competition, too, so it wasn't surprising that he became regarded as a demanding boss, who, like his father, grandfather, and great-grandfather, expected perfection in the furniture he sold. The result was a line of high-quality chairs, tables, and cabinets that earned the family business the respect of their customers. "You walk around our house and you'll see a Boeheim table here and a Boeheim hutch there," says Lee Boice, a retired history/physical-education teacher and golf coach at Lyons High School. "And you'll probably see furniture that was purchased from Boeheim's that was made 60, 70, 80 years ago in a lot of homes in the area. The craftsmanship was very good. The stuff was made to last."

The high quality of the furniture wasn't the only thing that earned the Boeheims respect, according to Boice. "Lyons, like most communities in America in the 1930s and '40s, was still kind of a prejudicial town, where people on the south side of the bridge—primarily the Italians— were looked down upon by the German- and Dutch-Americans, who lived on the north side and were considered the high society members of the community," Boice said. "To his credit, Jim Sr., never looked down on the Italians. He treated them as equals, sold them furniture, gave them jobs, and let them slide on their payments when they were experiencing tough times. It was, of course, the right thing to do, but I can tell you that not everyone was doing the right thing back then. There was definitely an ethnic bias, and it took a while for the melting pot to catch up to a lot of places, including Lyons."

Although he was involved in two of Lyons' most visible businesses— the furniture store and funeral home—and was active in a number of service organizations, including the Chamber of Commerce and local service lodge, Boeheim did not care one iota for the limelight. "He was what I would describe as austere," said Boice, who occasionally had Boeheim and his wife, Janet, over for dinner. "He was respected in the community, but there was an aloofness to him. A lot of people knew of him but didn't really know him, and that's the way he wanted it. I think it was a just what he was comfortable with. He was kind of a private person."

There were times when he could be downright nasty in public, especially at restaurants if his order wasn't just right. "There is a classic story of him once being upset because his dish came with parsley as garnish," recalled Tony Santelli, a lifelong friend of Jim Boeheim the coach. "And he took the parsley off the plate and threw it on the floor. He could be moody and intimidating. There were times he was tough to deal with."

His stoicism, punctuated by occasional outbursts of anger, was in stark contrast to his wife's personality. Janet Kay Knapp, who married Boeheim on December 6, 1941—the day before the Japanese attack on Pearl Harbor—was a tall, slender woman with brown hair, described in glowing terms by those who knew her as a kindhearted, nurturing person.

"I think she offset some of the hard edges of her husband," said Isabelle Hartman, one of young Jim's aunts. "I think she was the best thing to ever happen to him, because a lot of people regarded him as a prima donna. Janet was so generous and personable with everyone, even total strangers. To be honest, I don't know what she saw in him, but somehow it all worked out between them."

Interestingly, decades later, friends of James Arthur Boeheim Jr. would say that his second wife, Juli, had a similar impact on him, softening many of his hard edges.

CHAPTER 2

Like Father, Like Son

IN THE DECADES IMMEDIATELY FOLLOWING WORLD WAR II, Lyons, New York, was quintessential small-town America. Sort of Mayberry, R.F.D. plopped down on the banks of the Erie Canal—without Sheriff Andy Taylor and deputy Barney Fife, of course. Farmers would come to town to sell their fruits, vegetables, milk, and meat at street markets. Doctors made house calls. Residents flocked to businesses in the three-to-four-block downtown area, not yet lured away by the shopping centers and mega-malls that would sprout in nearby Syracuse and Rochester in the 1970s and '80s. Churches usually were packed on Sunday mornings. Youth and high school sports were supported rabidly, sources of community pride and identity. "Lyons back then was a real close-knit place," recalled Earl Buchanan, a retired teacher and superintendent who has called the Wayne County seat his home since the late 1940s. "Everyone knew everyone's name, and neighbors looked out for one another. Serious crime was almost nonexistent. Heck, nobody bothered to lock up their houses or their cars. It really was sort of an idyllic place, a great place to raise your kids."

Jim and Janet Boeheim thought so, too, and on November 17, 1944, they welcomed their firstborn, James Arthur Boeheim Jr., into this "idyllic place." It became apparent to the townsfolk early on that the apple hadn't fallen far from the tree. The boy everyone called "Jimmy" would be profoundly influenced—good and bad—by his domineering, hyper-critical father. From the get-go, Senior and Junior seemed to have a competition rather than a relationship. Father would teach son how to play a game, then proceed to beat him at the game as decisively as he could. "It was amazing to watch," said Tony Santelli, a lifelong friend of the famous basketball coach who went on to run a successful lumber business in Lyons and nearby Newark. "He was relentless. Here's this adult playing this six- or seven-year-old in ping-pong, and he's hitting the ball as hard as he can and is intent on not letting him score a single point. The old man was hard on Jimmy. Very hard."

The elder Boeheim believed the world was extremely competitive and that you had better become fiercely competitive, too, or it will eat you alive. "I had an aunt who let me win at cards, and that bothered me," the father once told a reporter. "No one is going to let you win as a man, so you better learn to win as a kid. Jimmy got his competitive edge from me." Although the two argued incessantly, they were in complete agreement about that point. "I got to be the competitor I am because my father beat me like a drum every game we played, all my life," the younger Boeheim said. "And every game we played, when I beat him, he wouldn't play me anymore. But I eventually got him in every game, except cards. It took a long time. I got him, starting in ping-pong, pool, golf. It took me a long time to catch him, but I finally caught him."

Although Jimmy's abhorrence for defeat was ingrained in him by his overbearing father, his athletic genes came from his mother. The long-and-lean Janet Boeheim walked with the grace of an athlete and had excellent hand-eye coordination. She became a top-notch golfer, winning several local club championships. She also was a loving, nurturing woman, and her encouragement helped balance the daily barrage of criticism that Jimmy received from his dad. "She was a beautiful person, an absolutely beautiful person," Santelli said. "She was always smiling. She was one of those personalities where the day was always rosy, even if it was minus-25 outside." Years later, in a rare moment of introspection, Jim Boeheim Jr. discussed the disparate personalities of his mother and father in an interview with the *Syracuse Post-Standard.* "I had very, very different parents," he said. "I do tend to be a little too much like my father. I hope I have some of the good qualities of my mother. My father and I, we're both opinionated, stubborn, and very, very competitive."

Barbara Boeheim, the coach's younger sister, occasionally witnessed the sparks fly between her father and big brother. But she also experienced her father's generosity and kindness. "That big heart that everyone saw in Mom was there in Dad, too," she said. "It was just more hidden beneath a tough, outer veneer. Me, being a girl, I'm sure I saw the softer side of Dad much more than Jim did." She also saw the softer side of her brother more often than others did. "We pretty much had your typical older-brother, younger-sister relationship," said Barbara, who is seven years Jim's junior. "He'd call me 'Brat,' and I would do annoying, little-sister things like turn off the lights while he was shooting baskets out back," she said, chuckling at the memory. "But it was all pretty innocent stuff. He actually was a great big brother and still is. When I was little, I remember some kid was taunting me, and Jim came running out of the house and yelled, 'You better leave my little sister alone or else.' He was very protective." Friends and relatives who knew both Senior and Junior say there is a great facial resemblance between the two. Especially when they are agitated. "When Jim glares at an official with that I'm-not-too-pleased-with-you look of his, I say, 'Wow, that's Dad,'" Barbara said. "Of course, Jim doesn't like hearing that because he saw that look from my dad a lot more than I did, and he didn't like it one bit."

Like his father, Jimmy tended to be shy and socially awkward. He was frequently described as an introvert by those who knew him, which might partially explain his obsession with solitary pursuits such as shooting baskets, hitting golf balls, playing pool, and fishing. When he was a youngster, it was common for him to head by himself after dinner to a spot where the Canandaigua Outlet emptied into the canal and fish until one in the morning. "Jimmy wasn't very outgoing," Boeheim Sr. said in an interview a few years after his son became Syracuse's head coach in 1976. "That's how I am. I don't like much attention. I'd rather not be in the spotlight, and neither would Jimmy." Barbara Boeheim theorized that her big brother's shyness may have contributed to his strained relationship with the press later on when he became a coach. "He's always been more of an introvert, so I think doing those interviews, especially after a tough game, was extremely hard for him," she surmised. "He was very uncomfortable being the focus of attention, and although he's clearly gotten so much better at it, I think it's still something that he doesn't enjoy—even when his team is playing well, which is usually the case. He'd rather the credit go to others. He's always been that way. And that's the way my dad was, too."

Another trait Jimmy inherited from his parents was a steel-trap mind. Jim and Janet were life master bridge players, who would compete in card tournaments around the country. "His father had incredible recall," said Santelli. "His dad would remember all 13 cards played in a hand in a game from 20 years ago, and I've noticed that Jimmy has the same recall when it comes to basketball. It isn't unusual for him to say that we lost a game back in 1982 when there were 12 minutes and 32 seconds left, and we were bringing the ball down the right side on a fast break." Bridge games between Jimmy, his parents, and uncles and aunts were rarely dull. Often, the competitive nature of the two Jims would result in an explosive finish, with decks of cards being tossed in the air. "Imagine the intensity of a bunch of Boeheims coaching against one another, and you'll have an idea of what those games were like," Santelli said. "His father was obviously a very good player, but—and I know his dad would never agree with this assessment—his mom was the best bridge player in the family."

Sports helped Jimmy overcome his awkwardness—part of which may have been caused by the fact he wore thick glasses and was tall and pencil thin. By high school, he had sprouted to 6'3" but weighed only 145 pounds soaking wet. During a pickup game the summer before his senior year, Jimmy peeled off his shirt, shocking the family doctor, who was sitting in the stands with the elder Boeheim. "My God," said the physician to Jimmy's dad. "Don't you feed that boy?" Jimmy's peers wondered the same thing. "He definitely was geeky-looking," said Mike DeCola, a lifelong Boeheim friend. "And you know how cruel kids can be about those things. But I think sports helped Jimmy feel connected to others and earn people's respect, because it doesn't matter how you look, it's how you play—and Jimmy proved he could play with the best of them at a lot of things."

Boeheim Sr. passed along his love of many sports, including golf, cutting down a set of clubs for Jimmy when the boy was about four or five. A few years later, the younger Boeheim and Santelli began forging their friendship at Sodus Bay Heights Country Club, a little nine-hole course north of Lyons where their parents were members. "We lived there some summers," Santelli recalled. "We'd drive up there with Lee Boice, who was the Lyons High School golf coach and a teaching pro. We'd put the flags out and do a few other chores for Lee, then play until it was dark and drive back home with him. There was one time, Jimmy and I played the course nine times in a single day. That's how crazed we were about golf."

Jimmy's father was equally crazed about the sport. He was among the driving forces behind the building of Wayne Hills Country Club, an 18-hole layout on the outskirts of town. Father and son would play often, and golf balls weren't necessarily the only things taking flight. Legend has it that Senior and Junior never finished a round of golf together—

the good walk often spoiled by angry words and flung clubs. "It got so that when people on the course heard the Boeheims were playing, they headed for cover," said the younger Boeheim. Jimmy eventually would beat his father and play varsity golf at both Lyons High and Syracuse University before becoming the coach of the final golf team his college alma mater fielded. His lowest handicap was a 2 in the late 1970s, around the time he won consecutive National Association of Basketball Coaches Tournament titles. "Jimmy wasn't a natural by any means," said Boice, a spry octogenarian who coached Boeheim in high school. "But he was a fierce, fierce competitor. And he had great focus on the course. He always would be looking for an edge."

Santelli can vouch for that. He estimated he has played more than a thousand rounds of golf with Boeheim through the years, and he joked that none of the matches were friendly. Santelli remembered a time when Jimmy became so incensed over a bad tee shot that he chucked his driver into a pond. The two often played dime-a-hole golf, and if a player birdied the hole, the other player paid him double. During one match, Santelli eagled the 17th hole and told Boeheim he would have to pay him triple. Jimmy exploded, telling his friend that they had never agreed to such an arrangement. Furious, Santelli shanked his tee shot on 18, enabling Jimmy to win the final hole. Afterward, a smiling Boeheim told Santelli that he knew they had agreed to pay triple for eagles, but that he was just trying to rile him up so that he would lose his concentration on the final hole. "He's not a good loser," Santelli said, shaking his head. "Never has been." Santelli recalled that "even when we lost, he would figure out a way to say we won. You might have had a tie, but he would say, 'We won more holes on the front than you won on the back...so, it really doesn't matter...we won today.' That's just the way he is."

Baseball was another sport the young Boeheim became passionate about. A die-hard Brooklyn Dodgers fan who attended a game at

Ebbets Field during the Jackie Robinson era, Jimmy was a sure-handed shortstop, crafty pitcher, and dead pull hitter without much power. "He didn't throw real hard, but he broke off some unbelievable curveballs," said DeCola, a catcher who played Little League and Pony League (15- to 16-year-olds) baseball with him. "And he was very smart— just like he was in every sport he played." Boeheim and DeCola made the Lyons Little League All-Star team in 1956. Many local residents believed the talent-laden squad had the ability to win the district and state tournaments and maybe even make it all the way to the Little League World Series in Williamsport, Pennsylvania. Unfortunately for them, their team was bounced out of the tourney before it even began because the secretary of the Lyons Little League failed to fill out the application in time. "It was such a shame because that team's roster was filled with gifted athletes, many who would go on to enjoy great success in high school and college sports," said Patricia Alena, a former history teacher and town historian whose father, Nick Sculli, coached the team. "To deal with the disappointment of not being able to play in the tournament, my dad arranged for them to play all-star teams from throughout the area, and they wound up winning all of those games by some pretty lopsided margins. And I remember Jimmy really shining as a pitcher."

One of the few organized sports Jimmy didn't play was football, although he loved the game. He was a die-hard Cleveland Browns fan, largely because of Jimmy Brown and the fact that Browns games were televised every Sunday. Although Boeheim was skinny, he more than held his own in sandlot games against his peers, excelling as a receiver. "Jimmy had a great set of hands, and he had a pretty good arm, too— he could throw it a long way and was accurate," DeCola recalled. "But he always had his sights set on basketball and [Lyons High School basketball coach] Dick Blackwell told Jimmy that if he played football, he wouldn't let him play basketball. It was a little selfish on Coach

Blackwell's part. But you couldn't blame him. He knew Jimmy had the potential to become one the best players he ever coached, and he didn't want to risk him getting hurt playing football and losing him for the basketball season."

Basketball was one sport in which Junior and Senior didn't square off. The elder Boeheim's shortened leg from his childhood bullet wound prevented him from playing hoops effectively against his son, and some theorize that Jimmy gravitated to basketball, in part, because it was a game at which his father was neither proficient nor an expert. Plus, shooting and dribbling a basketball were activities you could do solo, making them ideally suited to the son's loner personality. A fan of both the Syracuse Nats and Boston Celtics, the enterprising young Boeheim would pretend he was playing with his idols at the old Onondaga War Memorial or the Boston Garden by shooting a rolled-up sock into a pot he attached to the top of his bedroom door. His father bought him new basketball sneakers and a new ball so he could practice dribbling and shooting at the asphalt court at the elementary school near the Boeheim's home on 77 Williams St. "We lived right across the street, and every night after dinner my dad would be sitting in his chair near our picture window, and he'd say, 'There goes Jimmy again with his basketball,'" Alena said. "You could set your watch by it. Every night, my dad would announce that Jimmy was dribbling to the school again to shoot baskets. So, I guess any of us who witnessed that on a nightly basis aren't surprised in the least that basketball would wind up becoming Jimmy's life."

CHAPTER 3

The Making of a High School Hoops Hero

ALTHOUGH THEIR RELATIONSHIP often was prickly, Jim Boeheim Jr. believed that deep down his father loved him. And, when it came to sports—something which bound, and, occasionally, divided the two—Senior always made sure his son had the equipment and opportunities necessary to excel. "He coached Jimmy in Little League Baseball and got him started in golf," Jimmy's late uncle, Chuck Boeheim, recalled in an interview in the early 1980s. "I think he saw Jimmy do a lot of things in sports that he would have liked a chance to do. I think, at times, he was living vicariously through Jimmy. And although he didn't mention it much, if ever, to Jimmy, I know he was very, very proud of his son's accomplishments."

One day, when Jimmy was around 11 years old, Jim Sr. surprised the boy by installing a basketball hoop in the parking lot near the storage barn behind the Boeheims' home/funeral home. The father also put a light at the top of the pole, so his son would be able to shoot after darkness arrived. "I thought I died and had gone to heaven," the famed basketball coach said, beaming while recalling the moment. "Still one of the best things my dad ever did for me."

Word of the lighted basket behind the funeral home spread quickly, and in no time the court became a magnet for neighborhood kids interested in hooping it up with Jimmy. "It became our playground, our meeting place," said Mike DeCola, who has fond memories of those sunrise-to-sunset pickup games. "I like to joke that decades before they named the court after him at the Carrier Dome, Jimmy had his own unofficial court." And it was pretty much in use year-round. "It would be the middle of the winter, and Jimmy and his friends would be out there, shoveling it clear of snow, so they could play," recalled Earl Buchanan, a former Lyons teacher and superintendent. "And in the spring, they'd be dribbling through and around the puddles. I swear, every time I drove by the house, Jimmy and his crew would be playing games. You have to remember there weren't any video games back then, and you only had a handful of television stations, so kids spent a lot more time playing outside." Although inclement weather wouldn't stop games, funerals would. During calling hours, the boys would merely head across the street to the elementary school courts to resume play.

The games featured many of the players with whom Jimmy had begun playing organized basketball in the fifth grade and who would form the nucleus of the great Lyons varsity teams of the early 1960s. "By the time we got to high school, everybody knew everybody else's style of play like the backs of their hands because we had been playing with and against one another for years," DeCola said. "It became a real advantage for us."

Boeheim's court became not only an unofficial training ground for one of Lyons' legendary high school basketball teams but also the place where Jimmy picked up the nickname "Sid," after Sid Borgia, a colorful character who was the most recognizable NBA referee of the 1950s. "We gave Jimmy the name," said DeCola, chuckling, "because he liked to call fouls on people while he was playing. The thing is, Jimmy would only call fouls on other players, never himself. It's amazing, but in all the years we played, he never committed a foul. At least not in his own mind." What makes the nickname even more humorous is that years later, when he became Syracuse University's head coach, Boeheim gained a reputation for being one of college basketball's most persistent and annoying referee baiters. In fact, in one 1980s poll, college referees voted the whiny Boeheim among the 10 coaches whose games they least liked to work. Jimmy, though, wasn't bothered by the nickname his teen-age friends had pinned on him. In fact, he seemed to like it, often signing notes to friends "Sid" instead of "Jimmy."

Sports were huge in Lyons in the 1950s and '60s, and basketball was king, thanks, in large part, to Richard Blackwell, a decorated World War II paratrooper and 1948 Ithaca College graduate who helped establish the Lyons Lions as a high school powerhouse in Wayne County and throughout the Finger Lakes. Blackwell was born Gaston Richard on May 12, 1922, in Montreal, Canada. At age six, he was legally adopted by his sister, Eva, and her husband, Edwin Blackwell of Saginaw, Michigan, and changed his first and last names. In addition to being a standout athlete at Saginaw High, the young Blackwell became an accomplished piano player who fronted a swing band that performed at numerous high school and college concerts in the late-1930s. In 1941, he attended the Rochester Institute of Technology to study photography. While there, he met his future wife, Dorothy, who was an art student from Lyons. A year later, Blackwell enlisted in the 82nd Army Airborne and wound up seeing combat action in Germany and North Africa in World War II. During the D-Day invasion, he dropped behind enemy lines and was separated from his unit. Thanks to the French Resistance, he was able to escape capture by German forces. Blackwell also fought in the Battle of the Bulge and helped free a Nazi concentration camp. He was wounded twice during the war and wound up receiving two Purple Hearts.

After returning to the States in 1946, he married his college sweetheart in Lyons and resumed his studies at Ithaca College, where he received bachelor's and master's degrees in physical education. He briefly taught in Colorado before returning to Lyons to take a job as a physical education instructor and high school basketball coach. He wound up coaching hoops at the school for 15 years, capturing nine league championships while compiling a record of 210 wins and 80 losses for a .724 winning percentage.

Despite drawing from an enrollment of about 75 students per class, Blackwell insisted on playing in the Class-A division when the sectional tournament rolled around, meaning Lyons often went head-to-head against Rochester city schools with student bodies nearly 10 times bigger. "There was kind of a *Hoosiers* element to those matchups," said James Blandino, a lifelong Lyons resident. "It was little, old Lyons against the big boys, and Lyons more than held its own." In Blackwell's initial season (1951–52), he guided the Lions to an 18–0 record and the sectional title. Two seasons later, led by Chuck Austin, who was Boeheim's idol and claims to have taught young Jimmy how to play the game, Lyons repeated its large school crown. "There was a tradition of success that had been established," DeCola said. "And every class coming up wanted to build on that success and keep the tradition going."

Part of Lyons' success was predicated on a feeder system in which players began learning the varsity's style of play as early as the sixth grade. Boeheim fondly remembers Blackwell putting him and his fellow 12-year-olds through Saturday morning practices that often lasted four hours. "He really was an innovative coach, a guy ahead of his time," said the Syracuse basketball coach. "We were running fast breaks in high school before that style of play was fashionable and playing match-up zone defenses when everyone else relied solely on playing man-to-man." Blackwell would provide his players with detailed scouting reports on upcoming opponents. "It was like we knew what the other team was going to do before they actually did something," said DeCola. "That's how well prepared we were, thanks to Coach."

The man known as "Blackie" was a disciplinarian. He enforced strict curfews, occasionally driving around town in the evening to make sure his players were home. He also enforced a dress code, in which the players were required to wear dress shirts and ties on the bus during road games. And, in what clearly was a reflection of a different era in terms of acceptable school punishment, Blackwell occasionally pulled out a paddle—fondly known to students as his "Board of Education"—and gave those who misbehaved or were late to gym class or practice an attention-grabbing whack on the fanny in front of their peers. Violators would then sign their names on the paddle, and when the board became too full for any more signatures, Blackwell would retire it to his office and break out a new one. "Some kids would do things just so they could say they got their names on the paddle," DeCola said. "Certainly, this sort of thing wouldn't fly today, but it was accepted back then. And, to be honest with you, I think it worked. Coach whacked you just hard enough to make you think twice about doing something out of line again. And he increased the intensity of the whacking for repeat offenders."

DeCola said he and virtually everyone who ever played for Blackwell respected the coach's tough tactics and team-above-self approach. "I remember one time Jimmy came out to practice with a new pair of high-top sneakers," DeCola said. "The only problem was that Coach wanted us to all be wearing low-cuts. He went ballistic on Jimmy, and that was the last time Jimmy wore those sneakers to practice."

That incident, though, was one of the few times Blackwell laid into Boeheim, whom he regarded as a good kid and a gifted player. The coach loved Jimmy's focus and dedication to the game. The young

Boeheim was a true gym rat. Often when Blackwell headed back to his office after practice, he would hear the thumping of a basketball on the court. It would be Jimmy working on his shot. "I couldn't get him out of there," Blackwell recalled. "Other than playing sports, Jimmy did nothing. Absolutely nothing. That was it. He didn't date. He was wrapped up in sports. That was his whole life."

Patricia (Sculli) Alena, a varsity cheerleader during Boeheim's high school career, agreed with that assessment. Leafing through scrapbooks, yearbooks, and photo albums at her Lyons home, the retired history teacher couldn't find any pictures of Jimmy attending sock hops, proms, or other social events with his classmates. She did, however, dispel the long-held assumption that Jimmy never had a date in high school. She says he went on a date once with one of her cheerleading teammates— but only after the girl cornered him at his locker and asked him out. "I don't recall him ever going steady with anyone," Alena said. "He was too into sports to have time for girls back then. Basketball was his steady."

While others attended parties, Jimmy could be found shooting baskets or strapping on ankle weights and going out on two-mile runs through the streets of Lyons. In the summer, he would attend a two-week–long basketball camp north of Saratoga hosted by Basketball Hall of Famer Dolph Schayes and other members of the NBA's Syracuse Nats. "When I think of Jimmy," recalled Schayes, "I think about scraped knees. He was a great, great hustler. He would dive for balls on the blacktop. He was a good player, but what I remember most about him are those scraped knees." Boeheim remembered them, too. "I left a lot of skin and blood on Dolph's courts," the coach said four decades later, grinning ear to ear. "But I was young, and when you're that age and that focused, the only thing you care about is the game. Most of the time, I wasn't even aware I was bleeding."

Boeheim's intensity also still resonates with Buchanan. "Jimmy was very purposeful," he said. "He had a look in his eyes like an eagle.

His eyes were always on the ball and focused on what he was doing." Boeheim's gangly physique prevented him from moving gracefully, but it didn't stop him from becoming a prolific scorer. "It was like watching Icabod Crane, with those long broomstick legs of Jim's coming down the court," Buchanan said. "But when Jimmy shot the ball, it was fluid motion in action, like silk. Swish. Swish. Swish." Buchanan also recalled how personally Boeheim took the losses, which were few and far between during his scholastic career. "He never showed much emotion when they won," he said. "But when they lost, Jimmy would be despondent and introspective all week. It was like he was playing the game over and over in his mind."

Growing up in a funeral home might seem kind of weird and spooky, but Boeheim thought nothing of sharing his residence with the dead. A huge wall divided the family's big, brown brick house on Williams Street. On the front side were the corpses, whom Jimmy jokingly referred to as "the visitors," while on the other side resided Jimmy, his parents, and his younger sister, Barbara. "It was like having another building in your house," he said. "It was just like having an apartment next door. It was not a great situation, but you get used to it. You accept it." Jim Sr. did the embalming and his wife Janet did the makeup and hair. Jimmy would help out by delivering flowers to the cemetery, and when he turned 16 he got his driver's license so he could drive the hearse. But he never entered his father's embalming room. It became apparent early on that Jimmy had little interest in following in his dad's footsteps and continuing the tradition of the "burying Boeheims." "He was never much for undertaking," Senior said in a 1982 interview. "Sure, he helped out, but he didn't do it willingly. It might have been nice if he wanted to carry this on, but Jimmy has always been pretty quiet. He never wanted to be called 'Digger,' like Phelps [the former Notre Dame basketball coach and current ESPN analyst whose father also was an undertaker]."

Santelli recalled riding in the hearse with his friend. "I picked up a few stiffs [corpses] with him," he said, laughing. "That was interesting, to say the least. We'd be at a stoplight, and people would be looking at this hearse being driven by two teenagers." The Boeheims also operated an ambulance, and one time Jimmy was dispatched to pick up an expectant mother who had gone into labor. The young Boeheim drove at breakneck speed, but even Mario Andretti couldn't have reached this destination in time, as the woman gave birth before the ambulance arrived at the hospital. "Never again," Jimmy shouted at his father upon returning to the funeral home to clean up the mess inside the car. "This business is not for me." Years later, while struggling to get by on an assistant basketball coach's paltry salary at Syracuse, Boeheim contemplated returning to Lyons and becoming the fifth generation to run the family's undertaking business. But the more he thought about it, the more he realized that his heart wasn't into it.

Baskets, not caskets, were his passion.

• • •

Jimmy Boeheim clearly was one book you couldn't judge by its cover. At 6'3", 145 pounds with thick glasses, he looked like a librarian or even an undertaker instead of a highly competitive athlete. Nothing about his stature or appearance projected ferocity or intimidation. But Dick Blackwell realized early on that appearances definitely were deceiving when it came to Boeheim. The Lyons varsity basketball coach first became acquainted with skinny Jimmy while running youth basketball practices when Boeheim was in the sixth grade, and he immediately liked what he saw. The kid might have seemed awkward and did things in an unorthodox manner on occasion, but he also had a knack for being in the right place at the right time, and his grasp of the game's strategy was far superior to his peers. "I noticed from the start that he was a great student of the game," Blackwell recalled. "While others watched the game for entertainment and focused solely on the ball and the high scorer, Jimmy was dissecting the game, trying to understand what worked and what didn't. He saw the entire court and understood the importance of moving without the ball and seeking open spaces. He had boundless energy. He was in perpetual motion the minute the game began, always on the move."

Though he lacked great jumping ability—his teammates joked you'd be hard-pressed to slide a dime under his sneakers when he went "airborne"—he was a better athlete than people gave him credit for. "He had superb hand-eye coordination, which I believe contributed to him being a dead-on shooter from 12 to 15 feet," Blackwell said. Jimmy was especially accurate from the free throw line, where he canned 85 percent of his shots, including a school-record 14-for-14 one night versus Penn Yan. The depth of Boeheim's marksmanship and coolness under pressure was underscored during a foul-shooting contest when Jimmy was just 16. When one of the contestants made 24 of 25, everyone figured the competition was over. Everyone, that is, except the young Boeheim, who calmly stepped to the line and sank 25 of 25 to win the prize.

Jimmy's shot—more push than jump—wasn't pretty to behold, but you couldn't argue with the results. From 18 feet in, he was remarkably accurate. "He has the most uncanny shot of any player I've coached," Blackwell told reporters. "He's the best shooter I've ever had. He has more moves than any player I've ever handled. He has a good pair of hands and strong wrists, and he plays a strong defensive game, to boot." His intelligence and fearlessness helped compensate for what he lacked athletically. He often dove on floors or banged into gym walls in pursuit of loose balls. "Jimmy would drive to the basket and an opponent would push him into the wall, and Jimmy would just bounce back up and come back for more," Blackwell said. "You couldn't intimidate him. He was quite durable. I don't recall him ever missing a game in four years. He was very driven. I never, ever had to worry about Jimmy Boeheim giving it his all."

Blackwell promoted him to the varsity before his sophomore season, and although Jimmy didn't set the world on fire right away, he more than held his own against the upperclassmen, averaging a respectable 8.3 points per game for the 12–7 Lions. The experience prepared him to become not only a starter, but a star during his junior and senior seasons at Lyons. All those years of dribbling and shooting baskets paid off during the winter of 1960–61, as he averaged 19.3 points per game to finish a close second to George Valesente (20.3) in the race for the Wayne–Finger Lakes League scoring title. The Lions made it all the way to the big-school sectional semifinals that season, losing to Rochester's Franklin High School. Franklin was led by Trent Jackson, a magnificent three-sport athlete who would tie Jesse Owens' national high school record in the 100-yard dash and earn a spot on the United States Olympic Track and Field team in 1964 before playing briefly as a wide receiver in the NFL for the Philadelphia Eagles and Washington Redskins.

That loss, which capped an 18–2 campaign, was tough to swallow, but Boeheim and his teammates were confident their senior season would have a much happier ending, because the core of the team was returning. The Lions' preseason optimism was shared by the local newspapers. One preview noted that Blackwell "has more experienced talent than he really knows what to do with." The coach agreed. "That '61–62 club might have been the best I ever coached," he said. "We had great balance, great chemistry, great kids. The nucleus of that group had grown up playing together at the elementary school and at the court behind the Boeheims' funeral home, and they really liked one another. Jimmy clearly was the standout of the bunch, but this was by no means a one-man team. We had a bunch of really gifted athletes on that club. The parts fit together really well."

The starting lineup featured 5'10" guard Gary Tunnison, who averaged 8.6 points per game that season and served as the primary playmaker. Joe Holly, a ruggedly built 6'1", 195-pounder who earned honorable mention All-American status in football that fall from the *Sporting News*, and Don Oakleaf, a 6'5" center, were physical forces on the back line of the Lions' 3-2 zone defense and also helped control the boards, while Dave Fratangelo, a 6'2", 160-pound co-captain with Boeheim, averaged 11 points per game and did a little bit of everything. Boeheim, who would lead the team and league in scoring that season with 24.7 points per game, played a combination shooting guard/ forward. David Barnes, whom Blackwell said "would be a starter and a star on any other team in the league," was the first man off the bench.

Blackwell preached an attacking style on both defense and offense. He wanted his teams to dictate the action, which is why he often employed man-to-man, full-court presses, replete with traps, as well as a tough-to-penetrate 3-2 zone. Offensively, "Blackie" loved to see his players run the fast break, which was unusual at a time when many high school basketball coaches preferred a more methodical, less risky, pass-the-ball-several-times-before-shooting approach. The marriage of strategy and talent resulted in one of the most dominating seasons ever by a Wayne–Finger Lakes basketball team. Each time the Lions took the court, it wasn't a question of *if* they were going to win but *by how much*. Leading the way was young Jimmy Boeheim, who may have looked like a string bean but played more like a high school version of Bob Cousy and Jerry West. After Boeheim scored 16 and 34 points, respectively, in 23- and 53-point routs of Geneva DeSales that season, losing coach Bob Maher told reporters: "I'll be glad when Jimmy Boeheim graduates." That sentiment was shared by coaches throughout the league, who had no answers for stopping him and the Lions' juggernaut.

One of Boeheim's most spectacular performances occurred late in the season, when he scored 33 points in an 85–44 thrashing of Canandaigua on the road. In that game, the Lions sped to a 40–8 first-period lead—a remarkable feat, considering quarters were just eight minutes long and there was no shot clock, so teams could attempt to stall in order to hold the score down. Boeheim had 21 points during that first-quarter barrage and probably would have scored 50 had Blackwell not called off the dogs and benched Jimmy and the rest of the starters early in the third period. The Lions' march to an unbeaten league record also included easy victories against league rival Waterloo. An interesting side note to those games was that they pitted Boeheim, a senior, against Tom Coughlin, a sophomore. Coughlin also would go to Syracuse—on a football scholarship—and play in the same backfield as Orangemen All-American running backs Floyd Little and Larry Csonka, before establishing himself as a renowned college and NFL head coach who won Super Bowl XLII with the New York Giants. Boeheim wound up serving as Coughlin's resident advisor at SU. "The quietest, most mild-mannered guy I've ever known," Boeheim said, "the last guy you would think would be a tough football coach. The last guy." Lyons concluded the regular-season at 18–0 and entered the sectionals outscoring their opponents by a mind-boggling 31 points per game.

On February 11, 1962, the *Rochester Democrat and Chronicle* took notice, devoting an entire page of its sports section to the hoopmania sweeping Lyons, which was about 45 minutes east of the Flower City:

> *Grammar school youngsters babble about the team. High schoolers exult in the team's triumphs. Former grads strut proudly, proclaiming the team's accomplishments. Staid citizens shuffle off their cool reserve. Even the village fathers are excited.*
>
> *All of Lyons is roaring praise and enthusiasm for the Lyons Central School basketball team—the Wayne County village is alive, cheering its undefeated hoopsters.*

From Mayor Clark R. Gardner to the least of Lyons'
4,290 (latest population figure), the village is basketball
mad.

"The whole town's talking, thinking, rooting and
sometimes, I think, almost eating basketball," Gardner
said. "The U.S. is ready to send a man into orbit. Well,
most of this town already is in orbit."

More than 1,000 fans—nearly a quarter of the village's residents—
routinely shoe-horned their way into the high school gymnasium for
Lyons home games. And scores more, those who didn't arrive in time
to purchase the hottest sports ticket in the Finger Lakes, would wait
outside in hopes of receiving updates from the fortunate attendees
during breaks between periods. When the team headed to road games,
it would be accompanied by a caravan of five to six busloads of students
and numerous cars driven by adult residents smitten with their town's
hoop stars. The entourage made for sizable and vociferous cheering
sections at opposing gyms.

Lyons, which boasted about 75 students per graduating class, was
eligible to play schools of similar size in the Section V tournament.
But Blackwell wanted to be recognized as the best team in the region,
and he realized that status would be achieved only if the Lions beat
the Class-AA schools in Rochester. So, with the blessing of his athletic
director and superintendent, he arranged for Lyons to play in the
large-school division, and his teams always acquitted themselves well.
"He probably would have won a ton more sectionals had he decided
to stay in our classification based on enrollment," said Mike DeCola,
a reserve on that '61–62 team. "But he wanted to play the big guys,
and we players did, too. If we had played in the classification we were
supposed to in the sectionals, we would have won the title easily, but
we would have always wondered how we would have fared against the
biggest schools in our region."

Blackwell's first Lyons team in 1951–52 went 21–0 and won the Class AA crown with a 53–49 victory against East Rochester. Although the Lions lost two games during the 1953–54 season, they regrouped during the sectionals and defeated ER again, by a 45–43 score. The coach had plenty of reason to feel optimistic heading into the 1962 tournament, because he believed this team was as talented, if not more so, than his previous two sectional championship clubs. Sportswriters from the nearby "big" city of Rochester felt the same way. They had begun calling Blackwell's club the "Whiz Kids." The Lions certainly lived up to their new nickname in the sectional opener, as Boeheim scored a tournament-record 37 points to lead them to a 40-point victory against West High at the War Memorial in downtown Rochester. The game report in the next morning's *Democrat and Chronicle* by sportswriter Bill Vanderschmidt was effusive in its praise of Jimmy's record-setting performance.

> *While the smashing defeat of West High was accounted for largely by the superb team play of the winners, Jim Boeheim gave as great an exhibition of basketball as has ever been witnessed in the sectionals. He scored 37 of the 72 points made by Lyons, or five more than the entire West team managed.*
>
> *The tall, slender forward did everything but eat the ball, as they say in sports. Both offensively and defensively he was a thorn in the side of West High, while he was on the floor. His ball-handling won praise from the crowd.*

One Boeheim move in particular brought the crowd of about 4,600—1,500 of whom were from Lyons—to its collective feet.

Wrote Norm Jollow of *The Geneva Times*:

> *The game's most dazzling play came in the third period when Boeheim took a pass near midcourt, took a couple of dribbles down the sideline, ran up to a West defender,*

shifted the ball behind his back (à la Bob Cousy) and went around the defender easily to go up for a two-pointer.

No one was more impressed by the Harlem Globetrotters–like deception than Blackwell. "That's my old standby," the coach marveled, sounding like a proud father whose son had helped him peel away the years. "I used to be able to do that play well. It's not just fancy. You lose your man because he's overshifted."

The scoring barrage made Jimmy Boeheim the talk of the town, but it also made the painfully shy teenager hesitant to head outdoors the day after the game. His father finally convinced the reluctant hero to get out of the house, but Jimmy went out of his way to avoid downtown because he was uncomfortable being the center of attention. Instead, he grabbed his basketball and ran across the street to the elementary school and practiced shooting until darkness arrived. "Jimmy didn't like people congratulating him," Boeheim Sr. said. "He was low key. He didn't toot his own horn. All he wanted to do was win." On those rare occasions when the Lions wound up losing—just 10 times in 58 games during Boeheim's varsity basketball career—Jimmy would act as if the world had come to an end.

The Lions' seemingly inexorable march to a title and an unbeaten season continued in front of 6,950 spectators at the War Memorial in the semifinals, as Boeheim tallied 27 points in an easy 67–42 victory against Wellsville. That cakewalk set up one of the most highly anticipated high school games in Rochester history—a championship matchup between Lyons and East Rochester, each of whom entered the contest with unblemished 20–0 records. The fact that Blackwell's Lions twice nipped the Bombers in the sectional finals in the early 1950s only added to the drama and the pregame hype of the contest one local newspaper dubbed the "game of games."

A record crowd of 9,871 spectators stuffed the War Memorial on March 28, 1962. To this day, people who attended that evening's championship game claim that the announced attendance figure was on the conservative side and that at least 11,000 had sardined their way into the old concrete building that doubled as a bomb shelter overlooking the Genesee River. Still, the official figure was high enough to smash the arena's previous mark of 8,517 for the 1956 NBA All-Star Game. An estimated 3,000 fans from Lyons—nearly three-quarters of the village's residents—had journeyed by bus or car to Rochester to witness what they believed would be the crowning moment of a 21–0 season. "We've essentially shut our town down today," Mayor Gardner told reporters. "Our community clearly has fallen in love with this team." The spectators included Jim Boeheim Sr., whose chronic back problems as a result of his childhood gunshot wound forced him to attend the game in a wheelchair.

Rarely do such highly anticipated sporting events live up to their hype. But this clash of high school basketball titans proved to be even better than advertised. What transpired that early spring night was a classic game that still evokes strong emotions from the participants and witnesses nearly a half century later.

Sprinting to a 13–2 first-quarter lead that they extended to 25–13 at the half, it appeared the Lions were well on their way to another easy victory. But East Rochester junior Kenny Rice sparked a comeback, sinking three long shots at the start of the second half. And when Dave Schake and Todd Hahn tipped in rebounds at the beginning of the fourth quarter, Lyons' once seemingly insurmountable cushion was pared to two points. Midway through the period, the Bombers went on top for the first time, and the lead changed hands several times down the stretch. With about five seconds remaining in regulation, Boeheim fed center Don Oakleaf for an easy layup, and the game went into overtime after a 35-foot shot by East Rochester's Gerry Ballone clanged off the iron at the buzzer.

Boeheim wound up scoring four of Lyons' next six points, including a buzzer-beating basket as he was falling to the floor, knotting the score at 51 and sending the game into a second overtime. The second extra session saw Hahn, who had played a masterful defensive game against Boeheim, steal the ball from the Lions' star and score the decisive basket in a 58–57 victory. After winning 20 straight games—all by comfortable margins—Lyons' streak and season had come to a bitter end. And, so, too, had the high school careers of Boeheim and several of his teammates. "We're shocked, stunned," Blackwell said about 30 minutes later outside the locker room in the bowels of the War Memorial. "We still can't believe it. But as I told our kids, failure, like success, is a part of life." The philosophical words, though true, seemed to ring hollow even for Blackwell at that moment. "I can't get it through my head that we lost," he said to a reporter. "I'm like the kids, I guess. It just doesn't seem possible. I still say we have a great ballclub. You can't blame those kids. They have a lot of pride and a lot of heart. East Rochester has a good ballclub that knocked us down, little by little. At least they didn't clobber us."

For his efforts—a game-high 18 points versus East Rochester, plus his 54 points in his previous two playoff games—Boeheim was named the tournament's most outstanding player and was joined on the All-Tourney team by teammate Dave Fratangelo. The individual honors, though, were little consolation for Boeheim, who had been taught by his father from the moment he first picked up a ping-pong paddle as a toddler that there was no substitute for victory.

As had been the custom that season, the fans and cheerleaders gathered at Agnes & Johnnies, a family restaurant near the park in downtown Lyons, upon returning from the game. The players and their families made a brief appearance, then headed to the Boeheims for their traditional postgame pizza. But no one was in a mood to celebrate at either place. "It really was like a funeral," Jim Sr. recalled. "And, believe me, I should know what a funeral atmosphere is like."

Jimmy Boeheim had finished his brilliant high school career with 1,012 points—a 17.8-per-game average—and two league titles. But when he looks back on those days, it's the loss to ER that dominates his thoughts. "That—and the loss to Indiana [in the 1987 NCAA championship game]," he said, sighing, "are the two games I'll never get over."

After the devastating loss in his final high school basketball game, Boeheim's thoughts turned to golf. The success he had enjoyed on the court continued on the course, as he averaged about 43 strokes per 9 holes to lead Lyons to victories against Sodus, Newark, Clyde, and Ontario en route to the Wayne County high school team golf title and an undefeated record. "We had a lot of good players," said former Lyons golf coach Lee Boice. "But Jimmy was the leader. He set the tone with his competitiveness and his smarts."

Although regarded by his teachers and peers as extremely intelligent, Boeheim was a B student who didn't push himself in the classroom. "Jimmy was not very studious, except for sports," said Jim Boeheim Sr. "He could have done a lot better academically, but he was kind of lazy. If he had applied the same kind of energy toward his studies that he did toward sports, he would have been a straight-A student." In retrospect, the younger Boeheim agreed, adding, "I don't think I ever brought home a book in high school." So you won't find his name listed among the top 25 students, whose cumulative grades were listed in the 1962 school yearbook, which was called the *Lyons Tale*. Nor will you find him in the photo of those who made the national honor society. The yearbook's activity index showed that Boeheim had played three years of varsity golf and basketball, one year of junior varsity baseball, was a member of the Varsity Letterman's Club and yearbook advertising committee, and served two years as an intramural referee. "He didn't spend a lot of time studying or socializing," Senior said. "He often kept to himself. Sports were his life back then. Everything else seemed secondary."

Jimmy's love of basketball was underscored when his Lyons High School classmates asked him to sign their yearbooks. While most seniors signed near their individual class photos, Jimmy preferred to write his notes near the picture of him shooting on the varsity basketball page. Each senior picture in the *Lyons Tale* was accompanied by a rhyme. Predictably, the yearbook editors made sure that Jimmy's limerick focused on his hoop prowess:

> *"Call him Sid or call him Heimer,*
>
> *At basketball, there's no one finer."*

CHAPTER 4

Becoming an Orange Man

WHEN IT CAME TIME TO DECIDE UPON COLLEGES, Jimmy Boeheim was more concerned about where he would play his next competitive basketball than what he would major in or where he would earn his degree. Colgate, Cornell, and the University of Rochester had scouted him during his senior season at Lyons and were keen on him playing basketball at their respective schools. His father mailed in a $100 non-refundable deposit after Jimmy was accepted at Colgate. But the elder Boeheim might as well have taken a match to the money because stubborn Jimmy, over the objections of his father, had designs on playing at Syracuse University. "Part of Jimmy's competitive nature always has involved proving people wrong," said Boeheim's lifelong friend, Tony Santelli. "He wanted to play big-time college basketball, although, at that time, Syracuse basketball was in a big-time slump. Colgate and Cornell were actually better programs at that time."

In reality, just about every Division I basketball program was better than SU in those days. The Orangemen's fall from respectability had been precipitous. Led by Vinnie Cohen (24.2 points per game) and Jon Cincebox (11.8 rebounds per game), the 1956–57 squad had earned the school's first NCAA invitation—a much harder task back then because there were only 24 teams in the tournament. Syracuse made it to the East Regional finals, where it lost to a North Carolina team that would go on to defeat Wilt Chamberlain's Kansas Jayhawks in triple overtime for the national championship in one of college basketball's most memorable contests. Some believe that if the great and multitalented Jim Brown had continued playing basketball that season, as he had during his first two years at SU, the Orangemen might have gone the distance.

Coach Marc Guley's Orangemen remained competitive, with 14–9 and 13–8 records the next two seasons before becoming the dregs of college basketball. SU plummeted to 4–19 in 1960–61, ending its season with a five-game losing skid. But the worst was yet to come as the Orangemen lost their first 22 games in 1961–62 to extend their ignominious streak to a then-NCAA record 27 straight games. Students and people in the community were so turned off by the mediocrity that crowds for SU home games at the 7,000-seat Onondaga War Memorial routinely numbered in the low 100s. The Orangemen finally snapped their futility streak with a 73–72 victory at Boston College on March 3, 1962, but the damage had been done.

A month before the season ended, Guley announced that he would be resigning after the final game. It clearly was a wise and preemptive move because he was certain to have been fired anyway. A search committee was formed, headed by athletics director Lew Andreas, who had coached SU basketball teams to a school-record 358 victories and a mythical national championship during his 25 years at the helm. The credentials of more than 50 candidates were reviewed and, for the first time in the 60-year history of SU basketball, an outsider was hired as coach. The daunting task of raising the Orangemen from the ashes would fall to Fred Lewis, a successful basketball taskmaster who believed in rugged physical conditioning drills, just as Andreas had.

Lewis arrived on campus with a long and impressive basketball résumé. Born in Brooklyn in 1922, he had attended Madison High School, where he played for legendary basketball coach Harry

"Jammy" Moskowitz. Sparked by Lewis, who earned All-City honors at guard, Madison won 37 straight games and 53 of 54 over three years. "One thing that Lewis always had going for him was a tremendous outside shot," Moskowitz recalled in a 1965 interview with Syracuse University's student newspaper, *The Daily Orange*. "But he also had that ability to move with the shots. He was an all-around backcourt-man." The other thing that set him apart, according to Moskowitz, was his on-court swagger. "He had that feeling of confidence," Moskowitz said, "the belief that he could be just as good as anyone else."

Lewis' success continued at Long Island University, where he played for another legendary coach—Basketball Hall of Famer Clair Bee. During his sophomore season (1941–42), he scored a team-leading 567 points and earned All-Metropolitan honors. But a falling-out with Bee prompted him to transfer to Eastern Kentucky University. In two seasons with the Maroons, he finished second and third in the nation in scoring and twice earned All-America honors. The Sheboygan Redskins of the National Basketball League (a forerunner to the NBA) drafted him, and Lewis' ability to put the ball in the basket with regularity continued in the pros, as he finished second in the league in scoring while earning Rookie of the Year and all-star honors. He was traded to the Baltimore Bullets the following season and led them in scoring the next two campaigns before deciding to hang up his sneakers and begin his coaching career.

From 1950–53, he guided Amityville High School on Long Island to a 63–40 record. Lewis' dream, though, was to coach on the collegiate level, and that goal was realized in 1956, when he took the job at Hawaii University. After leading the Rainbows to a 21–2 record, Lewis returned stateside and took over as the head basketball coach at Southern Mississippi, which, at the time, was a small college program. His golden touch continued with the Golden Comets, as he guided them to a No. 3 national ranking in 1959–60 and a No. 2 ranking the following season.

Lewis' success there—an 89–38 record in five seasons—along with his reputation as a disciplinarian and an offensive innovator, paired with his recruiting connections in New York City, convinced Andreas and his committee that Lewis was the right man for the job.

To aid in the resuscitation of the Orangemen's morbid program, Lewis brought along his loquacious, energetic assistant, Roy Danforth. The man with the doctorate in education and his protégé would engineer a surprisingly rapid turnaround at a school where football reigned as Big Man On Campus and basketball was an unpopular stepchild. The Syracuse gridders, under Hall of Fame coach Ben Schwartzwalder, were just three years removed from their first national championship in football and just a year removed from charismatic running back Ernie Davis becoming the first African American to win the Heisman Trophy. Football was a source of pride on campus, a symbol of excellence. Basketball, meanwhile, was a source of ridicule— something students and the local populace followed with lukewarm interest to pass the time from the end of the football season until the annual spring game.

Interestingly, a building that opened in 1962 to enhance the football program would wind up enhancing the basketball program even more. Manley Field House was constructed to provide the football team with an indoor facility for bowl preparations in December when the weather became too rainy or snowy to use chewed-up outdoor practice fields. But Andreas also arranged for the arena with the dirt floor to become the new home of the hoops program. A raised basketball court was purchased, and bleachers, accommodating crowds of up to 8,000, were brought in. "It wasn't exactly the Taj Mahal," Lewis recalled. "But it wound up being a much more impressive venue than the War Memorial or State Fair Grounds or any of the small gyms we had on campus. It made recruiting easier, especially after we got things going and started drawing some decent crowds."

In the spring of 1962, toward the end of Boeheim's final year of high school, he climbed into the family's 1959 black Ford station wagon—the same one he drove to pick up funeral flowers—and drove to Syracuse to visit the SU campus. The teenager from the little town wound up getting lost in the big city. After asking several people for directions, he finally made his way to campus and saw the brand spanking new field house. Although it was still just a shell with a dirt floor, it might as well have been the Boston Garden as far as Boeheim was concerned—a cavernous arena big enough to house several Lyons High School gymnasiums. The awestruck teenager then met with Lewis and was immediately swept away by him. "There was just something about Fred's enthusiasm that appealed to me right away," Boeheim recalled. "He said he wanted to build a national program from the ashes, and I believed he could do it. He's the best recruiter I've ever known."

Lewis told Boeheim that he didn't have any more scholarships to offer but said that he could walk on, and if he produced, he would earn free tuition and board by his sophomore year. That deal was fine with Jimmy but not so fine initially with his father, who believed his son was taking a huge gamble and that Colgate and Cornell offered better opportunities to play. Jimmy's high school coach, Dick Blackwell, agreed with the elder Boeheim but kept his mouth shut when the teenager told him of his plans. "I was leery, too, about him going to Syracuse, because I didn't know if he could play at that level," Blackwell said in a 1996 interview. "But I never told him that, because I didn't want to discourage him. Jimmy was heady and determined. That's a pretty good combination."

The cornerstone of Lewis' first recruiting class was a young man out of Spingarn High School in Washington, D.C., by the name of Dave Bing. That Lewis was able to convince Bing to spurn scholarship offers from more than 200 other schools, including national basketball powerhouses UCLA and Maryland, in order to play basketball at a program that had won just six of its previous 47 games is one of the greatest recruiting upsets of all time. "Syracuse was not even on the list when Fred went down, but he was able to convince David that by coming here, he'd be able to build up the program," Boeheim said. "It was a miracle of recruiting in my judgment, to get a kid of that quality to come into your program."

Lewis said that he and Bing hit it off immediately. "I told him about how Syracuse basketball had been struggling, but between the two of us, we could turn it around." The idea of being the main catalyst in the revival of the program definitely appealed to Bing. "I welcomed that challenge," he recalled. But there were other factors that played a role in him accepting Lewis' scholarship. "SU officials were smart enough to schedule my visit in early May, so I had no idea about the way it snows and snows and snows in Syracuse," he said, chuckling. "I'm up there on a sunny, spring day, and the students are all over the place, wearing shorts and having a good old time, and I'm thinking to myself, 'Wow, it must be like this year-round.' Nobody told me how bad the winters are."

Lewis sealed the deal with Bing by having him chaperoned around campus by Davis, the SU football legend. "I was clearly awestruck," Bing said. "I had a chance to speak with him at length, and the thing I appreciated about it is that he didn't say to me, 'You need to come to Syracuse.' He was honest and frank. He told me about the good experiences and the bad experiences he had at SU. I walked away thinking, 'What an impressive human being.' And I thought that if SU could help develop a human being like Ernie Davis, then I wanted to go there and try to follow in his footsteps. The way he handled himself on and off the field with such dignity set a standard, I believe, for everyone at Syracuse to follow. It's such a shame that his life was cut short by leukemia [in the spring of 1963]. I would have loved to have had an opportunity to have gotten to know him better. I remember when I was getting ready to leave campus that weekend, he told me I had the opportunity to be the Ernie Davis of basketball. That was the clincher for me."

Bing's decision to continue his basketball career at Syracuse was greeted with disbelief by friends and relatives. "Most people in the neighborhood figured I had lost it," he recalled. "They figured I would go up there and never be heard from again. But I saw it as an opportunity to go up there and make a name for myself. Syracuse was atrocious in basketball, and I was intrigued by the prospect of trying to help a program get off its knees."

His arrival at the hilly campus overlooking the city of Syracuse and Onondaga Lake would change his life and mark the beginning of a remarkable, half-century run of basketball success at the school. It also would profoundly impact the life of the nerdy, small-town kid from Lyons who would become his college roommate and lifelong friend.

• • •

Phil Schoff was playing ping-pong with basketball teammate Richie Duffy in Watson Hall on the Syracuse campus at the beginning of his sophomore year when he met Jimmy Boeheim for the first time. "He was sitting there, watching us play, and he started talking to us about how he was going to play basketball at SU," Schoff recalled. "And I said, 'Really.' I knew the names of the incoming freshmen who had been offered scholarships, and I knew Boeheim's name wasn't on the list. So I said to Jimmy, 'I don't recall your name being on the list,' and he said, 'Well, I don't have a scholarship yet, but I will.' I remember thinking to myself, 'I doubt it, kid.' See, Jimmy wasn't exactly what I'd call a physical specimen. He had thick glasses. He looked frail, almost emaciated, nothing like a major college athlete."

Freshman Sam Penceal, a highly recruited forward out of New York City's Boys High, had the same reaction as Schoff during his first encounter with the bespectacled, string-bean teenager from the sticks. "Jim was so darn thin that you figured he wouldn't be able to stand his ground against a gentle breeze, let alone a basketball opponent," he said. "I remember his legs and arms being like toothpicks. He—not Pete Maravich—was the original floppy socks basketball player." But, unlike Pistol Pete, Boeheim's floppy socks weren't by design. "They were flopping," Penceal said, "because his calves were so skinny that his socks wouldn't stay up."

Other teammates experienced the same underwhelming first impressions that Schoff and Penceal did, making Boeheim's job of earning their respect and making the quantum leap from a small high school to a major college program all the more difficult. "You couldn't help but wonder if this guy was good enough he'd be there on a full ride like the rest of us," said Penceal, one of seven freshmen who had been given free tuition and board by SU coach Fred Lewis that fall because of their basketball potential. "And just about every one of us was from an urban area, so we just naturally figured that the competition we had faced was way fiercer than what Jimmy had faced. Looking back on it, he had a bunch of obstacles in his way that many of the rest of us didn't, which makes what he did wind up achieving even more impressive."

Not long after arriving at SU, Boeheim had a chance to discover firsthand what all the hype was about regarding Dave Bing, the hotshot recruit from the same Washington, D.C., neighborhood that had produced NBA legend Elgin Baylor. Bing, Boeheim, and several other players were shooting baskets in a creaky, claustrophobic gym overlooking Archbold Stadium one afternoon when they decided to pick teams and play a game. Boeheim drew the unenviable assignment of guarding Bing. Not since his toddling days when his father routinely clobbered him in ping-pong did Jimmy endure such a mismatch. "David kicked my butt really bad," he recalled. "He must have scored 30 straight on me. I remember walking off that court totally demoralized.

I really started to wonder if I had made the right decision coming to Syracuse. I really questioned whether I was good enough to play at this level. It was only later after seeing David do the same thing to every other player he went up against that I realized it wasn't necessarily that I was so bad but rather that David was so good."

Early on, Boeheim struggled to adjust not only to Division I basketball but also to life on a big campus. There were times when the shy teenager felt like an outcast. "Jim was very introverted, coming from a small town and all," Bing said. "I think he felt rejected to a certain degree. He didn't fit in. He definitely was a fish out of water. It was like he was starting out in some foreign country, even though he was only about 40 minutes from where he grew up."

Not having a scholarship didn't bother Boeheim until he learned that Lewis had made the same walk-on promise to two other freshmen. "Ol' Fred was a pretty smooth talker," he said, reflecting on the coach's recruiting ploy with admiration years later. "I was pissed when I found out. But, in retrospect, I think it wound up motivating me even more. I became determined to show Ol' Fred that I deserved that basketball scholarship."

To combat the loneliness and overcome his teammates' early perceptions of him, Boeheim immersed himself in his books and basketball. First-year collegians were not eligible to play varsity basketball in those days, so Jimmy and the other members of his recruiting class played on the freshman team, which was called the Tangerines, a clever takeoff on the varsity moniker, the Orangemen. At first, his coaches didn't know what to make of all the questions Boeheim asked. His insatiable desire to expand his basketball IQ initially threw them for a loop. "I thought he was being a smart aleck," Lewis said. "You'd tell him to do something, and he asked why. I didn't realize for a long time that he wasn't trying to be a wise guy, but really wanted to know what was going on. His questions made us better coaches." And their answers helped make him a better player. "He had what I'd call an 'eye for the ball,'" said Roy Danforth, Lewis' top assistant who later would become the head coach at SU and hire Boeheim to join his staff. "Rebounds and loose balls would wind up in Jimmy's hands because he studied shooters and angles and knew where missed shots would wind up. Plus, he was always on the move, always hustling." In fact, some compared him to a poor-man's John Havlicek because, like the Boston Celtics All-Star, the lanky Boeheim would be in motion the entire time he was on the floor, often wearing out defenders who didn't have the endurance to keep up with him. "He was like a marathoner," Penceal said. "No wonder he was so skinny."

But maybe the brightest thing young Boeheim did was take advantage of Bing's magnetic ability to attract two or three defenders. "I could do the math," he said. "If three guys were on David, then at least two of us should be open, and I made sure I got open because I knew David, with his great court vision, his unselfishness, and great passing ability, was going to find the open man." And shooting and finishing plays were two of Boeheim's greatest strengths. "He was a great garbage player," Danforth said. "After a game you would look at his stats and say, 'Hey, that guy killed us.' Jimmy learned fast. He just followed Bing around and took the ball when Bing couldn't shoot it." Slowly but surely, Boeheim began to win the respect of his teammates. One incident, in particular, spoke to his toughness. During one of the early freshman practices, he went one-on-one against Fran Pinchot, a bruising 6'3", 220-pounder who was on scholarship. Pinchot elbowed Boeheim, breaking his glasses. "I picked up the pieces, went to the locker room, and taped them up," Boeheim recalled. "And, then, I came back for more." Bing and his teammates were impressed. "Jim sent a strong message when he did that," he said. "He wasn't going to be intimidated. He wasn't going to back down."

Word about Bing's dominance in practice and scrimmages soon spread throughout campus, and on December 2, 1963, 3,069 spectators—nearly 10 times more than the average varsity crowd the previous two years—showed up at Manley Field House to see the frosh phenom's first collegiate game. Bing did not disappoint, scoring 23 points, hauling in nine rebounds, and handing out six assists as the Tangerines pummeled the Morrisville frosh 85–31. The varsity game followed, but nearly two-thirds of the spectators left, raving about Bing and his promising supporting cast as they headed back to their dorms. The embarrassing trend of Bing & Co. turning in big games and the spectators leaving before the varsity tipoff would continue throughout the winter. "I know the varsity guys weren't too thrilled about it, but we found it very encouraging to receive support like that right off the bat," Penceal said. "We players and those fans could sense that something big was about to transpire, and people naturally wanted to be a part of it from the ground floor up." Bing finished with a freshman-record 25.7 points per game average and 11.3 rebounds per game as the Tangerines went 13–4. Not included in that record were several closed-door scrimmages against the SU varsity. Although the upperclassmen had shown more spunk under Lewis, improving from 2–22 to 8–13, they proved no match for the Bing-led frosh, who routinely beat them in those practice games. "That, too, obviously gave us confidence about the future," Penceal said. "Things were looking up for SU basketball." And for Boeheim, too. After averaging about six points and five rebounds per game, he had proven to himself, his teammates, and his coach that he belonged. "Jimmy was very unassuming, but he definitely could shoot," Bing said. "He played away from the ball, and he was able to move well to get open. He loved the game, and he knew what his skill level was and what he could do. He also worked as hard as any of us, and by the end of the year, he had the respect of all of us."

That summer, Lewis made good on his promise and called Boeheim to tell him that he would be receiving the basketball scholarship that originally had been reserved for Pinchot, who had been thrown out of school after driving without a license and getting into an accident. The irony was not lost on Boeheim, who remembered how Pinchot had intentionally elbowed him in the face during one of the early practices that season. The skinny kid from little Lyons had once again managed the last laugh. Another group of skeptics had been converted.

Lewis noticed that Boeheim and Bing were developing a good chemistry on the court, so he decided to try to make their bond even stronger by having the two backcourtmates become roommates. Bing was less than excited at first. "When I saw Coach Lewis had made him my roommate, there was no question in my mind that I had drawn a deadbeat," he said. "You looked at him looking at you behind those glasses, and you just knew you weren't going to have any fun that season." Boeheim, though, had a different reaction to the news. He was ecstatic about the opportunity to room with the Big Man On Campus, but he also understood Bing's reservations. "Hey, I was a hick," he said. "I came here with two pairs of Hush Puppies and two pairs of pants. I was lucky to have him as a roommate. I was very argumentative, and I didn't know how to deal with people. Dave was very organized, very meticulous, and I was just the opposite."

The pairing of the dignified, neatness-freak African American from the big city and the geeky, self-admitted white slob from the boondocks indeed seemed like a reach. Boeheim and Bing were "The Odd Couple" before Felix Unger and Oscar Madison had television viewers in stitches with their immensely popular 1970s sitcom. "Dave's side of the room would be immaculate, everything in its place," Boeheim recalled. "My side looked like the demolition derby had just blown through." Boeheim's sloppiness annoyed his roommate, as did his study habits. "He had a gift," Bing recalled. "He was blessed with a photographic memory. So, the night before an exam, he would cram and memorize everything. I couldn't do that. I had to study for several days leading up to the exam. I envied him for being able to do that."

Given their disparate personalities and backgrounds, the potential was there for disaster. But the two wound up getting along famously and becoming the best of friends. When officials from the Naismith Memorial Basketball Hall of Fame asked Boeheim who his presenter would be at the 2004 induction ceremonies, the coach immediately answered: "Dave Bing." And during the opening of his acceptance speech, Boeheim paid homage to his friend and former classmate, saying: "When I was that walk-on at Syracuse who couldn't really play that well, Dave was there. And he always kind of looked out for me, as a good roommate should. He kind of got me through those years when I could just play a little bit. When you played with Dave Bing, you didn't have to be very good because two or three guys on the other team were guarding him."

Bing's influence on Jimmy went beyond the court. He joked that he had to smooth out the rough edges of his country cousin. "I had the job of urbanizing Jim Boeheim, in terms of his dress, music, slang, giving him insight on what it was like to live in the inner city," Bing said. "He never made his bed, never washed his clothes because he took them home and let his mother wash them, while the rest of us fended for ourselves. He was very opinionated. He never thought he was wrong. He was very argumentative. But we got along all right." Bing said he remembers many occasions when he and Jim would talk deep into the night. "We'd spend a lot of time, a lot of late nights, talking about life and talking about basketball and what our goals and objectives and desires were," he said. By then, it was pretty obvious that Bing would have a bountiful career playing the game of basketball, but he would tell Boeheim how his real dream was to eventually run his own business. "I want to be the one calling the shots some day," he told his roommate. And Boeheim talked about someday coaching basketball after first attempting to play it professionally. As it turned out, both of their dreams came true—Bing built his own successful steel company before becoming mayor of Detroit, and Boeheim became the most successful coach in Syracuse University history.

Though he had a reputation for being quiet and dignified, there was a devilish side to Bing that Boeheim and others became privy to. Bing loved to pull practical jokes on his teammates, then plead innocence. Boeheim occasionally fell prey to Bing's shenanigans, but one day in the mid-1960s, he paid him back tenfold. Boeheim invited Bing and two of his teammates home for Thanksgiving dinner in Lyons. As they traveled west along Route 31, Bing asked him what his father did for a living. "Oh, you know," Boeheim said, shrugging. "He works." It wasn't until the car stopped in front of the red brick colonial at 77 Williams St. that Bing received his answer. There, in the front yard next to a birch tree was a prominent white wooden sign with black lettering reading: BOEHEIM'S FUNERAL HOME. Bing felt his heart begin to race. "You mean, you live here...in that house," he stammered. "You mean you grew up in a funeral home, with the bodies and everything?" Boeheim grinned ear to ear and nodded his head. Bing said he did not get much sleep that night. "We were eating the turkey in the kitchen, and there was a body in the next room. I wouldn't walk around the house alone. It was terrible at night. All the guys were banging on the walls and creeping around on their bellies opening doors. I was petrified." The following year—at the urging of Bing the practical joker—he and Boeheim rounded up the freshmen players and drove to Lyons. Everyone but the first-year players knew that they were about to spend a scary night in the funeral home.

A new era in Syracuse basketball—a run that continues unabated today, nearly a half century later—was launched during the 1963–64 season, as Bing and his classmates made their Orangemen varsity debuts along with Chuck Richards, a prized player who had transferred from the U.S. Military Academy at West Point. SU won four of its first six games—twice as many victories as it had racked up two seasons earlier—but national notice that the Orangemen no longer were college basketball patsies wasn't served until just after Christmas at the Hurricane Classic in Miami, Florida. Powered by Bing, Syracuse opened with a 76–71 win against a Princeton team featuring that season's player of the year, Bill Bradley. Lewis assigned Penceal to cover Bradley, and the sophomore defensive specialist did a superb job, as Bradley finished with a season-low 17 points before fouling out midway through the second half.

The Orangemen then won the Classic with an 86–85 overtime victory against a Miami team featuring Rick Barry, who would go on to lead the NCAA and later the NBA in scoring. The winning basket was scored by Bob Murray, one of the few seniors to see much action that season. Interestingly, Murray also scored the winning layup in the final seconds of the next-to-the-last game of the 1961–62 season against Boston College to snap SU's 27-game losing streak. "I think that tournament proved to us that we could play with anybody," Penceal said. "Unfortunately, it also kind of led to us getting some big heads." Consecutive losses to St. John's, LaSalle, and Army brought the Orangemen back to earth. But they regrouped to win 11 of their last 14 to finish 17–7 and earn a berth in the National Invitational Tournament. Although they lost to New York University in the first round of the tourney, the season had been a rousing success, and Bing had brought national attention to the program that had entered that campaign having lost 54 of its previous 68 games. The sleek guard from the nation's capital had lived up to his advance billing, establishing a sophomore record with 556 points, a 22.2 points-per-game average, while also averaging 8.2 rebounds per contest. Boeheim, meanwhile, had seen plenty of action off the bench and finished with a respectable 5.2 points per game.

Expectations were understandably soaring heading into the 1964–65 season. Many believed Syracuse's second invitation to the NCAA tournament was within reach, but the Orangemen underachieved, falling to 13–10 and failing to reach the postseason. "We were going to get an invitation to the NIT because we had finished strong, winning 11 of our last 13," Bing recalled. "But it's my understanding that Coach Lewis didn't think we deserved to go, so we didn't go. It was a message to us. We'd better get our act together." No message, though, needed to be delivered to Bing, who continued to elevate his game and his standing in the eyes of NBA talent assessors. He averaged 23.2 points and 12 rebounds per game to earn All-East and second-team All-America honors. The junior gained national attention by scoring 33 points in a televised 104–81 victory against LaSalle, then rewrote the school record book with 45 points—including the final 11 SU points—in a 93–90 victory versus Colgate. Despite his exceptional performances that season, Bing was disappointed. "I want to go to a big-time tournament, the NCAA," he told the school newspaper, *The Daily Orange*. "I want to go all the way."

Though disappointed with the team's showing that season, Lewis remained bullish on the future of the program because of Bing. The star player had brought national attention to Syracuse and had a magnetic impact on recruiting, enabling the coach to lure future stars Vaughn Harper, Rick Dean, Richie Cornwall, and George Hicker to SU. "This was another area in which Dave was such an asset," Boeheim said. "He wanted to get good players here. For example, when Hicker came here to visit, he'd almost made up his mind where he was going to school, and it wasn't SU. He changed in one day, in one day here. And Cornwall signed before he left. Vaughn Harper, same thing. Dave was just a super guy, and the big thing about him was his character and his leadership ability. That's one thing that was missing when he graduated, more than anything else, that leadership ability, the capacity to hold young players together."

Lewis was confident that the team would rebound during Bing's senior season, and he couldn't wait to see what his star would do for his final collegiate act. "If there is a better guard in the college ranks, I would like to see him," he said. "Even better, I would like to coach him. Dave is as good a player one-on-one as we have playing college ball today. He has all the moves. If he has a fault, it would be that he doesn't shoot enough. Dave is always looking until the last split second for the other fellow, and sometimes that doesn't pay off. If Bing were a selfish player, he could average 35 points per game and be right up there with the nation's leaders. But we wouldn't win ballgames that way." Lewis was especially proud of Bing's all-around game, comparing his style of play to NBA legend Oscar Robertson. "He has the same ability to rebound and make that important pass," Lewis said. The Syracuse coach wasn't the only one singing Bing's praises heading into his final college season. Boston Celtics coach Red Auerbach and Eddie Donovan of the New York Knicks told Lewis that Bing was ready for the NBA and that they would draft him first if they had the chance.

Bing's sidekick wasn't attracting any attention from the pro scouts, but Boeheim clearly had won over his coach, who had made him a starter during his junior season. The former walk-on responded with a consistently solid effort, averaging 8.9 points and 2.5 rebounds per game. That's not to say, though, that Boeheim was always a coach's dream. In a 2005 interview with *Syracuse Post-Standard* columnist Bud Poliquin, Danforth recalled times when Lewis would grumble about how opinionated and stubborn the guard could be. "Freddie would always say, 'That dang Boeheim. I want to wring the kid's neck. He won't do this. He won't do that.'" Danforth said. "Boeheim could be difficult. Really, really difficult." Difficult to the point of not following his coach's instructions. "I remember one game," Danforth continued. "I don't know who we were playing, but it was close down the stretch, so Freddie calls a timeout, and he wants to run a particular play. But

Boeheim and Sam Penceal say they want to run another play. Freddie says, 'No. No. No. We're going to run this play.' So, Boeheim and Penceal go back on the floor, and they run their own play. Freddie could have killed them. But that was Boeheim. He always had an opinion, and he was never wrong."

The fast-breaking Orangemen opened the 1965–66 season with seven consecutive wins, scoring 100 or more points five times, to earn a No. 7 ranking in the national polls. The tone was set in a 118–68 rout of Buffalo State in the opener as Bing scored 23 points. That romp was followed by another 50-point blowout, this time against the University at Buffalo, as Bing, the man nicknamed "Duke," "Pops," and "The Capitol Comet," exploded for 43 points. In late December, Syracuse took its high ranking and unblemished record to the West Coast for the Los Angeles Classic. The first-round matchup between SU and fourth-ranked Vanderbilt qualified as a classic, as Bing and Vandy forward Clyde Lee showed why they were destined to become consensus All-Americans. Lee finished with 39 points and 25 rebounds to down the Orangemen 113–98, despite a school-record 46 points by Bing. SU rebounded from that defeat, whipping Northwestern 105–75 and eastern rival St. John's 113–97, as Bing edged Lee and UCLA's Mike Warren for tournament MVP honors. "Dave was absolutely spectacular in that tournament against some of the best teams in the country," Hicker said. "It was just an honor, really, to be a witness to him putting our team on his shoulders and carrying us the way he did."

Although Bing was clearly the star, the 1965–66 team was far from a one-man show. In reality, the Orangemen were a well-balanced, unselfish team with four players—Bing, Hicker, Boeheim, and Rick Dean—averaging in double-digit scoring figures and a fifth, Harper, just missing, with nine points per game. The team shot 50 percent from the field and averaged an NCAA-record 99.9 points per game during the regular season. They finished just one basket shy of the century mark average as Penceal passed up a last-second shot in a 122–88 rout of Colgate in the finale because he didn't want to rub it in against the overmatched Red Raiders. Bing gave Syracuse fans a vintage going-away present in that game, scoring 31 points and dishing out 12 assists in his Manley Field House finale.

Boeheim, who finished the season shooting 56.5 percent from the field, was the third-leading scorer with 14.6 points per game. Although he was overshadowed by his famous backcourtmate most of the season, there was one game—a 120–85 victory against Cornell in early February—when the postgame honors went to him. Bing finished the contest with 39 points and a modern-day school record 25 rebounds, but a committee presented Boeheim, who had 25 points and three assists, with the Varsity Club Most Valuable Player Award. The thinking was that Boeheim was more deserving because he scored 11 points in the first four minutes of the game as Syracuse sprinted to a 14–1 lead and never looked back. "Jim deserved it," Bing told Bud VanderVeer of the *Syracuse Post-Standard* afterward. "He broke the game open." Boeheim, though, said he would have cast his ballot, if he had one, for his roommate. "I stole it away from Dave," he said, sheepishly. Lewis and Danforth had to push Boeheim to go to press row after the game so he could receive the trophy from former Syracuse basketball and football All-American Vic Hanson. "He was too embarrassed to go up and get it, but the thing is, he really deserved it," Danforth recalled. "He scored all of his points in the early going when the game was on the line. Honestly, he was the MVP that night, but he was having none of it. We had to beg him to accept it—I mean, beg him—and he finally did." In postgame interviews, Lewis' pride in Boeheim was obvious. "Jim has been one of our most underrated players all year," he said. "I'm happy he received a break."

For the third straight season, the Orangemen finished with a flourish, winning 11 of their final 13 games to go 21–5. Not only did they earn one of the 24 NCAA tournament bids, but they also were rewarded with a first-round bye. The Final Four that year was being played at the University of Maryland, not far from Bing's hometown. "We definitely wanted to get there for Dave," Hicker said. "We wanted him to be able to experience a championship in front of his family and friends." Penceal said the Orangemen also were hungering for a trip there because former Syracuse All-American football player John Mackey, at the time a star tight end with the Baltimore Colts, had promised them he would host a big party at his home. "John was one of the black players, along with Ernie Davis and Jim Brown, who had been so good to us African Americans when we were up for our recruiting trip," Penceal recalled. "And now that he was a star in the NFL, we were looking forward to taking him up on his offer to enjoy a big Syracuse celebration at his house."

On March 11, in Raleigh, North Carolina, the Orangemen easily disposed of Davidson 94–78 as Bing turned in a typical Bing all-around performance, with 20 points, 12 rebounds, and eight assists. The victory advanced them to the East Region finals, where they would meet Duke. The Blue Devils, from nearby Durham, would have a decided home-court advantage, but the Syracuse players, especially Bing, were confident they could overcome the pro-Duke crowd and a height disadvantage. That confidence was tested early, as the Orangemen shot poorly at the outset and found themselves down by as many as 16 points in the first half. Despite the worst shooting night of Bing's career—he finished 4-for-14—the Orangemen clawed back, thanks, in large part, to Boeheim's spirited play. He scored 15 points, two of them coming late in the game when he drove into the teeth of the Duke zone for a layup that put SU on top 74–72. But that would be the Orangemen's last gasp, as the Devils, led by All-American forward Jack Marin and guards Bob Verga and Steve Vacendak, went on a 19–7 run to win 91–81 and advance to the Final Four.

The loss was tough to take, especially for Bing, who finished with just 10 points, nearly 20 below his average. He picked up his fourth foul early in the second half, and that, along with foul trouble by Harper, stymied Syracuse on the boards against the much taller Blue Devils. "That's probably the worst game of Dave Bing's life," Danforth said. "He plays a regular game and we're in. But what are you going to do? One bad game and about 80 spectacular games over three seasons. No player in SU basketball ever had an impact equal to Dave Bing's."

Bing's 28.4 points-per-game average remains a school record 45 years later. He shot 54 percent from the field, 80 percent from the foul line; hauled in 10.8 rebounds per game; and averaged nearly seven assists per contest. Not only did he earn first-team honors on every All-American squad, but he also became the first basketball player to receive Syracuse University's athlete of the year award—a clear sign that hoops was no longer a poor stepchild on campus and never would be again. "The success we continue to enjoy can be traced directly back to Dave Bing," Boeheim said. "He's the guy who got things turned around here. He raised this program from the ashes."

A writer in the student yearbook, the *Onondagan*, was equally effusive and much more flowery with his praise, reaching back four decades to find a basketball campaign that had created similar excitement on the SU campus. "Not since its 1925–26 team was heralded as the national champion has Syracuse basketball drawn such praise from athletic circles," began the article. "Praise for the Orange this season flowed like milk and honey from The Promised Land. Not only did the hoopsters compile an impressive 22–6 record. Not only did they lead in national scoring statistics for months. But Coach Lewis' squad came within two points of becoming the first college team ever to average 100 points per game during an entire season. And Dave Bing walked off with the Hill's first All-American honors in the 39 years since Vic Hanson."

The ending may have been bittersweet, but Lewis looked back with pride on what Bing and his classmates had accomplished. He knew when he recruited Bing that the potential for greatness was there. But he never truly expected much from Boeheim. To see the gangly kid from the small town progress from walk-on to scholarship player to a starter averaging nearly 15 points per game was every bit as rewarding. "He was the worst leaper I ever had," Lewis reflected years later. "But by the time he graduated I thought he was the most underrated player in the East."

"If you play the game," Lewis continued, "you know sometimes you go against somebody who doesn't look like they can do it. You think, 'This will be an easy game. I'll kill this guy.' And by the end of the game, he's beaten your brains out. That was Jim. He had a tremendous advantage. People looked at him and thought every step would be his last, but that last step never came."

CHAPTER 5

Landing His Dream Job

ALTHOUGH HIS COLLEGE BASKETBALL playing career had officially ended with that loss to Duke in the 1966 East Regionals, Jim Boeheim had no desire to put away his sneakers and enter the "real world" after receiving his bachelor's degree in social sciences in May 1966. He, Dave Bing, and several other graduating Orangemen began playing for highly competitive semipro teams that were sponsored by restaurants and other businesses in small cities throughout upstate New York. The games— particularly the ones in which Bing played—would pack high school gymnasiums, where patrons were charged a nominal admission fee.

On a really good night, Boeheim might make $100 and receive free food and drinks, but he really would have played for nothing because he truly loved basketball and the high level of competition helped keep his skills sharp. That latter point was important, because he had another career goal in mind that everybody but him thought was a pipe dream. He wanted to play in the National Basketball Association, and he knew the only way that was going to happen was by convincing a team to bring him to training camp so he could showcase his competitiveness and his basketball intelligence.

With an assist from former Syracuse Nats stars Dolph Schayes and Paul Seymour, Boeheim was invited to the expansion Chicago Bulls' camp. The Bulls were coached at the time by ex-Nats standout Johnny

"Red" Kerr, who was happy to take a look at Boeheim, based on the recommendations of his friends and former teammates. No one gave Bing's college sidekick much of a chance, but the scrappy Boeheim wound up surprising people once more, making it all the way to the last two cuts. Being let go was a huge blow, and Boeheim returned home to ponder his future. He briefly considered entering the family funeral business, but his heart wasn't in it. He ultimately decided that he wanted to coach, and the door to that career was opened when Lewis offered him a position as a volunteer assistant.

In addition to helping out with the basketball program, Boeheim was asked to coach the SU golf team. The avid duffer gladly accepted the additional duties. He had earned two varsity letters playing golf for the Orangemen, going 4–1 and 2–5–1 in two seasons of match play as the No. 2 player behind Barry Buchsbaum in SU's five-man rotation. He and Buchsbaum consistently shot in the mid-to-upper 70s for a team that went 7–3 and 5–3 against a schedule that included the likes of Colgate, Cornell, Army, Penn State, Yale, and Penn. "Jim was just like he is on the basketball sidelines," recalled Buchsbaum. "He was a whiner. The only difference was that he would be swearing at himself instead of the referees, because golf is an individual sport. He'd miss a shot and start cursing at himself. He was very hard on himself. But he was a lot of fun to play with and a great teammate."

Boeheim held the golf coach's position until the program was disbanded in 1973. "As far as the press knows, we were undefeated every year because I never called in our scores when we lost," he joked. In reality, the Orangemen went 18–13–1 in dual matches he oversaw, according to research by the SU Sports Information Department. Boeheim enjoyed the opportunity to coach in relative anonymity, without fans or media scrutinizing his every decision. "The pay was lousy, but the perks were great," he said. "Coaches got to play a round every time their team did, and you didn't have a bunch of reporters around you afterward, hounding you about why you did this and why you did that. Plus, you didn't have to deal with referees."

To pick up a few extra bucks and sate his desire for hoops, Boeheim spent his weekends playing for the Scranton Miners in the Eastern Professional Basketball League, the forerunner to the old Continental Basketball Association, which was just a rung below the NBA on the professional basketball ladder. The Miners were coached by Seymour, the former Nats star who still lived in Syracuse. On Friday nights, he and Boeheim would climb into Seymour's '66 Oldsmobile 88 and speed down Route 81 to Scranton for weekend doubleheaders. Seymour usually let Boeheim do the driving, and "lead-footed Jimmy" would turn what was normally a two-hour drive into a 90-minute trek. "Oh, Christ, how that car rocked when Jimmy was driving," Seymour recalled in a 1991 interview. "It was like a rocket." On their trips back to Syracuse, Boeheim would dissect the weekend games and occasionally question some of Seymour's coaching decisions. "Jimmy always had his own ideas about basketball," he said. "But we had a hell of a lot of fun talking basketball."

The Miners were owned by Arthur Pachter, a lifelong basketball fan who ran a successful automotive supply company in the area. He purchased the team in the mid-1960s after reading a story in the local newspapers about the financially strapped franchise being in danger of leaving town. "I wound up owning it for about 20 years, and it was a money-losing proposition the entire way," he said. "But I would have done it all over again if I had the opportunity, because it was a hell of a lot of fun."

Although it was the minor leagues, the caliber of play was extremely high. "You have to remember, back then you only had 12 or 14 NBA teams [as opposed to 30 teams today], and each one had only a dozen players on a roster," Pachter said. "Plus, you didn't have the option of playing in Europe or Australia or South America the way kids do today. So, we'd get a lot of guys who had been great college players but weren't quite good enough to make the NBA. And we had guys who would wind up getting signed later by NBA clubs and other guys who had played there but had been let go. It was a competitive, exciting brand of ball because you had guys who were hungry to keep on playing and maybe get a shot at the next level. They truly were playing for the love of the game and not for the money. I know that for a fact because I was one of the guys signing the checks, and they weren't making much at all."

Pachter recalls paying Boeheim—who was one of his more consistent players—about $100 per game during his rookie season. By the time he officially retired from the Eastern League six years later, the former Syracuse walk-on was making roughly $200 per contest. "And don't forget," Pachter said, "he wasn't getting mileage. So out of that $100, he had to pay for gas to travel from Syracuse to Scranton or, when we were on the road, to places like Hartford, Connecticut, or Camden, New Jersey, or Wilmington, Delaware. That's a long drive, especially on a winter night, traveling 270 miles back to Syracuse after a game in Delaware."

But Boeheim never complained about the poor pay. For him, the experience was priceless. "He probably could have made more money, but he never made a stink about it," Pachter said. "He knew we were squeezed financially just to keep the ship afloat, so he always just said, 'Pay me what you think is fair.' The dollars were never the thing with him. He truly loved to play."

That was underscored by the fact he never missed a game despite the distances he had to travel, often on treacherous roads. "There were guys who lived in the next town over who missed games," recalled Jack Seitzinger, a former public relations director for the Miners who went on to become a longtime sports editor at one of the Scranton newspapers. "But Jimmy Boeheim never did. There could be four feet of snow out there, and he'd find a way to get to the arena if there was a game being played."

Jim Blandino remembers working at his uncle's service station in Lyons one wintry Sunday morning in the mid-1960s when Boeheim pulled in to fill up his car. A blizzard was sweeping across western New York, the snow falling so heavily that you could barely see 10 feet in front of you. "It was so bad out that day that my uncle had considered not opening up the station," Blandino said. "But there's Jimmy, undaunted, the only vehicle—other than the snowplows—on the road. I asked him where he was going, and he told me he had a basketball game that night in Scranton. I said, 'Jim, there's no way in hell you're going to make it to Scranton in these conditions. Turn on your radio. They're telling people to stay off the roads unless it's an emergency.' He just looked at me and said, 'Well, I got a ballgame.' I filled his tank, and he paid me and took off. That was Jimmy. He could be as stubborn as a mule, and nothing was ever going to get in the way of him and a basketball game." Boeheim laughed when the story was recounted years later. "He's right," the coach said. "And there were times when I'd drive through those blizzards only to find that the game had been canceled."

Nearly a half-century later, Pachter has fond memories of Jim Boeheim showing up early for a Sunday night game in Scranton and plopping himself down on the couch in the owner's house to watch the NBA Game of the Week on the tube. "He was a 20-something who couldn't get enough of the game," Pachter said. "You just knew that somehow, someway it was going to wind up being his life's work." Boeheim wound up playing six seasons of minor-league basketball— his best campaign being 1968–69, when he averaged 23.4 points, 3.8 rebounds, and 4.5 assists per game to earn All-Star honors. He twice led Scranton to league titles and finished his career with a 17 points-per-game average. He was named honorable mention on the CBA's all-time team. (After Boeheim's playing days, the Eastern League officially changed its name to the Continental Basketball Association.)

Phil Schoff, a former Syracuse basketball player who spent time with the NBA's Atlanta Hawks, remembers going against Boeheim on several occasions in the Eastern League. "Jimmy was a very good Eastern League player," he said. "He was a very, very smart player. Even though he had filled out a little bit since when I practiced against him at SU, he still wasn't imposing. He was still the kind of guy you looked at and didn't think he could hurt you, but he could. I remember my coach saying, 'I want you to play Boeheim,' and he wound up doing very well against me. You'd turn your back on him for an instance, and he'd score a basket on you. Just a very, very heady player."

He clearly was a coach in the making on the floor. "We had guys on those clubs who went on to play in the NBA and ABA, but all of them deferred to Jim because they could see how intelligent he was about the game," Pachter said. "He definitely was the floor leader. That he wound up becoming a coach doesn't surprise me in the least."

After Boeheim's rookie season, Seymour left to take a job as the Detroit Pistons' head scout. He believed Boeheim had the ability and smarts to play in the NBA and asked him to come to the Motor City for a tryout. The offer was very appealing, particularly because it would have given him a chance to reunite with his old teammate and good friend, Dave Bing. But after much soul-searching, Boeheim told Seymour, "No." "I could have hooked on with the Pistons, but I tried to be realistic," he said. "As much as I would have loved to have played in the NBA, I realized it was time to move on."

Although he turned down Seymour's tempting offer, Boeheim continued to play Eastern League games on weekends for several more seasons. Pachter couldn't have been more pleased to have someone like him to depend upon. "Jimmy was a great guy and still is," he said. "I always joked with him that Syracuse University and me are the only two places he's ever gotten paychecks from. Yeah, I know, he worked for his father at the funeral home back in Lyons, but I don't think his old man ever paid him."

In 1968, while enrolled in graduate school at Syracuse, Boeheim's role with the basketball program began to expand. Following a messy 11–14 season in which Lewis had several publicized disputes with players and the administration, the coach decided to leave Syracuse to become the athletics director at the University of California at Sacramento. "It's not worth the aggravation to remain at SU," Lewis told reporters before leaving for the West Coast.

Lewis' departure opened the door for the gregarious, more personable Roy Danforth to become head coach, and he immediately added the hard-working Boeheim to his staff as his assistant. "To show you how different things were," Boeheim said, "I was Roy's only assistant, and I wasn't making a dime. But I understood that you had to pay your dues. I think a lot of young assistants these days don't understand that. It was a great training ground for me because I did everything from recruiting to running practices."

Besides assisting the varsity, Boeheim coached the Tangerines' freshman squad to a 16–2 record during the 1968–69 season. Three years later, his dedication to the program was rewarded when he was awarded a full-time salary and benefits. "Roy was the face of the program, talking to the media, overseeing things," said former SU center Bob Parker. "But Jim was the nuts-and-bolts, behind-the-scenes guy. He ran practices, scouted, recruited—you name it. The two of them seemed to work well together because Roy was a glib, personable guy who loved to talk, particularly to anyone with a notepad or tape recorder. And Jim was a guy who preferred to just deal with the basketball side of things. He didn't care for the other stuff the head coach was required to do."

In 1971–72—after two mediocre seasons in which the Orangemen went a combined 21–28—SU basketball began to soar under Danforth

and his up-and-coming assistant. Led by Bill Smith, a towering 6'11"
center from Rochester's Rush-Henrietta High School who led the team
in scoring (22.7 points per game) and rebounding (14.5 rebounds
per game), Syracuse went 19–7 and secured a spot in the National
Invitational Tournament, where it lost to Michigan in the first round.
The following season, Smith graduated, forcing the Orangemen to go
with a much shorter lineup. The lack of height clearly didn't seem to
bother the team that became known as "Roy's Runts." Unveiling two
new hotshots—Greg "Kid" Kohls and Bob Dooms—the Orangemen
improved to 22–6 and reached the second round of the NIT before
being eliminated by Maryland. Flashy guard Dennis DuVal and
rebounding forward Rudy Hackett powered SU to a 24–5 record and
its first NCAA appearance in seven years during the 1972–73 season.
The Orangemen beat Maryland in the first round before dropping a
69–68 heartbreaker to Pennsylvania. DuVal, known to the Manley
Field House faithful as "Sweet D" because of his silky moves and flair
for showmanship, averaged 20.6 points and Hackett 11.7 rebounds as
Syracuse went 19–7 the next year, losing in the opening round of the
NCAAs to Oral Roberts in overtime.

That set the stage for the 1974–75 season—one of the most
improbable and exciting campaigns in SU basketball history. Despite
the graduation of the entertaining DuVal, who would become the
city of Syracuse's first African American police chief, the Orangemen
figured to be an Eastern powerhouse again. Hackett, who had benefited
greatly from individual sessions with Boeheim, was back for his senior
year, as was Jimmy Lee, a deadly outside shooter. The two roommates
and co-captains would form a potent inside-outside combination that
would give opposing defenses fits. Supplementing them was Chris
Sease, a soaring small forward whose leaping ability had earned him
the nickname "Rocket Man." The offense would be run by a speedy and
creative point guard named Jimmy "Bug" Williams, and centers Earnie

Seibert and Bob Parker provided big bodies to help Hackett and Sease dominate the boards.

The Orangemen started fast, winning 11 of 13 games to earn the 20th spot in the Associated Press college basketball rankings. But a midseason slump in which they lost five of eight not only dropped them out of the polls but had many wondering if they had the stuff to make the NCAAs. "It was just one of those difficult stretches, but we had a pretty experienced team, so we didn't panic," Lee recalled. "With this being the final season for Rudy and me, there was no way we wanted to go out with a whimper. Fortunately, we got our slump out of the way and got hot at the right time."

The Orangemen closed with four consecutive victories to finish their regular season at 18–7. Their NCAA tournament fate would be determined at the Eastern Collegiate Athletic Conference playoffs in Buffalo against upstate rivals Niagara and St. Bonaventure, two teams they had defeated during the regular season. SU rolled over Niagara by 18 points in the first round but were only slight favorites heading into the championship game against a Bonnies team that had taken them into overtime before losing in their first meeting a month earlier. After that game, several Bonaventure players had told reporters that the Orangemen had been lucky to escape with a victory. Lee procured copies of the newspaper stories with the condescending comments and made sure each of his teammates saw them. Spurred on by the bulletin board fodder, SU crushed the Bonnies 100–81 as Lee (22 points) and Hackett (32 points, 21 rebounds) shined.

The victory earned the Orangemen an NCAA bid, but the selection committee didn't do them any favors, pitting them against Philadelphia-based LaSalle University at the Palestra, smack-dab in the middle of the City of Brotherly Love. But the SU players didn't seem bothered by the prospect of playing what amounted to a LaSalle home game. Hackett and Lee again were at the top of their games, combining for 50 points as Syracuse defeated the Explorers 87–83 in overtime. SU did catch a break at the end of regulation when a short jumper by Joe "Jelly Bean" Bryant bounced off the rim. "That gave us a second life," said Boeheim, who would go on to coach Jelly Bean's legendary son, Kobe Bryant, in the 2008 Olympics. "It also gave us confidence in the next two games we played, which also went down to the wire."

The next game would be in Providence, Rhode Island, against Dean Smith's powerful North Carolina squad. No one in the media was giving the upstart Orangemen any chance against the sixth-ranked Tar Heels, whose star-studded lineup featured future NBA players Phil Ford, Walter Davis, Mitch Kupchak, and Tommy LaGarde. But Smith voiced concern in the pregame press conference, telling the media, "We know Syracuse is a hell of a team. I think Roy has done a great job coaching that team, especially the way he's got them running the fast break. I think it's going to be a hell of a game."

Danforth and his players thought it would be, too. "I think we've got a good shot at North Carolina," he said when it was his turn to address the media. "They've got a hell of a club, but so do we. Sometimes you can be a little awed of a team from a conference with the ACC's reputation, but our players aren't going to be awed by North Carolina. That's not going to be a problem." And it wasn't. Riding the confidence built during their seven-game winning streak, the Orangemen gave North Carolina all it could handle and trailed by just a point at halftime.

What made that slim deficit even more impressive was that the Orangemen had gone toe-to-toe with their heavily favored opponent, despite receiving virtually nothing out of Hackett, who got into foul trouble early and spent the final six minutes of the half on the bench. "At halftime, Roy reminded our players that we were down by just one point despite the fact Rudy hadn't scored a single point," Boeheim said. "I thought that was a great point to make because it told our guys that not only can we play with North Carolina, even when we're facing a bit of adversity, but that we could definitely beat them."

SU stormed out to a lead in the second half, but North Carolina eventually regrouped. Leading by one with 30 seconds remaining, Ford attempted to inbound the ball but threw it away. After their successful inbounds, the Orangemen worked the ball around against the Tar Heels' zone. Lee passed the ball inside to Hackett, and four defenders immediately surrounded him. The 6'8" forward calmly zipped the ball out to Lee, who was positioned just beyond the foul line, about 18 feet from the basket. As he had done thousands of times in his life, Lee let fly with a jumper that found nothing but net to put Syracuse on top 77–76 with five seconds remaining. A deafening roar erupted in the Providence Civic Center, where the majority of the fans had clearly adopted the underdog Orange. Smith called timeout to diagram one last desperation play. On the SU bench, Boeheim told Parker, who would be guarding the player throwing the inbounds pass, to just stand there and jump up and down with arms extended. "He warned me not to move," Parker recalled. "But I got caught up in the excitement of the moment." Kupchak, who was inbounding the ball, began running down the end line in hopes that Parker would move with him and bowl over a stationary Tar Heel and be called for a foul. And that's almost what happened, but, fortunately for him and the Orangemen, no foul was called and Kupchak's pass to Mickey Bell bounced off his hands and careened out of bounds. Jimmy Williams was fouled on the ensuing inbounds and sank a free throw to make the final score 78–76. No one was more relieved with the result than Parker, who could have become one of the biggest goats in SU hoops history. "If they had called me for that foul, I think Coach Boeheim might have shot me," Parker joked years later. After the game, the referee admitted to reporters that he had blown the call.

The win advanced the Orangemen into the regional finals against a Kansas State team that was expected to do to them what North

Carolina didn't. But once again the clock failed to strike 12 for this Cinderella team. This time it would be Hackett who would make a game-saving shot that would etch his name into Orange lore. With five seconds remaining and SU trailing 76–74, Williams took the inbounds pass, dribbled the length of the floor, and flipped the ball to Hackett, who was stationed about five feet from the basket. He bobbled the ball before throwing up a left-handed shot that went through the cylinder as the buzzer sounded. The basket tied the game, and the Orangemen dominated in overtime and won 95–87, to earn their first trip to the Final Four.

Their luck finally ran out in San Diego, where they were trounced by Kentucky 95–79 in the semifinal, then lost a heartbreaker to Louisville in overtime in the consolation game of a Final Four that would be best remembered for legendary UCLA coach John Wooden winning his 10th and final NCAA basketball championship. The journey to college basketball's grandest stage made an indelible impression on Boeheim. "It wasn't as big as it is now, but it was bigger than anything we had experienced before," he said. "We definitely wanted to experience it again. But the big thing was not just getting back there but getting to feel what it was like to win it all."

Despite the loss of several prominent players from their Final Four team, the Orangemen turned in another solid season, going 20–9 in 1975–76. But after sprinting to an 18–4 start, they hit a slide reminiscent of the not-so-distant bad old days, losing their final four games of the regular season. As a result, they had to win the two-game ECAC tournament to qualify for the NCAAs—which they did. But there was no March Magic this time, as they were bounced out of the Midwest Regionals in the first round by Texas Tech 69–56.

About a month after SU's elimination from the NCAA tournament, Danforth informed athletics director Les Dye that he was resigning to take the Tulane University head coaching job. The timing of the resignation—just two weeks before National Letter of Intent Signing Day—caught many by surprise. Some critics surmised that Danforth had already made up his mind about bolting for the New Orleans college weeks before but had delayed his decision because he was a delegate for Democratic presidential candidate Henry "Scoop" Jackson and didn't want to leave until he had cast his ballot in the New York state primary. An editorial in the school newspaper, *The Daily Orange*, ripped Danforth for putting his own interests ahead of the program that had given him his first head coaching opportunity. Although the manner in which he departed may have irked some, there was no denying that Danforth had built upon the foundation Lewis had established. His squads had won 68 percent of their games and made it to four consecutive NCAA tournaments and the school's first Final Four. In his hastily called farewell news conference, Danforth thanked the university and the community and also put in a plug for Boeheim to replace him, saying, "He is as responsible for our success over the past six years as I am."

In retrospect, the promotion of Boeheim to the top spot seemed like a no-brainer. But the move did not come without a little drama. Before landing his dream job—the one he still holds nearly four decades later—Boeheim interviewed for the University of Rochester head coaching position that had become vacant when Lyle Brown, the Yellowjackets head man for 19 seasons, retired. "They were Division II back then," he said. "But they were talking about going to Division I." Boeheim walked out of that morning meeting believing that the Rochester job was his. But as he drove back to the Salt City for a meeting with the Syracuse University search committee, he knew, deep down, that the position he really wanted was the one open at his alma mater.

The Syracuse search committee of Dye, vice-chancellor Cliff Winters, trustee W. Carroll Coyne, and board chairman David Bennett were high on the 31-year-old Boeheim but thought it also might be wise to interview several men with Division I head-coaching experience. Among the candidates they discussed were Tom Young, who in just this third season at Rutgers had guided the Scarlet Knights to the 1976 Final Four, and Bill Blair, whose Virginia Military Institute team had lost to Rutgers in the East Regional finals. In a 2002 interview with Mike Waters of the *Syracuse Post-Standard*, Bennett recalled the name of Michigan assistant Bill Frieder also being broached.

"At that point, we said if we're talking about assistant coaches, we've got Jim about to come in here anyway," Bennett said.

The committee members didn't really know what to expect from Boeheim because he had kept such a low profile as an assistant. "He never took credit for the team's achievements," Bennett said. "But, now, it was his opportunity to tell us what he had done." Boeheim was aware that several outside candidates were being considered. But he also knew that he had the UR job in his hip pocket, and he wasn't afraid to use it as leverage. "They wanted to open the process up," he recalled. "I told them I was going to go to Rochester if I didn't get the job. I didn't want to wait around for the interview process. I strongly believed that if you had an assistant who's capable and been there and done the work, he should be given a chance in that situation."

Boeheim also stressed that there was a sense of urgency because National Letter of Intent Day was just around the corner and that prized recruits were about to be lost. He mentioned how the Orangemen were locked in a recruiting battle with St. Bonaventure University for the services of Roosevelt Bouie, a highly coveted 6'11" center from Kendall, a small town northwest of Rochester. Boeheim told the committee that he believed he had the inside track on landing him. "But time was of the essence," the coach explained. "If [the committee] was going to wait two more weeks before making a decision, we would have lost out on the guy who really could help the program take off."

Boeheim's interview went well, but the feedback the committee received from current and former players may have been the deciding factor. The player who spoke most passionately about Boeheim was guard Jim "Bug" Williams. "Jim Williams said, 'Coach Boeheim put in the 2-3 [zone defense], Coach Boeheim did this, Coach Boeheim did that," Bennett recalled. "They were not only very affirmative about him, but they wanted to make clear how critical he was to the team's success and how they thought it was obvious he should be the guy."

After Boeheim left the meeting, the committee deliberated for about 30 minutes before calling him back in to tell him the job was his. "It was not obvious that Jim would be the choice at the beginning of the two-hour meeting," Bennett said. "It was only when he spoke on his own behalf and the players spoke about him that it became clear that there was no point looking elsewhere."

Details of a three-year $75,000 deal were worked out quickly, and on April 3, 1976, the walk-on from Lyons was introduced as the seventh men's basketball coach in school history.

"We already felt that Jim was the best assistant coach in the country," Syracuse University chancellor Melvin Eggers said at the news conference introducing Boeheim. "The only question the committee had to decide was whether the pick would be Jim or an established coach. We received overwhelming support for Jim from the present members of this team and from several former players. Because of his keen basketball mind and his knowledge of what had to be done to keep Syracuse basketball at the top, the [search] committee quickly realized the best man for the job was right here." Boeheim told reporters he had always had his eye on the head coaching job and said he asked for a three-year contract because, "I wanted the opportunity to develop my own program." He also joked that, unlike his predecessor, he would avoid politics. Asked whom he was supporting in the upcoming Presidential election, Boeheim quipped: "Roosevelt Bouie."

Several newspaper stories about his hiring included a parenthetical explanation about how to pronounce his name (BAY-hyme). Reporters felt compelled to include that information because despite Boeheim's background as a player and six seasons as an assistant coach, he was somewhat of an anonymous figure even among Syracuse basketball fans, having been greatly overshadowed by his former teammate, Dave Bing, and his former boss, Roy Danforth. Interestingly, his name would continue to be botched by fans and sportscasters alike in the ensuing decades.

Boeheim thanked the athletic administrators at the University of Rochester, saying that his talks with them had been excellent. But he admitted Syracuse was the job he wanted all along, adding, "Everybody wants to coach where he played." With National Letter of Intent Day just a week away, Boeheim said he would immediately hit the recruiting trail in hopes of landing Bouie. "Anytime you have a coaching change at this late date, it will affect the recruiting situation," he said. "But I have seen all the recruits personally, at least once, so it should not make that much of a difference. Roosevelt Bouie is still our No. 1 kid. Our center position has been weak, and we need some support there." Boeheim also told the media, "There's no real difference in coaching philosophy between Roy and myself. I plan to stress defense a little more, but that's about it." Players wouldn't be the only personnel Boeheim would need to recruit. He'd also need to find two new assistant coaches, because Tommy Green, who also had worked on Danforth's staff at SU, had announced he was following his boss to Tulane.

News of Boeheim's hiring was cause for celebration in his hometown of Lyons. His parents were understandably thrilled, but the person most proud may have been Jimmy's mentor and former high school coach, Dick Blackwell. "He was really shy when I coached him," Blackwell said, reminiscing about Boeheim with Norm Jollow, a sportswriter with the *Finger Lakes Times*. "He would hardly look at you when you were talking to him. But I watched him being interviewed on TV, and he's really poised. He's matured, and if he comes off with his players and in recruiting as well as he did on TV, he should be great." Not long after watching the news conference on television, Blackwell wrote his protégé a letter telling him that there was no doubt in his mind that he would become a successful head coach. "There's never been anybody more dedicated," continued Blackwell, who joked that Boeheim must have been born with a basketball in his hands. "I'm sure all he dreams about is basketball. He didn't know anything else." The news of Boeheim's promotion didn't surprise Blackwell one iota. "I understand a couple of years ago, when Roy was thinking of going somewhere else, the Hardwood Club of Syracuse was reported to say they wouldn't mind losing Danforth but wanted to keep Jimmy. They knew how well he worked with the kids. I'll tell you this much: nobody will ever be more completely dedicated than he will. It's all he ever wanted to do."

Nearly a quarter of a century later, as the school prepared to honor Boeheim by naming the Carrier Dome basketball court after him, the coach was asked what would have happened if the SU search committee had wanted to interview another candidate. "I would've probably ended up in Rochester, and they'd be naming that court after somebody else," he said. Of the other candidates, Young stayed at Rutgers until 1985 before taking over at Old Dominion University. Blair left VMI that spring for the University of Colorado, where he spent five seasons before embarking on a long career in the National Basketball Association, capped by the head coaching job of the Minnesota Timberwolves. Frieder took over for the legendary Johnny Orr at Michigan and left for Arizona State in 1989 just as the Wolverines were beginning their run to the national championship. And Mike Neer, a former assistant at the Naval Academy, took the Rochester job, leading the Yellowjackets to 563 wins and a national title before retiring following the 2009–10 season. "It's funny how things worked out for each of us," Boeheim said years later. "One move can have a domino effect. It can impact an awful lot of lives."

The moves Boeheim made that spring recruiting players and assistant coaches would have a tremendous impact on the start of his Hall of Fame coaching career. Mission No. 1 would be to land Bouie. The top high school player in upstate New York had never warmed up to the fast-talking, chain-smoking Danforth, but he developed a quick rapport with Boeheim. "We were both from small towns in upstate New York, and he came across as laid-back and that appealed to me because I'm laid-back, too," recalled Bouie. The prized recruit had visited Georgia Tech and Santa Clara but had narrowed his choices to SU and St. Bonaventure by that April. He actually was leaning toward the Bonnies until he heard the news about Boeheim getting the SU job. "My coach at Kendall [Dick Reynolds] knew that I really liked Syracuse," he recalled. "He knew that I liked Coach Boeheim and I also liked [Bonaventure coach] Jim Satalin. One day, I came in to Coach Reynolds' office and he said, 'Roosevelt, did you see the paper?'" Reynolds turned over the *Rochester Democrat and Chronicle* sports section to reveal the story about Boeheim's hiring. "A phone call was made," Bouie said, "and Coach Boeheim came out, and I signed my letter of intent."

"I don't think people appreciate what a huge, huge get that was for us," Boeheim said. "Roosevelt tends to get overlooked by people when they talk about the impact certain players had on this program. But he played a big role in getting my career as a head coach off to a fast start."

Bouie was actually the second recruit from Boeheim's first class to commit to Syracuse. The first was a 6' sharpshooting guard from the North Country of New York State by the name of Hal Cohen. He had verbally agreed to SU's scholarship offer while Danforth was still the coach and didn't waver when Boeheim took over. "I'd known Coach Boeheim from camp and interacted with him more than Coach

Danforth," said Cohen, who had received national publicity after making close to 700 consecutive free throws during a high school shooting contest. "So when Coach Danforth announced that he was leaving, I still felt very comfortable. I knew Coach Boeheim was going to be the coach. It didn't really alter my thinking."

The other recruit Boeheim desired was Louie Orr, a 6'9" forward from Cincinnati who didn't attract a lot of attention because he was razor thin. But Boeheim knew a thing or two about razor-thin players and about how they could develop a lot physically during four years of college. He believed Orr would blossom into an effective scorer and solid rebounder while teaming with the taller, bulkier, shot-blocking Bouie.

But to seal the deal with Orr, Boeheim needed to fill out his coaching staff. The first assistant he hired was Rick Pitino, and the way he landed him is the stuff of legend. Boeheim had become familiar with the fast-talking Pitino when he was a college player, and he continued to be impressed with him when he ran into him at basketball clinics. "I knew he was an energetic young coach," Boeheim said. "He was the first guy I thought of."

So shortly after taking over as SU's head coach, he tracked down a mutual friend who told him that Pitino was in New York City getting married. Because Boeheim was in the Big Apple on a recruiting trip anyway, he decided to stop by the lobby of the old Americana Hotel and conduct a job interview.

Talk about bad timing.

The new husband had just carried his bride across the threshold.

"I had put her on the bed, and this was a very big moment for me," Pitino recalled with the timing of a stand-up comedian.

"Right then, the phone rings in our room. I hear this whining voice I didn't recognize. He says, 'Hey, Rick, this is Jim Boeheim.' He tells me that he'd like to interview me about the assistant's job at SU, and I started whispering into the phone, 'Jim, I just got married about two hours ago.'

"And he's a bachelor, and he didn't know at that time what was going on. He said to me, 'Look, I understand that, and please give your wife my apologies. But have to talk to you before you go on your honeymoon.'

"I said, 'Jim, that's fine. We're going to San Francisco for three days and Hawaii for four days and we're coming back and as soon as we get back, I'd like to talk to you, as well.'

"And he said, 'No, you don't understand. I'd like to talk to you before you go.'

"I said, 'Jim, you don't understand. We're leaving tomorrow morning. We've got an early flight out.'

"He said, 'No, I understand that. I'm at LaGuardia Airport now, and I'm taking a cab to the hotel.'

"And I said, 'Jim, no, you can't do that.'

"He said, 'No, I'm going to do that. I'm very persistent about this, and I'm coming in.'

"At the time, I was being considered for the Fordham assistant job, the head job at Wagner College, and now the assistant job at Syracuse.

"I went in and told my wife, 'There's a person that just hung up named Jim Boeheim. He was just named the head coach at Syracuse. An outstanding coach and he's going to do one of the great jobs in basketball.'

"She said, 'That's great.'

"And I said, 'But he wants to interview me as a potential candidate, and right now I think it'd be a good move to do it.'

"She said, 'Fine, when you get back, sit down and talk with the man.'

"I said, 'No, you don't understand. It's now 6:15 and he'll be here at 7 o'clock.' And I said, 'Call your mother on the phone and have a great conversation with her and don't worry. I'll be back in a half hour. I promise you. One half hour.' I said, 'Just relax and get unpacked.'

"And we went down about 7 o'clock. I came up a quarter to ten. And every half hour I was calling my wife to tell her I was going to wrap it up.

"And every half hour I kept telling him, 'Jim, all I want to do is get back upstairs.'

"And he kept thinking I was putting him off, and he kept going up $1,000. All I wanted to do was get upstairs before I ended this great honeymoon. And each time I said, 'Look, Jim, I have to think about it,' he said, 'How about another $1,000?'

"The best part is that Jim thought the only reason I was calling my wife was because I wanted him to up the ante," Pitino said. "He started by offering me a salary of $14,000. By the time we were done it was up to $17,500."

CHAPTER 6

The Louie & Bouie Show

BY THE TIME HE BECAME HEAD COACH in April 1976, Jim Boeheim already had established himself as an outstanding recruiter, especially in upstate New York. High school coaches respected his knowledge of the game and his work ethic, and prospective players and their parents liked his no-nonsense, honest approach. With the exception of Larry Kelley, who hailed from Connecticut, Boeheim's first starting lineup consisted of players recruited from across the state. Center Roosevelt Bouie was from Kendall, forward Marty Byrnes from Rochester, guard Jim Williams from Buffalo, and guard/forward Dale Shackleford from Utica. "Coach Boeheim," joked Bouie, "was pretty good at finding kids who wouldn't be intimidated by Syracuse winters." He also was pretty good at finding players who were overlooked by other coaches and would develop and flourish in his up-tempo offensive system. "Jimmy Boeheim has always had a good eye for identifying talent," said ESPN basketball guru Dick Vitale. "Yes, he's had some McDonald's and *Parade* All-Americans through the years, but he's more times than not been able to enjoy great success with players other coaches didn't think would amount to much."

His first recruiting class as a head coach reflects that. Though Bouie was 6'11" and a graceful athlete who could run the floor, the college basketball powerhouses shied away from him because he played at a small high school against inferior competition. "I did go against a lot of 6'2" and 6'3" centers in high school, which helped me dominate offensively," Bouie said. "But Coach Boeheim saw how well I was able to move and recognized that I would fill out some in college and work hard to maximize my potential." No wonder Boeheim made the 240-mile round trip from Syracuse to Kendall—often on treacherous, icy, snowy roads—roughly 40 times during Bouie's junior and senior seasons. "We didn't have a true center the year before," he explained. "I knew Roosevelt would give us an immediate presence in the middle." Though Bouie's offensive game needed plenty of work, his height and shot-blocking and rebounding skills prompted Boeheim to start him as a freshman. The big man didn't disappoint, breaking the school record for career blocks in just one season (91).

Louis Orr was a different story altogether. He didn't start right away because the Orangemen had veteran forwards and he needed to gain some strength. He hadn't been widely recruited because he weighed only 165 pounds, and many believed that he wouldn't be able to bang the boards against major college forwards, many of whom would have a 30- to 40-pound advantage. But Boeheim, who found out about the unheralded Orr from an SU alumnus in the Cincinnati area, looked beyond the forward's thin physique and was able to see a gifted athlete with an intense motivation to succeed. "I really liked him," Boeheim said. "He might have looked frail, but he could shoot and drive the ball to the basket, and he had tremendous desire."

The coach no doubt remembered how a certain skinny Syracuse basketball player had been sold short about 15 years earlier—a player by the name of Jim Boeheim. "Coach Boeheim has a way of viewing a recruit and visualizing, based on the kid's abilities and work ethic, how the young man is going to be like two, three, four years into his college career," said Orr, who wound up coaching under Boeheim and later became the head coach at Siena, Seton Hall, and Bowling Green.

"Some kids peak athletically their senior year of high school. Others haven't even scratched the surface of their abilities. Coach usually is able to figure that out ahead of time and know how a kid is going to develop and fit into Syracuse's style of play."

Though Orr wasn't a regular starter his freshman season, his play off the bench contributed greatly to the Orangemen's success and convinced Boeheim that he had found his first of many diamonds in the rough.

Boeheim's first season as a head coach would be a rousing success as Syracuse began establishing itself as a true Eastern basketball power. After losing its second game of the 1976–77 season, SU reeled off seven straight wins, including an impressive 76–75 victory on the road against national power Louisville. After an 11-point loss at Maryland, the Orangemen went streaking again, winning 11 straight and 15 of their final 16 to finish the regular season at 23–3. Despite the sterling record, Syracuse flew under the radar, failing to crack the Top 20. As Tony Kornheiser of the *Washington Post* wrote: "So Boeheim has his team of sleepers, a team so quiet it doesn't even leave footprints in the snow." The lack of a superstar may have contributed to the team's anonymity. As would be the case with most of Boeheim's teams, the '76–77 club was incredibly unselfish. Five players—Williams (14 points per game), Shackleford (12 points per game), Bouie (11 points per game), Byrnes (11 points per game), and Kelley (10 points per game) averaged in double figures scoring, while Bouie, Byrnes, and Shackleford took care of the boards, each averaging about eight rebounds per game. Orr provided solid play off the bench and was seeing almost as much playing time as the starters by the second half of the season.

Boeheim's first team also would be aided greatly by its unofficial sixth man—the fans. Bowing to negative publicity created by profane, unruly behavior, the university's administration had banished the student cheering section known as "The Zoo" to the Manley Field

House rafters. But, in its place, a new student group, known as "The Kennel Club," set up shop near the court. Instead of shouting obscenities, its members would bark at opposing players throughout the game. The annoying sounds were music to the Orangemen's ears as they went 12–0 inside the building that had become one of college basketball's toughest places to visit.

SU continued its winning ways in the postseason, defeating upstate rival St. Bonaventure at home in the ECAC upstate playoffs 85–72 and Old Dominion 67–64 in Norfolk, Virginia. The two victories secured an NCAA bid for the Orangemen, but the tournament selection committee, unimpressed with SU's strength of schedule, pitted SU against powerful Tennessee in a first-round game at the Mideast Region in Baton Rouge, Louisiana. The Volunteers, featuring the senior All-American combination of Bernard King and Ernie Grunfeld, were favored to roll past the Orangemen, but someone forgot to tell Boeheim & Co. that. Syracuse brought the curtain down prematurely on "The Ernie and Bernie Show" with a stunning 93–88 overtime victory, spurred in part by Orr's block of King's turnaround jumper late in the game. That shocking win made SU the favorite in its Sweet 16 matchup against an unheralded UNC-Charlotte team, but, as had been the case in the Orangemen-Vols game, the oddsmakers were way off target. Led by future Boston Celtics star Cedric "Cornbread" Maxwell, UNC-Charlotte crushed Syracuse 81–59. It was a disappointing way to end a 26–4 season, but Boeheim had reason to be optimistic about the program's future, with several starters returning, including the promising twosome of Bouie and Orr.

Boeheim's second season would follow a pattern similar to the first one. After losing their second game, like they had the year before, the Orangemen strung together 11 consecutive victories. One of those wins came against Michigan State and its budding superstar, Magic Johnson, in the finals of the first Carrier Classic 75–67 at Manley Field

House. That game would lead to an infamous tirade by Boeheim. Angered that reporters had voted Johnson instead of SU's Marty Byrnes the tournament most valuable player, Boeheim excoriated the media. The outburst resulted in a scathing column by *Syracuse Post-Standard* basketball beat reporter Rob Lawin, ripping Boeheim. The headline of the piece that was striped across the top of the sports section read: "A Perfect Case of No Class." Some point to that incident as the beginning of Boeheim's occasionally tempestuous relationship with the media.

A midseason slump saw the Orangemen lose three of five games. But led by the scoring of Byrnes, a senior forward who would pace the team with a 16.3 points-per-game average, they rebounded to win their final eight games and finish the regular season at 22–4. Another ECAC upstate matchup with St. Bonaventure loomed—this time at a neutral court in Rochester—and the Bonnies avenged the previous year's loss with a 70–69 victory. The deleterious effects of that defeat continued to be felt 10 days later as Syracuse lost its opening round NCAA game to Western Kentucky 87–86 in overtime. Although the season had ended with alarming suddenness, Orr had improved dramatically as a sophomore, finishing with 12.8 points and 7.8 rebounds per game. He and Bouie were developing a great relationship on and off the court and were ready to emerge as one of college basketball's most dominating duos during their final two seasons.

What most people don't know, though, is that Orr nearly transferred from SU before his sophomore season when his father died unexpectedly that October following surgery for lung cancer. "I never got to say goodbye," Orr recalled. "I went home the next day. Longest flight I ever had to take." While home in Cincinnati, he seriously considered transferring to Xavier so that he could be closer to his family. But the caring and concern of his teammates and coaches, along with the encouragement of his family, convinced him to return to Syracuse, and, in retrospect, he's glad he did. "Basketball helped me focus on something positive," Orr said. "At practice and during games, it took my mind off my grief."

Over the next two seasons, Boeheim's teams would begin to receive national recognition, with Bouie and Orr leading the way. The Orangemen began the 1978–79 season ranked ninth in the Associated Press poll and would climb as high as sixth toward the end of the campaign. SU opened its schedule with six consecutive wins before losing back-to-back road contests against 15th-ranked Illinois and 11th-ranked Kentucky. It would be more than two months before the Orangemen would lose again as they put together a 19-game win streak. Bouie and Orr were virtually unstoppable, combining for 28.4 points and 16.3 rebounds per contest—numbers that would have been even more impressive had they not spent so much time on the bench during second halves of blowouts.

It was during this time that some enterprising editors and designers on the student newspaper, *The Daily Orange*, came up with the concept of "The Louie and Bouie Show." "They took this photo of us running up the court together and drew a caricature of us with top hats and canes in our hands, like we were the leads in some old, vaudeville dance routine," Bouie recalled. "It was pretty creative and the students really took to it, but Louis didn't like it at first because he didn't like being called Louie. He wanted to know why it couldn't be 'The Louis and Roosevelt Show' even though he understood that it just didn't have the same ring to it." That the two of them would be forever linked in Orange basketball lore makes sense because they worked so well together. "We knew each other's instincts," Bouie recalled. "It was like we had a sixth sense and always knew not only where the other one was on the court but where he was going to be next."

Orr would receive a scare during the season when he injured his knee. He refused to go under the knife for fear it would end his season and instead opted to subject himself to a new procedure known as arthroscopic surgery. The operation was a success, and Orr wound up missing just one game. After trouncing St. Bonaventure by 12 points in the ECAC Upstate playoffs in Rochester on February 28, 1979, the Orangemen climbed to sixth in the AP poll. But their 19-game win streak came to an end a few days later in the ECAC Upstate-Southern playoff game in a 66–58 loss to Georgetown in College Park, Maryland. A week later, Syracuse defeated Connecticut by eight points in the opening round of the NCAA tournament but was knocked out six days later by Penn after Orr got into foul trouble. For the second time in Boeheim's three seasons as head coach, the Orangemen had finished 26–4 and had been eliminated in the Sweet 16. A pattern of sensational regular seasons followed by early departures—a trend that would hound Boeheim during the first decade of his coaching career—was being established.

Expectations were sky-high heading into the 1979–80 season—the final act of "The Louie and Bouie Show"—and the Orangemen lived up to them from the start. With Orr and Bouie combining for 32 points and nearly 17 rebounds per game, they won their first 14 games and 21 of their first 22 to climb to No. 2, their highest ranking in the four-decades-plus history of the AP college basketball polls. On January 13, 1980, Boeheim's club served notice in a nationally televised game that it was for real, defeating Purdue and its All-American center Joe Barry Carroll 66–61 in front of a hostile crowd in West Lafayette, Indiana.

That prompted *Sports Illustrated* to dispatch a writer and photographer to produce a cover story about the Orangemen. Unfortunately, timing is everything, and the lengthy feature wound up being bumped from the cover when the magazine editors decided to run it in the immensely popular *Swimsuit Issue*. The feature introduced the nation's sports fans not only to the lead actors of "The Louie and Bouie Show" but also the supporting cast. It included: guard Eddie Moss, the team's playmaker and defensive standout; guard Marty

Headd, the team's dead-on outside shooter; freshman forward Tony "Red" Bruin, a high school All-American out of Queens with a 42-inch vertical jump who turned down North Carolina and UCLA to come to SU; freshman forward Erich Santifer, a Detroit scholastic star who had survived a gunshot wound to the face; Hal Cohen, a senior guard who was a pre-med major; and Danny Schayes, a 7' center whose father, Dolph Schayes, was a former NBA star and is a member of the Naismith Memorial Basketball Hall of Fame.

Writer Mike DelNagro's story also described Boeheim as a hoops junkie. "I only think about basketball," the coach told *SI*. The reporter went on to write: "If he's not coaching or scouting a game or watching hoops on the tube, he's probably in his office taking in a game film. When the season ends in March, he hops in his Pontiac Bonneville and travels to New York, Pennsylvania, Connecticut, D.C., or Ohio all-star games." The story also mentioned SU's disappointing postseason record and Boeheim's response. "You can't judge a team by what it does in the NCAAs," the coach said, issuing a quote he would repeat numerous times throughout his career. "Everybody loses. Every team but one." In the article, Boeheim gives the impression that he believes the '79–80 team might produce different results than his previous three teams, telling DelNagro: "Sure, we're not unbeatable. But unlike before, we can match up with anybody." Bonnies coach Jim Satalin agreed with Boeheim's assessment. "I've seen DePaul, Notre Dame, and Ohio State," he is quoted saying in the story, "and the best team in the country is Syracuse."

Before the season, two decisions were made that would enormously affect the future of Jim Boeheim and his program. Providence coach and athletic director Dave Gavitt and SU athletic director Jake Crouthamel met with ADs from a handful of other prominent Eastern basketball schools to form a new conference. The belief was that a league that included the likes of Syracuse, Providence, St. John's, Georgetown, Seton Hall, Pitt, and Connecticut would be able to negotiate a lucrative network television contract and increase its revenues. The Orangemen had been a member of the unwieldy Eastern Collegiate Athletic Conference. But a smaller conference would provide greater bargaining power, especially if it included the elite programs. After many deliberations, the Big East Conference was formed.

The other major development—one which Boeheim vehemently opposed in the beginning—was the moving of home games from the bandbox that was Manley Field House into the cavernous new Carrier Dome, which was being built on the exact spot of the old Archbold Stadium on campus. The arena with the air-supported, Teflon-coated roof would be finished in time for the 1980 football season and the '80–81 basketball season. The plan called for placing the hardwood court in one of the end zones, bringing in some temporary bleachers, and dividing the dome with a hanging curtain. School officials believed they could average another 2,000 fans per game, adding $500,000 to the athletic department's coffers. The half-million dollars would help fund some of the non–revenue producing sports teams at the school.

Boeheim's resistance to the move was understandable. With nearly 10,000 fans shoehorned into its cramped confines, Manley had provided the Orangemen with an incredible home-court advantage. As an assistant and head coach, Boeheim had enjoyed winning streaks of 36 and 57 games there. Visiting teams clearly were intimidated there because the raucous fans sat so close to the action that they could count a player's nose hairs. "A coach is looking for any edge he can find for his team, and the proximity of our fans to the action at Manley definitely gave us an advantage," Boeheim said. "I didn't want to lose that advantage—no coach would. I also didn't believe we'd draw that many more people at the Carrier Dome. I thought we were going from one of the best atmospheres in college basketball to a place that even with 12,000 people would look empty." Boeheim didn't hold back in his meeting with SU vice-chancellor Cliff Winters in the spring of 1980 when the move was proposed. There were heated exchanges between the two before Winters slammed his fists on the table in anger and told the coach that the discussion was over and the move would be made. Boeheim left in a huff. The home-court advantage that was Manley would be leaving the program along with Bouie and Orr following the '79–80 season.

No ceremonies were held to mark the final game at Manley on February 12, 1980. Boeheim didn't deliver any rah-rah pregame speech about the building's significance in building the program. Words were not necessary, especially for seniors such as Bouie, Orr, and Hal Cohen, who had never experienced a loss in the arena and planned on keeping it that way. An unranked Georgetown team was in town to face the second-ranked Orangemen. Although Georgetown had joined the Big East, there was no rivalry between the Hoyas and SU at the time. In those days, St. Bonaventure and St. John's were the huge rivals. Georgetown was merely another team. But that would all change on this Valentine's Day eve.

As 9,251 fans looked on, Syracuse sprinted to a 28–14 lead with four minutes remaining in the first half. That cushion would reach 16 points after intermission, but a combination of frigid shooting by the Orangemen and torrid shooting by the Hoyas would turn the game into a nail-biter. Down the stretch, Georgetown began fouling SU players in hopes of stopping the clock. The strategy worked, as the Orangemen converted just 1 of 8 free throws. With five seconds remaining and the game tied at 50, Georgetown's sophomore guard Eric "Sleepy" Floyd hit two free throws to give the Hoyas their first lead of the night. SU inbounded the ball to Orr, who missed a 30-foot shot at the buzzer. "We were bummed because that was the last game in Manley, and we wanted so badly to close the place with a win," Bouie said. "It was a real downer."

After the game, Georgetown coach John Thompson rubbed salt in SU's wounds, announcing bombastically: "Manley Field House is officially closed." The hulking 6'11" Thompson instantly went from being an anonymous coach to enemy No. 1 among Syracuse basketball fans. Neither the Georgetown rivalry, nor the fledgling Big East Conference would ever be the same. "They [the Hoyas] came into town and ruined our party," Bouie said. "And then Coach Thompson made that statement. That just got people even more riled. From that point on, whenever he and his team came to town, the crowds really got on him. He became big, bad John, the guy they loved to hate."

Although the loss put an end to the Orangemen's home schedule, there was still plenty of basketball to be played. Syracuse rebounded with consecutive victories against St. John's, Niagara, and Boston College. Then, in the first Big East Conference Tournament, the Orangemen crushed UConn by 31 points before losing to Georgetown again—87–81. SU regrouped in the NCAAs, beating Villanova by 14 points in the first round. The victory made Boeheim the fastest coach in college basketball history to reach the 100 victory mark, but the milestone wouldn't be what he remembered from that season. Instead, he would stew over the way things ended—an 88–77 loss to Iowa. Hamstrung by foul problems, Bouie played just 19 minutes in the game, finishing with an impressive 18 points but just three rebounds before fouling out with 25 seconds to go. Orr was magnificent in his attempts to pick up the slack, barely missing a triple-double on the stat sheet with 25 points, 16 rebounds, and eight assists. Once again, the Orangemen posted a 26–4 record. Once again, the season ended several games sooner than they had hoped.

CHAPTER 7

Discovering a Gem in Pearl

ALTHOUGH THE CURTAIN HAD COME DOWN on "The Louie & Bouie Show," Jim Boeheim was hopeful there wouldn't be a huge drop-off following the graduation of Louis Orr and Roosevelt Bouie in the spring of 1980. Seven-foot center Danny Schayes, son of NBA legend Dolph Schayes, was back for his senior season and more than ready to start after spending three seasons locking horns with Bouie in practice and coming off the bench during games. The backcourt figured to be solid with the return of playmaker and defensive special "Fast" Eddie Moss and sharpshooter Marty Headd. Small forwards Tony "Red" Bruin and Erich Santifer were expected to be even bigger contributors now that they were sophomores.

But the main reason for Boeheim's optimism was the eligibility of Leo Rautins, who had transferred from the University of Minnesota the year before. Billed as a "white Magic Johnson" because of his guard-like dribbling and passing skills in a 6'8" body, Rautins was raised in the hockey hotbed of Toronto, Canada, but preferred hoops to pucks. "I grew up in a Lithuanian neighborhood, and basketball was our sport," he said. "It was something that was brought over from the old country. We grew up in a place where nobody was playing basketball except the Lithuanian kids. We'd go to tournaments in the States and play against other Lithuanian teams. We had an open gym all the time when kids normally didn't have one. That brought me to the game, and I wanted to play it better than anyone."

Few in Canadian high school basketball history wound up playing it better than Rautins, who had overcome a crippling muscular disease as a child that had almost cost him his ability to walk. By his senior year, the tall young man with the long, curly blonde hair, was being recruited by scores of college basketball programs in the United States. He eventually narrowed his choices to SU and Minnesota and decided to head to the Land of 10,000 Lakes after attending a Golden Gophers home game against Purdue. "It was the heyday of the Big Ten," he explained. "Williams Arena had 18,000 fans for the game. It was absolutely rocking. I thought it would be a cool place to play."

And it was—for a brief time, as he wound up leading a team featuring future Boston Celtics star Kevin McHale in assists. But, in Rautins' mind, Minnesota wasn't a cool place to go to college and get an education. "You never had to go to class," he said. "I wanted to go to school. I almost left during the season, but I decided to finish it out. Right after the season, I got out of there."

Rautins had planned to transfer to Marshall University because he knew Thundering Herd coach Stu Aberdeen and thought a smaller school with less of an emphasis on basketball would be a good fit for him, athletically and academically. But when Aberdeen dropped dead of a heart attack before Rautins enrolled, the young man changed his mind. Boeheim contacted Rautins and told him that a scholarship would be waiting for him at Syracuse. After deliberating with his family for a few days, he decided to accept Boeheim's offer.

Rautins wasn't eligible to play for the Orangemen during the 1979–80 campaign because of NCAA rules that required Division I transfers to sit out a season. But he was allowed to practice, and he impressed his coaches and teammates with his ability to see the floor and find the open man. "He was one of the original point-forwards, along the lines of Magic Johnson and Larry Bird," Bouie said. "That's commonplace now to see guys that tall handle the ball the way he did. But it was strange back then to see a big guy have guard-like skills. Leo was on the cutting edge of that trend. And it was impressive to see."

Despite his bountiful basketball gifts, Rautins' transition did not go smoothly during the 1980–81 season. He struggled, as did his teammates, coaches, and SU fans, as they attempted to adjust to the move from the cozy, intimidating atmosphere of Manley Field House—a true college basketball pit—to the cavernous confines of the Carrier Dome. Though attendance jumped by a few thousand fans per game and SU maintained its home-court dominance by going 10–3 under the air-supported bubble, there was a perception that games were more sparsely attended. "Even when we had 15,000—which is still a pretty good crowd for most college games—it looked half-empty," Rautins said.

The Orangemen, based largely on their previous season's record, began the campaign ranked 19th in the country. However, after a 7–1 start, mostly against their overmatched upstate New York opponents, they began to stumble and fell out of the polls. One of the low points of the season occurred on January 26, 1981, when SU lost 74–71 at St. Bonaventure to drop to 10–6. On the return trip from Olean to Syracuse that night, Boeheim summoned Rautins to the front of the bus and informed him he was being benched. "I told him, 'I understand; I'd bench me, too,'" Rautins recalled. "The only thing I asked was that I'd like a chance to get my job back and try to understand why I'm playing the way I'm playing." Boeheim promised he would give him another chance down the road if he worked on reducing his turnovers and improving his defense.

About the only consistent performer for the Orangemen throughout the season was Schayes, the senior center, who wound up leading the team in scoring (14.6 points per game), rebounding (8.3), and blocked shots (2.2). "The fact I had gone against the best center in college basketball every day in practice for three years clearly aided my development as a player and resulted in me having a solid season my senior year," Schayes said. "Roosevelt was so athletic and so intense. He made me work very hard for everything—baskets, rebounds, loose balls. In a way, the games were the easy part for me because I knew I wouldn't be meeting any one as tough as Roosevelt." The funny thing is that Dolph Schayes, the former NBA star with the Syracuse Nats, had advised his son not to go to SU because he didn't want him to be constantly subjected to unfair comparisons with him. The elder Schayes also believed that playing college basketball in the same town where he had played high school hoops (at nearby Jamesville-DeWitt) would result in additional pressure. But Danny Schayes was dead-set on attending Syracuse, and, in retrospect, said he has no regrets. Following his senior season, he was drafted 13th overall and spent 18 seasons playing for various NBA teams.

Schayes' senior heroics weren't enough, though, to prevent Boeheim's fifth SU squad from suffering through a mediocre regular season. After their hot start, the Orangemen lost 10 of their final 18 games to finish with a disappointing 15–11 record. That March, for the second time, the Big East Conference was staging a postseason tournament, and Commissioner Dave Gavitt decided Syracuse would be the host school as part of a rotation system that would move the tourney to a different Big East city each season. This system, though, was in effect just three years. After being played in Hartford, Connecticut, in 1982, the tournament found a permanent home in New York City's Madison Square Garden.

Although the Orangemen had gone 11–3 in the Dome during the '80–81 season, basketball pundits weren't giving them much of a chance of winning the three-day tournament because Syracuse had ended the season on a sour note with four losses in its final five games.

But Boeheim had seen much better things out of a more confident Rautins in practices and games down the stretch, and he believed the sophomore forward was ready to fulfill his potential. "It was like the whole season had been erased, and we were entering a new season on our home floor," Rautins recalled. "Even though we had lost a bunch of games toward the end of the regular season, we were playing better together as a team. We had a real chemistry developing, and I had this weird feeling that we were ready to gel." Rautins was so confident about his and his team's prospects that he called his parents in Toronto and told them to drive down for the tournament. They were reluctant at first because they had attended games during that season, and it had been difficult for them to watch their son struggle. "It took a while on the phone to convince them to come," Rautins said. "I told them, 'No, really, you've got to come on down for this. Something good is about to happen.' Call it intuition or whatever, but I just had these positive vibes that they wouldn't be disappointed."

Syracuse disposed of St. John's in the first round, but Rautins injured his knee when Redmen center Wayne McKoy barreled into him while driving to the basket. Rautins managed to finish the game but was in obvious pain and had to spend much of the night and next morning with an ice pack affixed to his knee. Though still gimpy the following day, he helped Syracuse defeat Georgetown 67–53 to earn a berth in the title game against Villanova. Before taking the court against the Wildcats that Sunday afternoon, Rautins iced his knee once more, then had his leg wrapped tightly in an ace bandage by trainer Don Lowe. "I felt like a mummy, but once I got on the court, I didn't really feel the pain," he said. "The adrenaline had taken over. Ever since I was playing as a kid back in my Toronto neighborhood I had dreamed about a game like this. I wasn't about to miss this."

Villanova had beaten SU twice that season, so the Orangemen knew the road to the tournament title was not going to be easy.

Syracuse led by two at intermission and by six with 10 minutes to go, but Rollie Massimino's squad clawed back and a mistake by Rautins helped the Wildcats force the game into overtime. Eddie Moss made two free throws with 1:04 left in regulation to give SU an apparent three-point lead, but Rautins was whistled for an early entry into the lane, wiping out the second free throw. Nova's Alex Bradley then hit a foul-line jumper with 20 seconds remaining to tie the score, and that's the way it stayed when the buzzer sounded.

In the first overtime, Villanova seemed destined to win after opening a 70–64 lead. But Moss hit a short jumper, and after Wildcats center John Pinone missed the front end of a one-and-one, Moss fed Schayes for a layup to make it 70–68 as the crowd of 15,213 roared its approval. After a timeout, sophomore Erich Santifer—in the starting lineup for the tournament because Marty Headd had suffered a broken wrist in practice earlier in the week—stole the ball from Tom Sienkiewicz. Santifer drove in and missed the layup, but Moss was there for the tying tip-in. When neither team scored again, it was on to the second overtime.

This time, SU took charge, going up by four with 1:06 remaining. But Sienkiewicz nailed a jumper, and after an Orange turnover, Bradley knocked down an 18-footer to knot the game at 78 with 18 seconds left. Santifer had a chance to win it, but he missed a jumper and Moss' attempt at a game-winning tip-in rolled off the rim as the buzzer sounded once more.

The third overtime wound up being a game of stall ball in this era just before the institution of the shot clock. Schayes won the tip, and the Orangemen held the ball for more than three minutes before Schayes was fouled. He made both shots, only to see Stewart Granger tie the score at 80. SU went into stall mode again. Boeheim called a timeout with eight seconds to go and drew up a final play. It called for Rautins to inbound the ball to Santifer, who was supposed to penetrate toward the basket and then kick it back out to Rautins near the top of the key for the final shot. Rautins wound up taking the final shot, but the play didn't unfold the way Boeheim had drawn it up. "This is the benefit of knowing your teammates, I guess," said Rautins. "Because when Erich got the ball I knew it wasn't coming back. He's a big competitor. He got the ball, and just the way the defense played him I knew he was going to try to make a play. Aaron Howard was covering me on the inbounds, and he made the mistake that a lot of players make—he forgot about the inbounds passer. He turned to see where the ball went and kind of moved to the ball. As soon as Erich got the ball, he put it on the floor and started going toward the foul line. I knew what he was going to do, so I just went to the basket. Sure enough he shot it and the ball bounced literally right into my hands."

Rautins put it immediately back in for the go-ahead score with two seconds remaining. Massimino immediately called a timeout. Just one problem. Villanova didn't have any remaining. The Wildcats were called for a technical foul, and Schayes sank it to cap an 83–80 victory in triple overtime. Although the Dome was half-empty when Rautins put Santifer's miss back in, the noise was incredibly loud. Among those jumping up and down in the stands were Rautins' parents. "I had hit some game winners before, but this was the Big East tournament," Rautins said. "Coming from where we came from as a team and where I had come from individually, putting it all together was pretty cool." Few were happier for him than Boeheim, who had kept his promise of giving Rautins a second chance. "I give Leo an awful lot of credit for the way he handled things," his coach said. "Some guys, when they lose their starting job, sulk and make things worse for themselves and their teammates. But Leo used that time to correct the things he hadn't been doing well, and when an opportunity came again, he was ready to respond."

The Orangemen's surge to the Big East tournament title had been impressive but not impressive enough in the eyes of the NCAA tournament selection committee. Those were the days before the conference champion received an automatic invite, and the committee put more stock in the way SU had closed its regular season than on winning a league tournament on its home court. So when the berths were announced that March, the Orangemen were left out in the cold. "The thing that hurt most was that we really believed we had finally gotten things together and were playing as well as anybody in the country," Rautins said. "We really wanted a chance to go into the NCAAs in 1981, because I think we could have gone a long way. But it was not to be."

Instead, the Orangemen would have to strut their stuff in the National Invitational Tournament, which was still regarded as a prestigious second choice because the NCAA's field was only 48. "We definitely were on a mission in that tournament," Schayes said. "We picked the right time of the year to get really hot." That they did. What was nice about that year's NIT for the Orangemen was that they were able to play their first three games at home. And they took full advantage of their Dome-court advantage, mowing through Marquette (88–81), Holy Cross (77–57), and Michigan (91–76) to reach the tournament's final four at Madison Square Garden. After beating Purdue in the semifinals, the Orangemen's magic ride came to a halt as they lost to Tulsa 86–84 in overtime to finish with a 22–12 mark. The season may not have played out the way Boeheim had wanted, but he was extremely proud of the way that squad performed while winning seven of eight postseason games. "There was a case of a team going through a lot of ups and downs and really coming through when it counted most," he said. "I was very pleased with the way they came together and played as a team in that tournament."

The encouraging finish, coupled with the return of Rautins, Bruin, and Santifer, made Boeheim optimistic about the 1981–82 season. However, the regular season followed a pattern similar to the previous campaign. Paced by Santifer, who wound up leading the team in scoring (17 points per game) and rebounding (5.6 per game), the Orangemen sprinted to a 7–2 start, then stumbled and lost four of their final six games to finish 15–11. Once more they would be forced to win the Big East tournament in order to have any hopes of receiving an NCAA berth. It did appear that they might be peaking at the right time again, as they built a double-digit lead in the opening-round game against Boston College at the Hartford Civic Center. But they wound up frittering away that seemingly comfortable lead and lost to the Eagles 94–92. The loss occurred despite a remarkable performance by Rautins, who finished with 20 points on 9-for-11 shooting from the field, nine rebounds, and six assists. It was so impressive in the eyes of the media that Rautins wound up making the All-Tournament team. For the second consecutive year, the Orangemen received an invitation to the NIT, but this time their hearts didn't seem to be into it. After beating St. Peter's, they lost to Bradley at the Dome to finish 16–13. It remains, by far, the worst record ever recorded by a Jim Boeheim–coached team.

Boeheim's penchant for discovering unheralded talent was underscored again in 1982 when he recruited Rafael Addison, a slender 6'7" forward from Snyder High School in Jersey City, New Jersey, who had attracted just scant attention. "He was the prototypical Syracuse small forward," the coach said. "He was a very good player. He could shoot it. He could rebound a little bit. He could put it on the floor. He had pretty good size and was an above-average shooter." Addison would prove once again that Boeheim not only had a keen eye for talented players but also an understanding of how the players fit into his system and a vision for how they could grow and improve while in that system. Addison would finish his SU career in 1986 with 1,876 points to rank second at the time behind all-time leader Dave Bing.

The player known as "Raf" had a solid freshman season in 1982–83, averaging 8.4 points in just 18.5 minutes of play per game. But the Orangemen would ride the experienced trio of Santifer, Rautins, and Bruin to rebound to a 21–10 record and a return to the NCAA tournament for the first time in three years. Once again, Santifer led the team in scoring, with 17.8 points per game, and Rautins' well-rounded skills blossomed as he led the team in rebounding (7.3 per game) and assists (6.2 per game), becoming the first Orangeman to lead the team in both categories since Bing 17 seasons earlier. On January 10, 1983, Rautins became the first Big East Conference player to record a triple-double, with 12 points, 13 rebounds, and 10 assists in a 97–92 loss to Georgetown. A little more than a month later, he duplicated the feat, with a 13-point, 11-rebound, 13-assist performance in a 108–88 win over Boston College. "I took pride in filling up the stat sheet like that because I always strived to be a complete player," he said. "I worked on every aspect of my game. I didn't want to just be known as a scorer or a playmaker or a rebounder. I wanted to be known as a basketball player."

The '82–83 Orangemen opened impressively again, reeling off 11 straight wins, including a stunning upset of No. 9 Houston in a 92–87 scoring fest at the Dome. The string of victories convinced the pollsters to rank SU as high as ninth. But the Orangemen were brought back to reality by a visit to Chapel Hill, North Carolina, on January 8 when the Michael Jordan–led North Carolina Tar Heels thumped SU by 23 points. The Orangemen played .500 ball the rest of the season, but their 9–7 finish in conference play along with a victory over 15th-ranked Georgetown in the Big East tournament was enough to earn them a berth in the NCAAs. The selection committee had actually done the Orangemen a huge favor by placing them in the East Regional, because if they won their two games in Hartford, they would return home for the regional semifinals and finals in the Carrier Dome. "It looked like we had a clear path to the Final Four because of the home-court advantage and everything," Rautins said. "But the reality was that we really didn't have a great team that year. We just didn't have a lot of size. Nothing against our center, Andre Hawkins, but he was something like 6'5", 6'6" at most. I was our biggest guy at 6'8", and I was our playmaker. People were upset when we didn't take care of business that year. But we honestly weren't as good as people were making us out to be." After beating Morehead State in the first game in Hartford, SU lost to Ohio State 79–74. A rematch against Jordan and the Tar Heels in the Dome never materialized. As it turned out, though, Dean Smith's North Carolina squad would leave Syracuse disappointed, losing to underdog Georgia in the regional finals.

Rautins, however, would depart Syracuse a happy and rich man. The forward with the ball-handling and passing skills of a point guard had been able to showcase his overall game during his senior season, and the NBA scouts had paid rapt attention. The Philadelphia 76ers drafted Rautins in the first round and were hopeful that he would do for them what Magic Johnson had done for the Los Angeles Lakers and Larry Bird had done for the Boston Celtics. But injuries prevented his NBA career from ever taking off, and after a few years with the Sixers and several years in Europe, he returned to the United States, settled in Syracuse, and began a career as a broadcaster for Toronto Raptors games. Nearly a quarter-century later, he would make another significant contribution to the SU program when his son, Andy Rautins, became a star player for the Orange.

The most significant victory for Syracuse basketball during the '82–83 season would be scored away from the court. On February 20, 1983, during a halftime interview of a nationally televised game between St. John's and DePaul, Dwayne "Pearl" Washington told CBS commentator Al McGuire that he would be attending Syracuse. "I can't underscore how big a moment that was for our program," Boeheim said. "I believe at that point we officially went from being an Eastern program to a national program. Everybody knew who the Pearl was. I'd get off of a plane in L.A. and somebody would say, 'There's Pearl's coach.'" He was the guy who opened the door for us and enabled us to land recruits not just from the East Coast or the Midwest but from the entire country."

Boeheim was right about the Pied Piper impact Washington would have on SU's recruiting and the fact that his legend was already well established before he ever set foot on the hardwood court beneath the Dome. The chunky, 6'2" guard with the wicked cross-over dribble and the deceptive Globetrotter-like moves had been electrifying fans and demoralizing defenders for years on the asphalt, bent-rimmed playgrounds of New York City. His hoop dream began as a four-year-old in Brownsville—a section of Brooklyn that one writer said "looks like bombed-out London during World War II." Even though his talent was evident right away, Washington didn't enjoy playing the game at first. "My older brother, Beaver, really is the only reason I kept at it," he said. "He told me he was going to beat me up if I didn't stay with it. He told me I had this gift, and he wasn't going to let me squander it. Looking back, I'm glad that he threatened me that way because he saw something in me that I was too young to notice, when it came to basketball."

By age 10, Washington was playing against and dribbling past the likes of NBA stars World B. Free and Sly Williams in pickup games. Beaver Washington said he recalls scrimmages on the courts at King Towers in Harlem where the crowds were so big that some people had to climb trees or head to the roofs of nearby tenements to catch a glimpse of the young basketball magician. His mounting legion of fans already were calling him "Pearl" because his nifty moves were reminiscent of Earl "The Pearl" Monroe, the former Big Apple basketball legend who had entertained many on these same courts before becoming an NBA star with the Baltimore Bullets and the New York Knicks. Some also referred to Washington as "Black Magic" and "Pac Man," after a popular video game of the day in which you attempted to gobble up as many dots and ghosts as possible.

If there was a weakness in Pearl's game, it was his outside shooting. But his ability to penetrate against virtually any defense more than made up for those deficiencies. In an effort to force Washington to work on his jumper, Boys and Girls High School coach Paul Brown would occasionally put seven men on defense in practices. It didn't matter. Pearl still found a way to get to the basket. "Dwayne can't be stopped when he has it in his mind to score," Brown said, sighing. "He shoots layups against seven-man zones."

Pearl's legend would grow exponentially in high school. People raved about how, as a sophomore, he slashed his way to 16 first-quarter points in a game against a team of Boston scholastic all-stars that featured intimidating, shot-blocking center Patrick Ewing. It would be the first of several classic battles between him and Ewing, who would play for Big East rival Georgetown. During his junior season at Boys and Girls High—the same school that produced basketball heroes Connie Hawkins and Lenny Wilkens—Pearl scored 39 points in an upset of Camden, New Jersey, at the time the top-ranked team in the nation. That same season, Washington had an 82-point game.

By his senior season in 1982–83, more than 300 colleges were recruiting him, perhaps none more fiercely than North Carolina State, which was coached by the flamboyant Jim Valvano. When Washington stepped off the plane in Raleigh, North Carolina, for his official visit, he was greeted by Wolfpack assistant coach Tom Abatemarco, who suddenly began tearing off his sport coat, tie, and shirt to reveal a red T-shirt reading, "Welcome Pearl." During his tour of the North Carolina State campus, Washington was treated to more theatrics. He was brought to the darkened basketball arena. The instant he walked through the doors, a light flickered on revealing a Wolfpack jersey bearing Washington's name and number draped over a chair at center court.

The New York tabloids only fueled the hype and hysteria. People throughout basketball chimed in with their accolades. Utica College coach Larry Costello, who had won an NBA championship as a player with Wilt Chamberlain and as a coach with Kareem Abdul-Jabbar and Oscar Robertson, called Washington "a miniature Oscar Robertson. He can do what he wants on the basketball court. You just can't guard him one-on-one. And he sees the entire court so well." High school super-scout Howie Garfinkel called him "the best high school guard from the East since Calvin Murphy." Al Menendez, a scout for the New Jersey Nets, said, "If Pearl would have played for us last year, we would have beaten the Washington Bullets in our playoff series." Syracuse assistant Brendan Malone, a New York City native, called him "the best guard I've ever seen coming out of the city. Pearl can penetrate a crowded, rush-hour train in Manhattan and come out of the car without picking up a foul." And Boeheim gushed about Pearl's charisma, saying: "He doesn't disappoint. People come in with expectations about him, and they always leave happy."

Despite all the headlines and air time devoted to him, Pearl remained remarkably grounded. "With all the publicity he's received," Brown said, "Dwayne still is what I call a down-to-earth kid."

The hype, though, did go to his head in a different way. The barrage of recruiting letters and phone calls became so overwhelming during the first part of his senior year of high school that he began developing migraine headaches. Originally, he had intended to wait until the end of the season to make a decision about which college he would attend. However, those plans changed. "I wanted to get it over with because it was really starting to weigh on me," he said. "That's why I decided not to wait any longer." During his nationally televised interview with McGuire he explained his reasons for choosing Syracuse. "It is the right school for me for all the right reasons," he said. "They have a great communications department, and that is going to be my major in college. Someday I'd like to be a TV sportscaster. Syracuse also is in the Big East, which is my favorite conference. It has a great schedule, and it's close enough for my family to see most of my games."

Boeheim, who had been recruiting Washington for four years, couldn't have been more elated. He understood completely the ramifications. This clearly was a seminal moment in the history of the program and the university. "Dwayne is unusually strong and mature for his age, so he won't have any difficulty fitting right in at the college level," the coach said. "Also, his running style of play fits in perfectly with ours. He'll be a terrific addition to our team and will make all our players better."

Reflecting years later on his decision to go to SU, Washington cited Boeheim's low-key approach. "You experience a lot of phoniness and B.S. when you are recruited by as many programs as I was," he said. "The thing many coaches don't realize is that kids are usually smart enough to see through that stuff. Coach Boeheim kind of let the program and the school sell itself. He wasn't overbearing, throwing some huge sales pitch my way." Ever the entertainer, Pearl admitted the opportunity to play basketball in front of huge crowds inside the Dome also was a major appeal. "It was the largest stage I'd ever seen," he said. "What other school are you going to go to where you're going to play in front of 32,000 to 33,000 people? It really was amazing to come up there and see a place that big. I wanted to play on that stage." Pearl's decision resulted in 2,000 additional basketball season-ticket sales at SU and guaranteed a record six 30,000-plus crowds during his freshman season in the Dome. "Dwayne has gotten everyone excited," Boeheim said at the time. "If I were a fan, I'd pay to see him, too."

For every high school phenom who makes the transition to college superstardom, there are scores of others who fade into oblivion, never to be heard from again. However, Washington, who had been a man among boys in gyms and playgrounds throughout the Big Apple, was confident he'd be able to bridge the talent gap between scholastic hoops and the rugged Big East Conference. "People ask me if I'm feeling pressure because everybody is expecting so much from me this year, and I tell them 'No,'" Washington said on the eve of his college debut. "After all the recruiting and media coverage I've had since I was an eighth-grader, I know I can handle this."

Boeheim was confident he could, too. But in his comments to the media before Pearl's first practice, the SU coach attempted to lower some of the enormous expectations being placed on the freshman point guard's broad shoulders. Boeheim, a master psychologist, was sending a message not only to the fans and media but also to Pearl himself. "He had no competition in high school," the coach began. "He'll be pushed here in practice, which is something he needs. He was a great player on the high school level. Now, he's got to start all over again to prove to everybody how great he is here. He may be our best player and he may be our sixth best. Remember, last year's most-recruited freshman in the Big East was Villanova's Harold Pressley, and he averaged less than five points.

"Pearl must improve his shooting if he's going to realize his potential," Boeheim continued. "He also must cut down on his turnovers and not let himself get too lazy when the game isn't close. He's very strong and quick and he can go left or right equally well, and he has that little extra instinct to make the right play. Still, defense should be his strength, and we'll push him on that. He can be as good as Eddie Moss on disrupting with defense. We're looking forward for him to do that." Everything he said was true. In reality, though, even the outwardly cautious Boeheim was having difficulty curbing his enthusiasm. He knew deep down he would be coaching the most charismatic and gifted player SU had seen since Dave Bing two decades earlier. And he couldn't wait to see the Pearl work his wizardry in orange.

Although he had dazzled Dome denizens, teammates, and opponents while leading the 'Cuse to an 11–3 start his freshman season, Washington didn't truly become a bona fide Syracuse sports legend until game 15 against Boston College on January 21, 1984. It was on that night, beneath the Teflon big top, that the Pearl hit "the shot heard 'round the college basketball world." Minutes after Washington's almost nonchalant, buzzer-beating halfcourt shot had given Syracuse a stunning 75–73 victory and touched off "fandemonium" in the Dome, his teammate, Sean Kerins, proclaimed: "The Pearl has arrived."

With a nine-point lead with 15 minutes remaining, it didn't appear as if the Orangemen were going to need any last-second heroics to down their Big East rival. The Eagles stormed back to take the lead briefly, but Kerins converted two corner jumpers and passed to Rafael Addison for a dunk to give SU a 73–69 cushion with 53 seconds remaining. Moments later, BC forward Jay Murphy tipped in a missed shot to cut the deficit to two. With 26 seconds to go, Kerins missed the front end of a one-and-one, and Boston College grabbed the rebound. The Eagles brought the ball upcourt and tied the game on Martin Clark's put-back with four seconds left. Addison had failed to box out on the play, and to make matters worse, Clark was fouled, giving BC an excellent chance to win the game. But Clark's free throw attempt fell off the rim and into Kerins' hands. "At that point," Boeheim said, "I figured we were going into overtime." His sentiments were shared by the 30,293 spectators who had stuffed the Dome.

Kerins passed the ball to Pearl, who dribbled past Clark and let fly with the shot just as he passed the half-court line. The 45-footer swished through the basket just as the horn sounded. With his fist raised in celebration, the beaming Washington continued running off the court and through the tunnel leading to the locker room. It was a wise decision, because it enabled him to avoid the stampede of delirious fans who leaped over tables and chairs at press row to flood the court. Some, no doubt taking a cue from their football brethren, attempted unsuccessfully to rip down the basket that had graciously accepted Pearl's game-winner. "The thing that people forget is that was back in the day when storming the court wasn't commonplace the way it is today," Addison said. "That was a spontaneous reaction. The people did it based on the emotion of the moment. It wasn't something they had been planning, the way it's often done today. I've never seen a scene like it." Neither had Boeheim, who ecstatically leaped about four feet into the air and did a victory jig on his way to the locker room. "I never jumped that high when I was playing," he said afterward. "I could have slam-dunked the ball tonight."

"When I got the ball there wasn't much time to pass, so I shot instead," said Washington, who finished the night with 20 points and seven assists. "I knew it was straight on when I let it go, but I didn't know if it was going to be short or long. When it went in, I almost fainted." Then, flashing an ear-to-ear grin, Washington joked, "Not bad for a guy who supposedly can't shoot from the outside, huh?" Not bad, indeed. "If anyone can make a shot like that, it's Dwayne," Boeheim said of his steely nerved freshman. Washington's teammates concurred with their coach's assessment. They had seen him perform similar heroics in practice. "That's the kind of thing people expect from Pearl," said center Andre Hawkins. "He's a winner. He finds a way to win."

Interestingly, the USA cable network, which was televising the game, almost missed the climactic moment. When Washington was furiously dribbling up the floor for the last shot, a producer in the control truck outside the Dome tried to anticipate which camera angle to use. He thought for a moment that Pearl might opt to throw a long pass instead of shoot. According to one production assistant: "He almost switched to another player upcourt. Could you imagine if we had missed a shot like Washington's? Heads would have rolled."

Nearly three decades since his Nikes last squeaked against the Carrier Dome hardwood, Washington continues to be asked about his famous shot. "I never tire of talking about it," he said. "That shot made me a permanent part of Syracuse basketball. I had so many great moments during my playing days there, but that one's hard to top." Boeheim agreed. "That was a historic moment for our program," he said. "The instant that thing went through, there was an explosion in the building. As long as they play basketball at Syracuse, people will always talk about that shot." It was, as Kerins said, the moment the Pearl officially "arrived."

The victory against 16th-ranked Boston College enabled the Orangemen to crack the Top 20 the following week. They would remain there for the rest of Pearl's career. Syracuse finished 23–9 overall and placed second in the rugged Big East at 12–4. Washington led the Orangemen to the Big East Tournament finals, where they lost to Georgetown 82–71 in overtime in Madison Square Garden. With Syracuse ahead by three points with 3:52 left in regulation, the Hoyas' Michael Graham threw a punch at SU center Andre Hawkins as the latter fell to the floor with a rebound. Hawkins was awarded a two-shot foul, but Boeheim felt the officials should have called an intentional foul on Graham, which would have given the Orangemen the two free throws plus possession of the ball. Hawkins made both shots to extend the Syracuse lead to five, but Boeheim was still fuming about his team not receiving possession, and his anger only grew when Washington was later called for a five-second violation. Ignoring postgame protocol, the livid Boeheim stormed into the media room before the winning coach and lambasted the way the game had been officiated, punctuating the outburst by throwing a folding chair. "I didn't really throw the chair," he said with a smile, years later. "It was more of a toss. But, yes, I was ticked. I really felt at the time that the officials had cost us that game. I definitely let my emotions get the better of me, but I've

gotten a lot better with that over time. Just ask any veteran official."
Despite the loss, SU received an NCAA bid for the sixth time in eight
years under Boeheim. The 'Cuse won its first-round game against
Virginia Commonwealth before losing to Virginia in the second round
of the East Regionals.

Boeheim will be the first to tell you how rigorous the recruiting
process is, how he and his staff often court players for years, only
to be told by many of them that they are going to play their college
basketball elsewhere. To this day, Boeheim, the avid fisherman that
he is, laments the big ones who got away. The most painful one to
wriggle off his line was Sam Perkins, who played high school ball in the
Albany, New York, area. Boeheim logged more miles on the Thruway
than a New York state trooper while recruiting Perkins. But all those
four-hour round-trips from the Salt City to the state capital were for
naught, as Perkins wound up choosing North Carolina over Syracuse.
Perkins teamed with Michael Jordan and James Worthy at Chapel Hill
to win a national championship for Dean Smith. Boeheim can't help
but wonder if he might have won the big one earlier, had Perkins opted
to wear Syracuse orange instead of Carolina blue.

Of course, Boeheim has reeled in more than his fair share of
prized catches through the years, and no recruit came more easily than
Rony Seikaly, a 6'11" center who showed up one day unannounced
at the coach's Manley Field House office. A native of Lebanon who
was raised in Greece, Seikaly had a brother attending nearby Colgate
University. The family bought him an apartment in Syracuse because
the older Seikaly got bored with life at Colgate, a small liberal arts
university about an hour southeast of SU in the middle of nowhere.
The Seikaly brothers also had a sister who briefly attended SU. One
day in the summer of 1983, Rony showed up to watch some games at
the basketball camp run by Boeheim and his staff. The young man had
never played hoops before, but he quickly fell in love with the game.

That prompted him to pay Boeheim a visit one day. "I had no idea who he was, but when a 6'11" kid knocks on your door, you listen because you can't teach height," the coach joked.

They watched Seikaly play in some pickup games and realized immediately that the kid was a diamond in the rough. "It was obvious from the way he ran the floor and leaped that he was a very gifted athlete," Boeheim said. "But it also was apparent that he was way, way behind most kids his age as far as basketball instincts. We knew he was going to be a project, and it was going to take a lot of work on his part to try to play catch-up. It was going to depend on him and how hard he wanted to work."

Boeheim turned Seikaly over to assistant coach Bernie Fine, SU's designated teacher of big men, and Fine began sculpting a basketball player from a lump of clay. The basketball education of Seikaly would not always go smoothly. The young man had been raised in an affluent family and in a different culture. He wasn't used to being yelled at and pushed. "I think Rony definitely was a little spoiled," Boeheim said. "We certainly had our moments where we would be exasperated with him and he would be exasperated with us. But, to his credit, he responded. And looking back, he became one of the best players in the history of our program."

Boeheim and Fine not only had to give Seikaly a crash course on basketball, but they also had to toughen him up so he would be able to endure the rugged demands of major college and professional basketball. "When I first got to Syracuse, I didn't know a two-shot foul from a one-and-one," Seikaly said in a 1988 interview with the *Syracuse Herald-Journal*. "All I did was run around out there, dunking and blocking shots. Other than that, I had no idea what I was doing."

Although Seikaly was extremely raw and inexperienced, he started every game during his freshman season (1984–85). It was a fiery baptism, to be sure, as the great athlete with the raw basketball skills went up against the likes of Patrick Ewing, Ed Pinckney, and Bill Wennington in the Big East. Seikaly proved to be a quick learner and tougher than probably even he believed he was. He wound up leading the Orangemen in rebounds (6.4 per game) and blocked shots (59, second all-time only to Roosevelt Bouie among SU freshman centers).

Paced by the surprising Seikaly, the sharpshooting of Rafael Addison (18.4 points per game), and the leadership of floor general Washington, Syracuse opened the season 8–0 and climbed as high as fifth in the national polls. One of the highlights of the campaign would occur during an emotionally charged nationally televised game against the Hoyas on January 28, 1985, in the Carrier Dome. Georgetown came to town ranked second in the country. SU was ranked 11th. Early in the game, Patrick Ewing was fouled while attempting a shot against Seikaly. As the Hoyas senior center released his free throw, an orange, flung from the stands, smashed against the backboard. John Thompson waved his team off the floor as public address announcer Carl Eilenberg reminded the raucous crowd of 32,229 that the game could well be suspended. The referees took their time before resuming play in hopes that the tumult would subside. It didn't, so Thompson brought his players back to the bench. Boeheim, disappointed by the boorish behavior and obscene chants of the SU student section, grabbed the microphone this time. "I just want to say that any time the next orange is thrown on the court, we're going to ask for an intentional technical foul," he said. "And if I hear that chant one more time after a free throw, that's going to be a technical foul, too. On us." The crowd roared its approval, and no further incidents occurred.

Thompson's crew led 63–62 when the Orangemen got the ball back on a turnover with 16 seconds remaining. Boeheim called a timeout and essentially told his team to get the ball to Pearl, and Pearl would do the rest. Washington dribbled to the foul line and, with Hoya defender Michael Jackson draped to him, knocked down a 15-foot jumper with eight seconds to go. Georgetown failed to score on its final possession, and Pearl had added another unforgettable moment to his already impressive collection. Boeheim's role in drawing the line between enthusiasm and savagery was widely praised by the national media covering the game. Wrote *Philadelphia Daily News* sports columnist Mark Whicker: "It was quite a gesture. Would Memphis State's Dana Kirk do that for Louisville? Would Maryland's Lefty Driesell smooth the waters for Dean Smith and North Carolina?" In his postgame press conference, Boeheim claimed that SU fans usually were well-behaved. "But I'm tired of that [profane foul-shot] cheer," he said. "I think it's bush, and I've wanted to get it out of this building for a long time. I hope we did that."

The Hoyas would exact their revenge a month later, beating Syracuse in the regular-season finale and in the Big East tournament semifinals. The 15th-ranked Orangemen wound up in the NCAA East Regionals in Atlanta, where they defeated DePaul before losing to Georgia Tech 70–53 in what essentially amounted to a home game for the Rambling Wreck.

The Orangemen were extremely optimistic going into the 1985–86 season. Addison and Washington remained the heart of the team, but the supporting cast appeared to be much stronger than the year before. Seikaly figured to make even greater contributions in what essentially amounted to his second season of organized basketball. Junior guard Howard Triche, a physical defender who had played his high school basketball locally, and Greg Monroe, a brilliant shooter from Rochester, would team with Washington in the backcourt, and 6'9" forward Wendell Alexis would provide some scoring and help Seikaly on the boards. "That team really had everything you could ask for, talent-wise," Addison recalled. "We had guys who could fill it up from the perimeter. We had guys who could rebound and get you points underneath. And we had a great, great leader in Pearl. I expected us to go to the Final Four and maybe even win the national championship."

The pollsters agreed. They voted Syracuse No. 4 in their preseason poll, and the Orangemen didn't disappoint, winning their first 13 games before suffering back-to-back losses at Georgetown and Louisville in mid-January. But SU's great expectations took a tumble during a game at Seton Hall on February 5, 1986. While scrambling for a loose ball, Mark Bryant of the Pirates fell on Addison's ankle. Syracuse wound up winning that game easily 84–61, but Addison would be hampered by the injury the rest of the season. He gamely attempted to play through the pain. However, it was obvious he couldn't attack the basket the way he had, and his average plummeted. "Looking back, I probably should have sat out a game or two to try to let it heal," he said. "But I'm a competitor and we were heading into the heart of the Big East schedule and I didn't want to let my team down." With Addison hobbled, Pearl took it on himself to carry more of the scoring load. He would finish with a team-leading 17.3 points per game and help the Orangemen to a 23–4 regular-season record. "When Raf went down, Dwayne showed once again what a great player he is," Boeheim said. "He literally put that team on his shoulders and carried us down the stretch. And he took it to another level when we went to the Big East tournament that year."

That he did. The New York City playground legend played some of his most memorable games in Madison Square Garden. After disposing of Boston College 102–79 in the opening round of the Big East Tournament on March 6, 1986, Syracuse found itself once more matched up against the Hoyas. The teams had split their regular-season series, and much was made in the New York tabloids about the bad blood that had developed between Washington and Georgetown center Patrick Ewing during the 1985 Big East semifinals. In that game, the two exchanged elbows to the ribs, prompting Ewing to throw a roundhouse right that barely missed Pearl. The two were assessed technical fouls but were allowed to remain in the game, and the riled-up Hoyas went on to beat the Orangemen by nine. This time, though, Washington would deliver a knockout punch of a different kind, scoring 21 points as SU edged Georgetown 75–73 in overtime. "What you have to remember," Boeheim said, "is that Georgetown team played suffocating defense. There were *teams* that struggled to score 40 or 50 points against them, and there's Pearl scoring 21 on them and just dominating them from start to finish. They had no answer whatsoever for him. It was one of those nights where he was unstoppable." Despite being spent from that performance, Washington put on another show in the finals against fifth-ranked St. John's the following night and was unstoppable again until his attempted game-winning shot was blocked by Walter Berry. Although his team didn't win the crown, the media covering this Garden party voted Pearl the tournament MVP.

The next day, the NCAA selection committee presented Pearl and his teammates another gift when they placed the eighth-ranked Orangemen in the East Regionals in the Carrier Dome. Some in the national media squawked about this obvious advantage—and a few years later, the NCAA changed the rules, prohibiting tournament teams from playing on their home courts. Nobody in Syracuse, though, was complaining. Everyone just assumed that the Orangemen had been given a two-game pass into the Sweet Sixteen. In the first round, SU annihilated overmatched Brown 101–52, setting up a second-round matchup with the Naval Academy. The teams had met in the Dome early in the regular season, and despite the presence of All-American center David Robinson, the Midshipmen were throttled by 22 points. A similar result was anticipated in the return match, but Navy had different plans. Not only did they upset the Orangemen on their home court, they beat them handily 97–85. "David Robinson played a superb game, but they really didn't have anybody else," Washington lamented.

"One guy should never be able to beat five guys. I don't care how good he is. We just played a horrible game."

Around this time, news came out that Ohio State had received permission from SU athletics director Jake Crouthamel to speak with Boeheim about the Buckeyes' open coaching position. The phone conversation between Boeheim and Ohio State AD Rick Bay didn't go very far. "They were interested somewhat and I was interested somewhat, but we didn't continue the discussion," said Boeheim, who would have received a considerable salary increase by taking over the Buckeyes program. "I've been in one place too long [10 years], and I didn't want to get involved in a job discussion now. And we've recruited a lot of kids who expect me to be here."

Not long after the stunning loss to Navy, SU basketball fans received more bad news: Pearl announced that he was going to skip his senior season and turn pro. He wound up being selected 13th overall by the New Jersey Nets in that year's NBA draft. Boeheim backed his decision to leave. Though Washington wound up receiving a lucrative multimillion dollar contract, the magic he had displayed on the playgrounds, in high school, and at Syracuse disappeared when he turned pro. He spent just three seasons in the NBA, averaging 8.6 points and 3.8 assists per game. His lack of conditioning and poor outside shooting (18.4 percent from beyond the three-point arc) finally caught up to him. "I kind of lost my love for the game when I turned pro," he said. "It wasn't fun anymore. It became a job."

Years later, at Boeheim's urging, Washington came back and finished the 31 credit hours he needed to complete his degree. He also became the third person in SU basketball history (Dave Bing and Vic Hanson were the first two) to have his number retired.

Though he never guided the Orangemen to a Big East title and had only limited success in three NCAA appearances, Washington made a lasting impression on the program. During his three seasons, Syracuse won 71 games and lost 24. In an interview with *Syracuse Post-Standard* beat reporter Mike Waters, Boeheim cogently summed up the Pearl's impact.

"Everybody says Patrick Ewing and Chris Mullin made the Big East, but I think Pearl made the league," he said. "They were the best players, but Pearl was the player that people turned out to see and turned on their TVs to watch. We had the highest-rated games every year because Pearl was here. All of our games on TV were the highest-rated. Whenever it was us and Georgetown or us and St. John's or us and whoever, those were the games people watched.

"And they were watching him. We were okay, but we weren't the best team. We weren't even close to the best team in the league in those years. His three years, we were just okay. If we were the highest-rated games on TV, it was because of Pearl."

New York City may have had the House That Ruth Built, but Syracuse had the House That Pearl Filled. His impact on the Dome's turnstiles and the SU athletic department's coffers was enormous. In the first three seasons the Orangemen played basketball in the Carrier Dome, they averaged 16,440 fans, 18,851, and 20,401. In Pearl's first season, per-game crowds jumped to 22,380, then, in 1984–85, Syracuse led the nation in basketball attendance for the first time, with an average crowd of 25,870. The following season—Pearl's final on the Hill—they successfully defended their attendance crown and set a new NCAA record by jumping to 26,255 fans per game. Thirteen times in his three seasons, Pearl played in front of crowds in excess of 30,000. As Boeheim said: "Pearl's the reason there was that guy in line waiting to buy that 31,000[th] seat." And the reason vendors on campus had an easy time selling those "On the eighth day, God created the Pearl" T-shirts.

CHAPTER 8

A Dagger in the Heart

THE MAN WHO WOULD REPLACE the legendary Pearl Washington arrived at SU with a chip on his shoulder the size of the Carrier Dome. And who could blame him? Despite leading his high school team to a 31–0 record and earning player of the year honors in the basketball hotbed of Washington, D.C., during his senior season, Sherman Douglas had been lightly recruited. A product of Spingarn, the same school that had produced SU legend Dave Bing and Los Angeles Lakers superstar Elgin Baylor, Douglas' dream had been to stay in the D.C. area and play for Georgetown. But Hoyas coach John Thompson didn't show much interest in the small shooting guard with the awkward-looking outside shot because Georgetown already had an abundance of talented guards on its roster with more on the way. "I was especially disappointed when they didn't recruit me because they played my type of basketball—full-court pressure and lots of running," said Douglas, who averaged 26.6 points and 8.1 assists per game his senior season. "Georgetown was kind of like home, and I wanted to stay home. But they didn't want me."

The Hoyas weren't alone in that sentiment. Until Syracuse became interested in him, most major college programs shied away from Douglas because they believed he wouldn't hold up against the rigors of a Big East or Atlantic Coast Conference schedule. Even Boeheim, who began recruiting Douglas only after New York City point guard

Greg "Boo" Harvey failed to meet SU's academic requirements in 1985, had reservations. Initially, he didn't know if Douglas would be a worthy four-year successor to the Pearl or merely a one-year stopgap. What he and his staff had known was that the meter was running on Pearl's college career the instant he set foot on SU's campus and that they desperately needed to get someone in so they could teach him how to run the show before Washington departed following his junior year.

Shortly after receiving the news about Harvey's failure to qualify, Boeheim dispatched assistant coach Wayne Morgan to Washington, D.C., to check out David Butler, a highly regarded junior at Coolidge High School. While chatting with Coolidge coach Frank Williams about players in the capital region, Morgan couldn't help but notice how animated Williams became when talking about a small, overlooked point guard at Spingarn. Morgan called Boeheim, who told him to stay an extra day so he could scout Douglas. "Wayne came back raving about Sherman's incredibly quick first step," Boeheim recalled. "He also liked his competitiveness. He told me that Sherman didn't say much off the court, but he had an awful lot of fire in him on it."

Morgan's scintillating reviews were enough to convince Boeheim to offer Douglas a scholarship, and the guard who had scholarship offers from only Old Dominion and Rutgers reluctantly accepted. "Don't get me wrong," Douglas said. "I wanted to play in the Big East and Syracuse was a great program, but I was concerned about playing time. I knew with Pearl already there that my opportunities were going to be limited because he was a durable guy who would be out there 95 percent of the time." Despite his sensational senior season, Douglas began to wonder if he had what it took to play at college basketball's highest level. "I had self-doubts coming out of high school," he said. "I had confidence I would make a good point guard, but after not being recruited, I began thinking that maybe I wasn't as good a player as I thought." Interestingly, the more Boeheim studied Douglas, the more he thought that SU might have discovered another diamond in the rough. "Sherm was a little small, and he played the two-guard in high school, and at the time, you had Georgetown, Nova, St. John's, and Syracuse with point guards," the coach said when asked why Douglas wasn't recruited more heavily. "But when Harvey didn't work out, we were lucky that Sherm was still available."

It didn't take long for Douglas to prove his mettle to himself and to his teammates and coaches. In his first practice against Washington in October 1985, he didn't give an inch. "Dwayne had a considerable size and strength advantage on Sherman, and I remember him knocking Sherman on his butt about four or five times that day," Boeheim recalled. "Each time, Sherman got right back up and played tenacious defense against Dwayne. Heck, he even went after [6'11" center] Rony Seikaly. Sherman had no fear." The unknown was intent on establishing himself on a team of well-knowns. "I wasn't one of the top players in the country, and Syracuse had a lot of them," he recalled. "I didn't want them to think I was a pushover."

Few were more impressed or appreciative of Douglas' tenacity and work ethic than Washington. "He made me work more than most of the guards I faced in the games that year," Pearl said. "He got after it from the start of practice till the end. Going against Sherman was like going against Georgetown on a daily basis. He was relentless." And his teammates respected that he refused to back down against perhaps the nation's most dynamic offensive guard. "The truth is that no one liked to guard Pearl in practice because it was exhausting," said SU guard Greg Monroe. "But Sherman didn't care. He was always up for it. He took it as a personal challenge. Those practices were like his games. Reputations didn't matter to Sherman. He just loved to compete. And some of the best competitions I saw in my time at Syracuse were him and Pearl going one-on-one."

Splitting time at the point and shooting guard positions his freshman season, Douglas averaged 5.4 points and 2.1 assists in 11 minutes per game. But the limited playing time bothered him, and his situation didn't figure to get better his sophomore year because many already had anointed incoming freshman Earl Duncan, a Los Angeles high school phenom, as the true successor to Washington. "Transferring seemed like the thing to do," Douglas said. "But I really didn't have any place to transfer to. Nobody wanted me coming out of high school, so who would want me after one year as a college backup? If I had left, I'd probably have ended up back home in D.C., flipping burgers at McDonald's."

When Washington made the decision to declare for the NBA draft after the disappointing 1985–86 season-ending loss to David Robinson and Navy in the NCAA tournament, Douglas became more determined than ever to prove that he was ready to become the Orangemen's floor general. A natural shooting guard, Douglas honed his dribbling and passing skills and began studying the intricacies of the SU full-court and half-court offense. A few weeks after Washington's announcement, the news broke that Duncan failed to qualify for enrollment, making Douglas' path to the starting job even clearer.

But skeptics remained in the media and even among his teammates and coaches. Boeheim loved Douglas' fire and work ethic, but he was concerned about the pressure the young man would face following in the footsteps of the most publicized player in school history. "The situation Sherman walked into reminded me of what it must be like to play center field for the New York Yankees," the coach said. "Every guy who plays that position automatically is expected to be Joe DiMaggio or Mickey Mantle. I was worried that everyone would expect Sherman to be the next Pearl Washington. I didn't know how he would handle it."

The incredibly motivated Douglas handled it better than anyone could have imagined, averaging a team-high 17.3 points per game and breaking Washington's single-season school record for assists with a Big East Conference–leading total of 289. He became the first Syracuse sophomore to score more than 600 points in a season and guided the Orangemen to a school-record 31 wins and within two points of a national championship. "People asked me about the pressure I would be facing, but they forgot that I was taking over a team filled with great players," Douglas said. "I actually think I had it easier than Pearl because he was expected to carry more of the load by himself. The expectations were sky high on him even before he arrived. Few were counting on me to do anything. I was surrounded by talent, and I just felt my job was to make sure I got the ball into the hands of the right people. And on the occasions when that wasn't possible, I wanted to take advantage of the scoring opportunities that came my way."

Despite the losses of Washington, high-scoring forward Rafael Addison, and dependable forward Wendell Alexis, Boeheim's cupboard was hardly bare. Douglas may not have played a lot, but he was battle-tested and had learned a great deal from going head-to-head with Washington every day in practice. Rony Seikaly, the athletic but raw center from Lebanon and Greece, was ready to make a quantum leap during his junior year, and sharpshooting guard Greg Monroe and reliable guard-forward Howard Triche were primed for solid senior seasons. The three upperclassmen felt extra motivation from the disappointing way the previous season had ended. The lessons from the loss on their home court to a Navy team they had crushed during the 1985–86 regular season had been learned. "It had been a case of us getting caught looking ahead," Seikaly said of the previous season's NCAA flame-out. "We weren't just thinking about our next game. We were thinking two games ahead. Everyone expected it to be us and Duke in the Eastern regionals." The lower expectations for the season after Pearl were fine with Seikaly. "The situation is just the reverse of last year," he said. "This year, we are going to go farther than people expect."

Seikaly was confident of that, not just because of his belief in Douglas but also because of his belief in freshman forward Derrick

Coleman, a 6'10" rebounding machine from Detroit who had spent several summers working for Dave Bing at his steel company in Motown. The conventional wisdom was that Bing influenced Coleman to play basketball at Syracuse, but Coleman claimed that wasn't the case. "To be honest, the first few years I worked at Bing Steel, I didn't even know Dave Bing had been an NBA player, let alone a great NBA player," he said. "The thing that impressed me was that here was this distinguished-looking black man who owned his own company. That's what struck me. I thought that was so cool because the only successful black role models I had been exposed to were athletes."

Bing's conversations with the young man rarely touched on basketball. Instead, he emphasized the importance of a college education. "Even after Jim had started recruiting him, I told Derrick, 'I don't care what college you get your degree from as long as long you get one,'" he said. Initially, Syracuse was one of the few schools recruiting Coleman. But after his junior year, the young man's thin body began to fill out, and every school was after him. "It ultimately came down to Michigan State and Syracuse," Coleman said. "And I figured if Syracuse University could produce a man with the class of Dave Bing, then that's where I wanted to go. By that time, I had learned all about Dave Bing's records at Syracuse. I joked to him that I was going to go to SU and break his records. He said he didn't care as long as I got a degree." Coleman would receive his degree and rewrite the record books before becoming the first Orangeman to be chosen No. 1 overall in the NBA draft. But his days at Syracuse would be filled with controversy, and, occasionally, tested the limits of his coach's patience.

That Boeheim had built Syracuse into a national program was underscored when he landed a highly publicized recruit from California who would contribute off the bench as a freshman that season. Stephen Thompson, who also went by Stevie, grew up in Los Angeles' rough Compton neighborhood and established himself as a two-time city player of the year at Crenshaw High School, which had produced a number of famous athletes through the years, including former New York Mets slugger Darryl Strawberry. A 6'3" guard with a 44-inch vertical leap and an uncanny knack for slicing through defenders and shutting down high scorers, Thompson had attracted the attention of more than 100 schools. Many expected him to stay on the West Coast. But, thanks to the power of television, Thompson had become familiar with Syracuse's entertaining fast-break style. He eventually whittled his list to two schools, and SU won out over Duke after Thompson took a tour of the Carrier Dome. "Call it perfect timing," he said. "The way it worked out, my last campus visit was to Syracuse, and I remember being blown away by the Dome. Had it not been for that visit I might have become a Duke Blue Devil instead of a Syracuse Orangeman. That's the kind of impression that building made on me."

Thompson had lost just two games during his career at Crenshaw, and both of those losses were to schools outside the state of California. So it's understandable why he expected the winning and the titles to continue when he arrived at Syracuse. Before the start of his freshman season, he told Rony Seikaly: "Man, we're going to win the national championship." The junior center just laughed at the bold prediction. "I didn't know any better," Thompson said. "At Crenshaw, we won two city championships and two state championships. I thought that's the way it was. I didn't know any better." Remarkably, his new team would come within a basket of making him a basketball Nostradamus.

The Orangemen wasted little time showing people that Life After Pearl would be just fine. Syracuse won its first 15 games and climbed as high as fifth in the national polls before losing 91–88 at Michigan. The 'Cuse would finish the regular season 24–5 and top the Big East with a 12–4 record. Although he had not played the point full-time since his sophomore year of high school, Douglas made a smooth transition back to his old role. Nicknamed "The General" for his floor leadership,

Douglas paced the team in scoring and was among the nation's leaders in assists and steals.

The '86–87 Orangemen were a remarkably balanced team, with all five starters averaging in double figures in scoring. Seikaly became a dominating force inside, hitting 57 percent of his shots from the field while averaging 15.1 points and 8.2 rebounds. Coleman lived up to his advance billing, averaging 11.9 points and a team-leading 8.8 rebounds. When teams sagged inside in an attempt to neutralize Seikaly and Coleman, the Orangemen merely kicked the ball out to senior shooting guard Greg Monroe, who made 44 percent of his shots from beyond the three-point arc. And Monroe, who had experience playing the point, took some of the ball-handling pressure off of Douglas, averaging four assists to go along with his 12.9 points per game. Howard Triche, a 6'5" small forward, was a shut-down defender, a dependable rebounder (4.8 per game), and a pretty good fifth scoring option as evidenced by his 11.8-point average. Slashing freshman guard Stevie Thompson (5.1 points per game), bruising center Derek Brower (3.2 points per game, 2.9 rebounds per game), and defensive forward Herman "The Helicopter" Harried were the top options off the bench.

The 10th-ranked Orangemen disposed of Villanova and Pitt in the Big East Tournament before losing to seventh-ranked Georgetown 69–59 in the championship game at Madison Square Garden. "Despite that loss, we felt good about our chances in the NCAAs because we knew if we could play with Georgetown and the other teams in our conference, we could play with anyone," said Monroe, a senior co-captain. "Coach told us after that game that our big guys had to start hitting the boards hard, and they did. Everybody stepped it up, especially Rony. He was a man possessed in that tournament."

Monroe was on target with his assessment as the 6'11" Seikaly literally carried his team through the NCAA East Region and into the

On each of the main roads leading into Lyons, New York, you will find orange signs honoring hometown hero Jim Boeheim. (SCOTT PITONIAK)

Boeheim (back row, far left) was the star of a powerhouse Lyons High School basketball team that went unbeaten until the last game of his senior year, when the Lions fell in the 1962 sectional finals. Coach Dick Blackwell (center, kneeling) had a profound impact on Boeheim. (COURTESY OF LYONS HIGH SCHOOL)

Boeheim's senior class photo from the 1962 Lyons Tale high school yearbook. The caption reads, "Call him Sid or call him Heimer, at basketball there's no one finer." (COURTESY OF LYONS HIGH SCHOOL)

No one at Syracuse expected much from the skinny Boeheim when he walked on to the freshman basketball team in the fall of 1962. But Boeheim wound up earning a scholarship by his sophomore year and teamed with All-American guard Dave Bing to lead the Orangemen into the NCAA tournament during their senior season. (COURTESY OF THE SYRACUSE UNIVERSITY ATHLETICS DEPARTMENT)

Dave Bing, still regarded as the greatest basketball player in SU history, soars to the basket as Boeheim positions himself for a pass or rebound. The backcourt mates combined for nearly 42 points per game during the 1965–66 season as the Orangemen led the nation in scoring with just under 100 points per game. (COURTESY OF THE SYRACUSE UNIVERSITY ATHLETICS DEPARTMENT)

Boeheim, like many coaches from the 1970s, was not known for his sartorial splendor. He jokes that the plaid sports jackets have long since been burned. (©2011 BY JOHN DOWLING)

Many of Boeheim's assistant coaches went on to become head coaches, including Rick Pitino, pictured here on the Syracuse bench during the 1976–77 season. (©2011 BY JOHN DOWLING)

The first four teams Boeheim coached at Syracuse went 100–16, thanks in large part to Louis Orr (55) and Roosevelt Bouie (50), the prime recruits who became known to Orange fans as "The Louie & Bouie Show." (COURTESY OF THE SYRACUSE UNIVERSITY ATHLETICS DEPARTMENT)

Pearl Washington, shown here dribbling upcourt ahead of Navy All-American center David Robinson, was the recruit who turned Syracuse into a national program. (COURTESY OF THE SYRACUSE UNIVERSITY ATHLETICS DEPARTMENT)

Boeheim was at first adamantly opposed to the move of SU home games from cozy Manley Field House to the cavernous Carrier Dome. But it wound up being a huge boon as the Orange routinely led the nation in attendance and have attracted more than 30,000 fans on nearly 70 occasions. (COURTESY OF THE SYRACUSE UNIVERSITY ATHLETICS DEPARTMENT)

Boeheim, shown here during a game in the late 1980s, is well-known for his sideline histrionics. (COURTESY OF THE SYRACUSE UNIVERSITY ATHLETICS DEPARTMENT)

Boeheim's second wife, Juli, is credited with softening some of the coach's rough edges and bringing out his gentler side. (COURTESY OF THE SYRACUSE UNIVERSITY ATHLETICS DEPARTMENT)

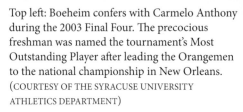

Top left: Boeheim confers with Carmelo Anthony during the 2003 Final Four. The precocious freshman was named the tournament's Most Outstanding Player after leading the Orangemen to the national championship in New Orleans. (COURTESY OF THE SYRACUSE UNIVERSITY ATHLETICS DEPARTMENT)

Top right: After coming oh so close on several occasions, Boeheim finally had a chance to snip a piece of the net after Syracuse defeated Kansas in the 2003 NCAA Championship game. (COURTESY OF THE SYRACUSE UNIVERSITY ATHLETICS DEPARTMENT)

Right: Boeheim holds aloft the NCAA championship trophy at a celebration in the Carrier Dome that attracted more than 25,000 fans. (COURTESY OF THE SYRACUSE UNIVERSITY ATHLETICS DEPARTMENT)

Assistant coach Bernie Fine (background) has been by Boeheim's side for the Syracuse legend's entire head coaching career and also was the student manager of the SU teams Boeheim played on in the mid-1960s. (COURTESY OF THE SYRACUSE UNIVERSITY ATHLETICS DEPARTMENT)

Several of Boeheim's former players joined him in Springfield, Massachusetts, in 2005 for the coach's induction into the Naismith Basketball Hall of Fame. Pictured from left are: Allen Griffin, Billy Owens, Hakim Warrick, Jason Hart, John Wallace, Damone Brown, Lawrence Moten, Boeheim, Sean Kerins, Rafael Addison, Derrick Coleman, Mike Hopkins, and Roosevelt Bouie. (COURTESY OF STEVE SLADE/SYRACUSE UNIVERSITY ATHLETICS DEPARTMENT)

Boeheim served as an assistant to U.S. head coach Mike Krzyzewski as the Americans captured Olympic gold at the 2008 Games in Beijing. Among the players on the U.S. team were Carmelo Anthony, LeBron James, Kobe Bryant, and Dwayne Wade. (JESSE D. GARRABRANT/ NBAE/GETTY IMAGES)

The SU student section at the Carrier Dome had a fun time displaying the Boeheim "Big Head" during the 2009–10 season. (COURTESY OF THE SYRACUSE UNIVERSITY ATHLETICS DEPARTMENT)

The two former backcourt mates and roommates— Bing, the mayor of Detroit, and Boeheim, the SU basketball coaching legend— reminisce. (THE POST-STANDARD/ STEPHEN CANNERELLI)

Final Four. The NCAA tournament selection committee made the Orangemen a second seed and gave them a gift by placing them in the East sub-regionals in the Carrier Dome. Seikaly scored 22 points as Syracuse defeated Georgia Southern 79–73 in a first-round game that was closer than most had expected. The junior center came up big again in the second round, scoring 23 points as the Orangemen trounced Western Kentucky by 18 points to advance to the Sweet 16 at the Meadowlands in East Rutherford, New Jersey. Seikaly clearly was on a roll, averaging nearly 10 points more per game during the tournament than he had during the regular season. For the first time in Boeheim's illustrious career his team had advanced into the third round, and as the final buzzer sounded in the Western Kentucky game, Seikaly tip-toed behind Boeheim and dumped a water bucket full of Gatorade on the coach. In the postgame press conference, the center told reporters, "I heard he had a monkey on his back. To get the monkey off his back, we washed it off." Boeheim laughed before delivering a humorous rejoinder. "Rony shot that water bucket like he shoots free throws," the soaked coach joked. "He got half of me." "Good one, Coach," said Seikaly, a 60 percent free throw shooter. "You got me."

Neither Georgia Southern nor Western Kentucky had a big man to match up against Seikaly. But that would not be the case in SU's third-round game against the University of Florida, when Seikaly would square off against Dwayne Schintzius, a cocky 7-footer who was regarded by many as the nation's best center. A few days before the game, Schintzius told reporters he wasn't that impressed with Seikaly. Thanks to Coleman and walk-on Joel Katz, the newspaper clipping found its way into Seikaly's locker. The motivational ploy worked, as an upset Seikaly went out and scored 33 points and pulled down nine rebounds in an 87–81 victory against the Gators.

Two days later, Seikaly was at the top of his game again, finishing with 26 points and 11 rebounds in his matchup against North Carolina All-

American J.R. Reid as Syracuse shocked the No. 2 ranked Tar Heels 79–75. "It was as if it all started making sense for Rony during that stretch," Boeheim said of the prodigy, who only three years earlier had shown up at the coach's summer basketball camp saying that he was interested in playing some hoops. "Everybody could see from Day 1 that he was a great athlete, but his basketball I.Q. was about 25. All he seemed to know how to do was dunk the ball. But he worked hard with Bernie [Fine] to learn the game. And I think it all started to come together during that postseason." Fine, whom Boeheim entrusts to work with the team's big men, wound up being the buffer between player and head coach. In fact, it was Fine who talked Seikaly out of declaring himself eligible for the NBA draft following his sophomore year.

"We have a funny relationship," Seikaly said when asked about Boeheim at the 1987 Final Four in New Orleans. "He kept saying that he saw in me a great player, that by my senior year I would be the No. 1 pick in the draft. But I thought, 'How could he believe that when he's yelling at me all the time?' I'd never been yelled at before or told what to do. I was hard to understand. Soon, I would get down on myself, and then I would get mad and just do the opposite of what he told me." But Seikaly said he began to understand Boeheim's approach better after reading John Feinstein's best-selling book, *A Season on the Brink*, a behind-the-scenes look at the Indiana basketball program and its volatile coach, Bobby Knight. "I saw that coaches go through a lot of the same things with their players," he said. "And they all just want the best out of them."

The relationship between Boeheim and Seikaly would remain strained for several years. While playing in the NBA, Seikaly reopened old wounds, publicly ripping the methods employed by his old coach. But the two eventually buried the hatchet, and Boeheim was instrumental in bringing back Seikaly on January 13, 2007, to take part in a ceremony in which his number was retired. "You hope that over time your players realize that you did what you did because you were trying to bring out the best in them," Boeheim said. "In hindsight, I probably should have done a better job of understanding that because Rony was from a different culture he might interpret things differently. I would definitely have handled it differently if I had it to do all over again. But he did wind up having a great career here and a great career in the NBA, so I think it probably worked out okay."

Although Seikaly was named the East Region's Most Outstanding player, Tar Heels coach Dean Smith was just as impressed with Douglas. "They lost Pearl," Smith said, "but in many ways they may be better than if Pearl had stayed." Smith went on to say in his postgame press conference that Syracuse was probably the favorite to beat at the Final Four because of its balanced attack. The Basketball Hall of Fame coach also took time to praise the coach who beat him. For Boeheim, the victory was extra sweet because it silenced, at least temporarily, the fans and members of the media who had criticized his coaching ability. In his first 10 seasons, he had coached several sensational teams, but none had advanced beyond the Sweet 16. And the way the previous season had ended—with a loss on their home floor to a Navy team SU had pummeled during the regular season—gave Boeheim's detractors additional ammunition. To get this far, with a new point guard, no less, was a testament to his coaching abilities. He had implored his big men to hit the boards more fiercely after being out-rebounded 47–30 by the Hoyas in the Big East championship game, and they heeded his call. During their run to the Final Four, the Orangemen were the chairmen of the boards, out-rebounding Georgia Southern, Western Kentucky, Florida, and North Carolina by sizable margins.

Syracuse had expected a rematch with Georgetown, the Southeast Region's top seed, in the semifinals in New Orleans. But a funny thing happened to the Hoyas on their way to the French Quarter—they were upset by Big East rival Providence College 88–73. That meant

SU would face the Friars a third time and that Boeheim would be matching Xs and Os with his good friend and former assistant, Rick Pitino. The Orangemen had beaten them by four points in Rhode Island and by nine points in the Carrier Dome, but Boeheim was concerned about facing them a third time, particularly after watching the Friars shoot the lights out against Georgetown's normally tenacious man-to-man defense. Pitino's team wasn't nearly as athletic as the Hoyas or Orangemen but made up for its deficiencies with deadly three-point shooting.

Boeheim emphasized to his players the importance of hounding the Friars' shooters, particularly hotshot guard Billy Donovan. "Defense," he told them, "will determine whether or not we win this game." The Orangemen clearly took his words to heart. Providence missed 10 of its first 12 shots, including nine in a row, and wound up converting just 36 percent of its attempts as SU cruised to a 77–63 victory in front of an NCAA-record crowd of 64,959 at the sold-out Louisiana Superdome. Douglas was the catalyst on the defensive end, limiting Donovan to a season-low eight points on 3-for-12 shooting. "Really, our offense was out of sync," Douglas said of the Orangemen, who shot below 50 percent for the first time in the tournament. "It was a sloppy game. But it was our defense that won it. People think Syracuse plays no defense, because we fast break so much. They forget we have the best field-goal percentage defense in the Big East." In addition to shutting down Donovan, Douglas scored 12 points, handed out six assists, and hauled in 11 rebounds—an amazing stat considering he was the shortest player on the floor. "When Sherman Douglas, a 6' point guard, gets 11 rebounds, well, we can beat anybody," said Seikaly, who finished with 16 points and six boards. Despite SU's offensive struggles, once again all five of its starters scored in double figures, with Greg Monroe leading the way with 17 points. Still, it was the defense that impressed Pitino the most. "For them to hold this team to 63 points means they're playing great basketball," he said after watching his Friars score their lowest total in more than two months. "They definitely have a great chance at the national championship."

Boeheim, though he didn't say so publicly, also liked his chances, even though the Orangemen would be slight underdogs heading into the program's first-ever NCAA title game on March 30, 1987, against third-ranked Indiana. Coach Bobby Knight's Hoosiers had outlasted a three-point barrage by Jerry Tarkanian's University of Nevada–Las Vegas Running Rebels in a 97–93 victory in the other semifinal. Although not as athletic as Syracuse, Indiana boasted a balanced team, and its coach had won two NCAA titles before. "Everybody expected it to be a great game," Monroe said. "And it was—until the final four seconds."

In a finish that still haunts Boeheim and Syracuse players and fans to this day, Keith Smart swished a 16-foot baseline jumper over Howard Triche's outstretched arms to propel Indiana to a 74–73 victory in front of more than 64,000 spectators in the Superdome and millions more on CBS' national telecast. Smart, a junior college transfer from Baton Rouge, Louisiana, had worked as an usher at New Orleans Saints games as a teenager. His game-winner capped a magnificent homecoming in which he scored six of Indiana's final seven baskets and 17 of his 21 points in the second half to capture Final Four Most Outstanding Player honors.

The thing that made the loss even more painful for Boeheim and his players and fans was the sense that the Orangemen had the game in their grasp during the final minute and let it slip away. Boeheim had coached a masterful game, matching Xs and Os with his exalted counterpart. Syracuse deployed multiple defenses to deal with Hoosiers guard Steve Alford, and the strategy worked, as a combination of Douglas, Monroe, Triche, and Thompson limited the All-American to 23 points, 10 fewer than he scored in the semifinal victory over UNLV. The harried Alford managed just one basket during the game's final eight minutes. The use of a 2-3 zone, man-to-man, occasional traps, and a box-and-one enabled SU to hold the Hoosiers to 18 points below their NCAA scoring average. "We used four different defenses," Boeheim said. "We just kept switching off, and I think we confused them a little and slowed them down a bit."

After a first half that saw a dozen lead changes, the second half featured several scoring runs. With 13 minutes to go, SU went up 52–44 on Triche's 18-foot jumper, but the Hoosiers came back and took the lead by scoring 10 straight. The game remained tight till the end. Triche nailed a short jumper with 57 seconds left to put the Orangemen up 72–70, and Indiana wound up fouling Triche 16 seconds later. The senior hit the first shot to extend the lead to three points, but his second free throw clanged off the rim and the Hoosiers quickly got the ball to Smart, who weaved his way through the Orangemen defenders to cut the lead to one. Indiana immediately fouled Derrick Coleman on the inbounds, and the confident freshman, who already had put together a sterling performance with eight points and 19 rebounds, headed to the foul line with 28 seconds remaining. "I thought, 'There it is,'" Seikaly recalled. "I thought Derrick was going to sink both ends of that one-and-one and we were going to win the national championship." On the bench, Stevie Thompson, the freshman who had predicted an NCAA title back at the start of practice more than five months earlier, had the same thoughts.

But Boeheim knew an "eternity" remained. Concerned about how easily the speedy Smart had beaten his defenders down the floor on Triche's miss just moments earlier, the coach decided to concede the rebound and have his defenders already positioned near the Indiana basket. As Coleman bounced the ball a few times at the foul line before launching his shot, only one thought crossed his mind: "Just make the damn free throws." He let it fly and knew immediately that it was going to bounce off the right side of the rim. "My hands were sweaty," he explained after the game. "And as I threw it up, I knew it was off right. I said, 'Damn! It's off.'"

Indiana grabbed the rebound, brought the ball up the floor, and worked the clock down to about seven seconds. The Hoosiers' first option, of course, was to attempt to get the ball in the hands of Alford, but Douglas stuck to him like a coat of paint. They also attempted to get the ball inside to Daryl Thomas, who was covered closely by both Seikaly and Coleman. Instead of attempting a difficult shot over his taller defenders, Thomas passed over to Smart, who dribbled toward the baseline and let loose with the shot that would be replayed ad nauseum during every NCAA tournament that followed. Triche, who had helped deny Alford the ball, tried valiantly to get over on Smart, but it was too late.

In the stunning moments that followed, Douglas attempted to get a timeout from the officials, but one wasn't awarded until just one second remained. "I tried to get them to look at the monitors," he said. "But they refused. Smart took the shot with five seconds to go. The difference between three seconds and one second is huge. With three seconds you can set up a play. With one, you have no chance."

Coleman's desperation heave was intercepted at midcourt by—you guessed it—Smart, and the final buzzer sounded on one of the most riveting and disheartening basketball games in Syracuse history. "It was like somebody had stabbed you in the heart," Monroe said. "And it all happened so fast. One second, you're ready to celebrate. The next second, you're saying to yourself, 'What just happened?'"

While the joyous Hoosiers players piled on Smart out on the court, the disconsolate Syracuse players walked around in a stunned daze. The two head coaches met in front of the scorer's table and shook hands, and Knight told Boeheim that his team would be back and would win it all someday. Boeheim thanked the Hoosiers legend but was too devastated to want to think about anything but getting far away from basketball and the hurt he was feeling. Unfortunately, he and his team had to remain on the court not only to receive their runners-up trophy but also to watch the victors receive the championship hardware and cut down the nets. Then, after a short cooling-off period, the Orangemen and their coach had to rehash what had just transpired with the scores of reporters covering the Final Four. "It doesn't feel good," said Boeheim, who looked as if he had just gone 15 rounds with Mike Tyson. "I've never had a loss that felt good. I guess this'll hurt a little bit more because there's more importance to this game than any other. But there is only one team better in the country than us, and that's not by much."

Boeheim's decision to not have any of his players in the lane while Coleman was attempting his one-and-one was called into question. The Syracuse coach, though, said he would have done the same thing all over again, citing the earlier missed free throw by Triche in which Boeheim placed three Orangemen in rebounding positions only to have Smart beat them back down the floor for an easy bucket. "If I made a mistake," he said, "it was at the earlier free throw, and they wouldn't have gotten a basket in transition."

Although Smart's final shot was what everyone remembered, one of the keys to the Indiana victory and the Syracuse loss was the Orangemen's futility at the free throw line, where they converted just 11 of 20 shots (55 percent) and missed the front ends of two one-and-ones, costing them potentially four points.

Smart proved to be the difference in more ways than one, taking up the slack for Alford, who was the center of attention all night, particularly on that last possession. "I just took what was given to me," Smart explained. "Syracuse was sagging inside and covering Steve tight, so he was looking for me and that worked. It's great to have a player like Steve because it opens up so much for the team."

Knight was effusive in his praise of the Orangemen at the postgame news conference.

"Syracuse did an excellent job of changing defenses and had us standing around a little bit," Knight said. "As a result, we were pressing a little bit more than we should and not really getting the ball where we wanted throughout the ballgame. They did a helluva job defensively."

Two days after the title game, thousands attended a welcome-back rally for the team near Syracuse City Hall. One of the fans hoisted a blue-and-orange sign that seemed to sum up the community's sentiments. It read: "TO US, YOU WON."

In the weeks that followed, Boeheim received hundreds of supportive letters from SU fans, thanking him and his team for the joyous journey to the Final Four. The coach and his players appreciated the kind words, but it proved to be a difficult off-season, as they attempted to get over the fact they had come within two points of winning the most important game of their lives.

CHAPTER 9

From Peaks to Valleys

THE VIDEOTAPE OF THE 1987 NCAA TITLE GAME was stuffed somewhere on the cluttered shelves in Jim Boeheim's Manley Field House office. And that's where it would stay for years because the Syracuse basketball coach had no desire to view it. As he prepared for a new basketball season seven months later, he was still agonizing over the squandered opportunities and the dagger-in-the-heart ending of that last-second loss to Indiana. "I don't know if I'll ever watch that game," he said, admitting that he had seen snippets of the tape. "That game just hurts too much. I think about it. I see the players. I can probably see every play in my mind still. But I have no interest in watching it." Neither did his players. "Someday I can tell my kids about playing [in the championship game]," said junior point guard Sherman Douglas. "I can show them a tape of me playing there…and turn it off for the last minute of the game."

Clearly, not nearly enough time had passed to heal their wounds. As sophomore forward Derrick Coleman had indicated, it wasn't merely the loss but the way it had happened—with SU failing to finish the deal at the foul line in the final minute. "We were so close; we had it in our hands," he lamented. "But we let it slip away. I'd rather lose by 15 or 20 than lose by one shot." All these months later, visions of Keith Smart's 16-foot baseline jumper as the clock wound down were still dancing in their heads, gnawing at their souls. "I really felt we should have won that game," Boeheim said. "A couple of unlucky things happened. We got out there and played defense. They threw up a bad shot and won."

Luckily for him and his players, the Orangemen were about to embark on another season, and they would do so armed with several experienced stars amid enormous expectations. The Big Three—Douglas, Coleman, and center Rony Seikaly—were back and hungry for a return to the Final Four and a shot at redemption. The idea they might be able to complete unfinished business at Kemper Arena in Kansas City the following March was being trumpeted not only by the admittedly biased citizens of Orange Nation but also by the unbiased members of the national media. SU clearly had reached heights it had never before experienced, finding itself atop the preseason polls of *Sports Illustrated*, the *Sporting News*, and the Basketball Writers Association of America. The *Sporting News* even splashed a photo of Seikaly, the senior center, standing next to a superimposed No. 1, on the cover of its college basketball preview issue.

Douglas embraced the challenge, fueled by the painful memory of the lost title. "We had the whole summer to think about that last game," he said. "And that's going to push us. I try not to think about what happened, but I can't help it. I know when my college career is over that could have been my best chance at a national championship." His words would be as prophetic as the words of former Duke University coach Bill Foster, who had experienced how enormous—and unrealistic—the expectations can become the year after reaching the NCAA championship game. In an article in the *Syracuse Herald-Journal*, Foster said that "every team that tries to repeat—either as a runner-up or champion—seems to end up an underachiever. Those players very easily fall into a trap of resting on their laurels, maybe not consciously but subconsciously."

Even Greg Monroe, who had graduated after helping SU reach the title game, was concerned that maybe the bar had been raised too high in a mid-sized city whose identity was so closely tied to Orangemen hoops. Monroe, then playing minor-league ball in the Continental Basketball Association, worried that too much pressure would be placed on Boeheim. "He's a great coach, and he deserves a lot more recognition," Monroe said. "But the pressure goes with the territory, and there's going to be a lot of pressure on this team. This year will either make or break him as a great coach."

As it turned out, the Orangemen's reign atop the college basketball world did not last long, as they opened the season with a 96–93 overtime loss to third-ranked North Carolina at the Hall of Fame Tipoff Classic in Springfield, Massachusetts, on November 21, 1987. Then, after two wins at the Great Alaskan Shootout in Anchorage, they lost 80–69 to 17th-ranked Arizona in the tournament's championship game. The Orangemen rebounded from their 2–2 start by reeling off 10 consecutive victories. They finished the regular season at 22–8 and were second in the Big East with an 11–5 mark. They entered the conference tournament ranked 11th in the nation, and after defeating Boston College, Seton Hall, and Villanova to cop the title, there was a sense that this immensely talented team might be peaking at the right time and ready to live up to the preseason hype. The Big Three of Seikaly (16.3 points and 9.6 rebounds per game), Douglas (16.1 points per game; 8.2 assists per game), and Coleman (a team-leading 11 rebounds per game) had been consistently good and had been bolstered by sophomore Stevie Thompson, who had a breakout season, averaging 14.1 points per game, despite not possessing an outside shot. "We thought we were primed to make another run at it," Coleman said. "But things just didn't work out." At the NCAA East Regional in Chapel Hill, North Carolina, Syracuse opened with a 69–55 victory against North Carolina A&T but was stunned by Rhode Island 97–94 in the second round. A few months after that upset, Seikaly was chosen by the Miami Heat with the ninth overall pick of the NBA draft. The talented but raw recruit who had showed up unexpectedly at Boeheim's office five years earlier would spend 11 seasons in the NBA, playing for the Heat, the Golden State Warriors, the Orlando Magic, and the New Jersey Nets.

While the departure of Seikaly to the NBA in 1988 was a big story in Syracuse, an even bigger story concerned an arrival. Reinforcements were on the way, as, for the second time in his career, Boeheim landed the national high school player of the year. Though Billy Owens, who led his Carlisle High School team to four Pennsylvania state championships, didn't generate the tsunami of interest that Pearl Washington's arrival had several years earlier, it still was a huge get and another indication of just how much of a national program SU had become. Orangemen football coach Dick MacPherson indirectly assisted in the landing of the star recruit, because a few years earlier Coach Mac had convinced Billy's older brother, Michael Owens, to come to Syracuse to play running back. "I was seriously considering North Carolina and Villanova, but I didn't want my parents having to travel to two schools in opposite directions in order to watch me and Michael play," said the younger Owens. "I also was obviously intrigued about being able to play in the Dome, and SU had proven it could contend for a national championship. I wanted to be a part of that."

The 6'8" Owens arrived with the ball-handling skills of a guard, the shooting range of a small forward, and the physical rebounding strength of a power forward. "Billy was the best high school player I ever saw," Boeheim said. "He and Pearl were the only No. 1–rated players we ever signed out of high school, and I would give a slight edge to Billy because of his size." Owens also received the edge from *Sports Illustrated*, which plopped the freshman-to-be on the cover of its basketball preview issue before he had played his first college game.

Actually, Owens was supposed to share cover honors with the nation's other top-rated incoming freshman, Alonzo Mourning of Georgetown. But Hoyas coach John Thompson wouldn't give Mourning permission to be featured, so Owens flew solo.

Owens was intrepid during his early practices at SU, going toe-to-toe with junior forward Derrick Coleman. "They were really intense, and you wondered if their egos were going to clash," Douglas said. "But what happened immediately was mutual respect. They became the best of friends, and they still are to this day." After having been *the* man for four seasons in high school, Owens was quite content to defer to the established stars, and the result was a wonderfully balanced attack and a season that turned out better than most thought it would. SU went from No 8 to No. 2 in the nation after sprinting to a 13–0 start.

The Orangemen opened with a convincing 92–76 win over LaSalle, and in the third game of the year, they crushed 20th-ranked Indiana 102–78 at the Big Apple NIT, handing coach Bobby Knight one of the worst losses of his career. Though the victory didn't atone for their title game loss two seasons earlier, it was satisfying and featured one of the most memorable plays in SU history when Douglas grabbed a loose ball and hiked it, football-style, through his legs, to a streaking Thompson for a basket. It would be one of 326 baskets "The General" would assist on during his senior season when he garnered consensus All-America honors. "We've had a lot of great passers at Syracuse, but he was the best," Boeheim said. "He could do the conventional and the spectacular pass equally well. And nobody has ever been better at throwing the alley-oop pass." Indeed, his lobs to a leaping Thompson or Coleman near the basket were things to behold and quite demoralizing to opposing defenders, who usually were caught flat-footed. "The thing is, we didn't practice them," Douglas said. "It's all a timing thing. I'd be out at halfcourt, and I'd give Stevie a look, then let it fly. People give me a lot of credit, but it's like in football—a quarterback is only as good as his receivers, and I had some guys with great leaping ability and great hands."

Douglas wound up reaching double-digits in assists 14 times that season, his best passing night coming in a 100–96 victory against Providence in front of 32,096 fans in the Dome on January 28, 1989, when he dished out an NCAA-record 22 assists. Six of the baskets came on his alley-oops. Although Douglas was good at setting others up, he also knew when and how to set himself up to score. When teams laid off him, expecting him to pass, he made them pay, averaging a team-leading 18.2 points to go along with his school-record average of 8.6 assists per game. "The amazing thing about Sherman was that he was able to keep Billy, Stevie, and Derrick happy while scoring 18 points a game himself," said longtime SU assistant coach Bernie Fine.

Douglas' value to the team was underscored when he missed two games in January with a back injury. Syracuse lost both contests. Douglas' favorite receiver was Thompson, who took his game up another notch, averaging 18 points. Coleman, meanwhile, continued to be one of the nation's premier rebounders, with 11.4 per game, and Owens did his share to help both Douglas with the ball handling and Coleman with the rebounding, averaging 13 points, nearly seven rebounds, and 3.1 assists per game. Shooting guard Matt Roe kept opponents from sagging down low with his three-point shots, future NBA player David Johnson provided some offense off the bench, and 7' center Richard Manning came in to help out on the boards.

It all added up to a 25–6 regular-season record that included an 18–1 mark inside the Dome—the final home win coming 82–76 in overtime against the Hoyas. The bitter rivals would meet a week later in the Big East championship game in the Big Apple, with Georgetown emerging victorious 88–79. The defeat dropped the Orangemen to seventh in the polls, and they were sent to the Midwest Region in Dallas, where they cruised past Bucknell by 23 points and Colorado

State by 15. At the Sweet 16 in Minneapolis, Syracuse beat sixth-ranked Missouri, setting up a highly anticipated regional final against third-ranked Illinois. The game, featuring eight future NBA players, wasn't decided until Thompson's long three-point attempt fell short at the buzzer, preserving an 89–86 Illini victory that had been sparked by the second-half play of Kendall Gill and Kenny Battle.

The game brought the curtain down on a pleasantly unexpected 30–8 season and on the remarkable career of Douglas, the lightly recruited afterthought who left Syracuse as the NCAA's career leader in assists and as the Orangemen's all-time leading scorer (2,060 points). Though he no longer holds the top spot in either of those categories, his legacy remains solid. That June, the Miami Heat made him the first pick of the second round, and he spent a dozen seasons in the NBA. Besides the Heat, he also played for the Boston Celtics, Los Angeles Clippers, Milwaukee Bucks, and New Jersey Nets. On March 9, 2003, his No. 20 jersey was retired at the Carrier Dome. "He's had an amazing career," Boeheim said. "Bing was a one-of-a-kind player because he could do so much. Sherman's like that, too. He plays both ends of the court. He's inside and he's outside. He's the greatest passer I've ever seen."

Clearly, Douglas' replacement was the main issue heading into the 1989–90 campaign. Fortunately for Boeheim, he wouldn't also have to answer the "Who is going to replace Derrick?" question, because Coleman put an end to the speculation that he would declare for the NBA draft shortly after the loss to Illinois. Coleman had hurt his back during the regular-season finale, which explained why his numbers dropped a tad in the NCAAs. Despite his slight decline in the tournament, Coleman still was projected to be a Top 10 pick, and had he asked Boeheim's advice the coach probably would have told him to turn pro. But the senior-to-be already had made up his mind to stay. "He just said he was going to be the fifth or sixth pick in the draft, and he said he wanted to be the first—that's it," Boeheim recalled. "That's the only discussion we ever had about it." Coleman said there was another reason why he decided to stay all four years: "I loved college, and I knew you only get one shot at being young," he said. "I figured the money would still be there, and if I played like I felt I was capable as a senior, there would be even more money waiting for me."

Boeheim had been blessed with seven seasons of dependable and occasionally spectacular point-guard play, thanks to Pearl and The General. But now he was facing a dilemma. Rather than throw freshman Michael Edwards in there at the start, he decided to move Thompson to the point with the proviso that Billy Owens would take some of the ball-handling pressure off of the senior guard. Interestingly, despite the loss of Douglas, the pollsters liked the Orangemen so much they made them preseason No. 1. Unlike two seasons before when they lost their opener, this time they held onto the ranking into the next calendar year. One of the early season victories was a 78–76 decision against sixth-ranked Duke in Greensboro, North Carolina, fueled in large part by Coleman's 19 rebounds. Boasting a balanced and powerful lineup that included Kentucky transfer LeRon Ellis at center, Coleman and Owens at the forwards, Thompson at the point, and David Johnson at two-guard, the Orangemen cruised to 10 straight wins before being upset by hot-shooting Villanova 93–74. Interestingly, the SU lineup included two players from California, one from Pennsylvania, one from Louisiana, and one from Michigan. "We had come a long way from the early years when we relied heavily on recruiting kids from upstate New York and the city," Boeheim said.

That January began with the release of Jim Boeheim's first instructional video, titled *Boeheim on Basketball*, and it included a little comic relief. When the coach turned the topic of conversation to free-throw shooting, the Orangemen's traditional blemish, he deadpanned: "We've had a little problem in the past, but I know I know how to shoot free throws." The man who converted a modest 69.5 percent of his foul shots during his SU career then was shown at the charity stripe, sinking 33 in a row without any splicing or retaping. "I think I may be the designated free throw shooter," he said into the camera. "That might be what we need. We're going to get our big guys fouled, and I'm going to come off the bench and shoot free throws."

After a January stretch in which the Orangemen played sloppily while losing three of five games, Boeheim needed more than a designated free throw shooter. In an effort to reduce the turnovers and get the offense running more smoothly, the coach abandoned the experiment with Thompson, moving the senior back to shooting guard and inserting freshman Michael Edwards at the point. The move worked brilliantly, as Syracuse won 10 of its final 12 regular-season games to finish 22–5 and atop the Big East at 12–4. The Orangemen clinched the conference title with a dramatic 89–87 overtime victory against Georgetown in the Dome on March 4, 1990, in front of a national television audience and an NCAA on-campus record crowd of 33,015 that included esteemed filmmaker Spike Lee and baseball legend Ernie Banks. It marked the first time SU had taken the season series from the Hoyas, prompting Owens to make motions with an imaginary broom at center court after the final buzzer sounded.

With a little more than seven minutes remaining in the first half, Georgetown coach John Thompson was ejected after receiving technical fouls from three different officials, resulting in what amounted to a 10-point play for Syracuse. Big, bad John, who loved playing the villain in this basketball passion play, incited the huge throng by waving his trademark towel as he trudged to the locker room. Thompson's tirade and the ensuing technical free throws and baskets turned a three-point SU deficit into a 43–36 SU lead. But even without the presence of the 6'10" Thompson on their bench, the Hoyas took the game to the limit and then some. The bizarre contest was sent into overtime when

Owens was inexplicably fouled by Sam Jefferson near halfcourt with one second remaining. Jefferson calmly drained both free throws to tie the score at 81. Another freshman, Michael Edwards, also turned in a huge performance, with 18 points. Owens, Edwards, and Coleman were a powerful trio, combining for 68 points, 19 rebounds, and 15 assists. In his postgame news conference, Thompson was in an almost jovial mood, telling reporters: "I let my competitive juices overflow. I made a mistake, and that's it. It won't happen again—I don't think. I've never gone three-on-one with the officials before." Then, smiling, he told the media to tell the Syracuse fans that he would see them in New York a week later.

By averaging 29,919 fans per game, Syracuse had established a new NCAA basketball record and had topped the nation in attendance a sixth straight season. Despite the huge crowds and thrilling victory against their despised rival, not everything was rosy in Orange Nation. A day before the Georgetown game, a new book was released that would rock the Syracuse basketball program. *Raw Recruits*, co-authored by respected *Sports Illustrated* reporters Alexander Wolff and Armen Keteyian, claimed that SU had benefited from its relationship with New York City "street agent" Robert Johnson, who reportedly had steered several prospects, including recently recruited center Conrad McRae, to Syracuse. It also alleged that Syracuse players had been provided with money and free sneakers, as well as discounted use of cars and airline tickets. Before heading to New York for the Big East Conference tournament, Boeheim spoke with *Syracuse Herald-Journal* sports columnist Bud Poliquin and adamantly denied the allegations. "I've been associated with Syracuse basketball since 1962," the coach said in that March 6, 1990, interview from his Manley Field House office. "That's 27 years. The NCAA has never called us about anything we've done. We never have, to my knowledge, and never will, break a rule to get a player."

Boeheim, then, went on the offensive, attacking the credibility of *Raw Recruits*. "The book claims to portray abuses in college basketball," he said. "The book, to me, portrays abuses in journalism. They draw conclusions without presenting a fact. To say we're successful in recruiting—and then to say we've done it because we've cheated—is ludicrous. There are a lot of conclusions drawn without a single fact. I see no facts. Read me a fact. The book is about perception. That's what the book is about." During the interview, Boeheim acknowledged that Johnson, an acquaintance of his since the mid-70s, had a murky reputation. He said he spoke to Johnson about a dozen times per year, and Poliquin pointed out in his column published the following day that Johnson had sat in the ritzy seats behind the SU bench and had been spotted in the team's locker room after games. "The only thing I've ever talked to Robert Johnson about is that he cannot give anything or do anything on behalf of Syracuse University because he doesn't work for us," Boeheim said. "He has no connection in that regard with us. He does like Syracuse. I know that. But as far as us being associated with him in any way, we're not."

Though only several pages of the book were devoted to the Syracuse program, the damage had been done. The allegations would prompt the *Syracuse Post-Standard* to launch an exhaustive seven-month investigation resulting in a scathing two-part, award-winning series titled *Out of Bounds*. The newspaper's allegations of even more NCAA violations convinced the school to perform its own in-house investigation, which eventually led college sports' governing body to penalize Syracuse's basketball, lacrosse, wrestling, and football programs.

Despite the storm clouds, Boeheim was able to focus on basketball in New York, guiding his fourth-ranked Orangemen to the 1990 Big East finals, where they lost to Connecticut. SU crushed Coppin State by 22 in the opener of the NCAA Southeast Regionals and nipped

Virginia by two to advance to the Sweet 16 in New Orleans. But the 'Cuse's season came to an unceremonious end in an 82–78 upset loss to Minnesota. "It was very, very disappointing because I thought we had a great team and a great chance at making it to Final Four and winning it all," Coleman said. "If you had told me after reaching the title game my freshman season that we wouldn't make it back there again, I wouldn't have believed you." Although their college careers didn't end the way they had envisioned, Coleman and Thompson had established themselves as the winningest combo in school history. They guided the Orangemen to a school-record 114 victories— including 11 in the NCAA tournament—in four seasons. Thompson, despite not possessing a jump shot, left SU as the school's third-leading scorer, while Coleman ended his college career as the Orangemen's all-time leading scorer (2,143 points) and as college basketball's all-time leading rebounder (his total of 1,537 rebounds has since been surpassed). Thompson would bounce around pro basketball's minor leagues for a few seasons before becoming a college coach.

Coleman, meanwhile, was named the national player of the year after his senior season and would fulfill his goal of becoming the No. 1 overall pick in the 1990 NBA draft when he was selected by the New Jersey Nets. He averaged 16.5 points and 9.3 rebounds during his 15-year pro basketball career, averaging more than 20 points and 10 rebounds per game three different seasons. His off-court problems also were part of his Syracuse and NBA legacy. At SU, he was at the heart of a brawl with Cornell players during a game as a sophomore and pleaded guilty to non-criminal charges for being involved in a fight and a break-in during his junior year. Boeheim, though, believes Coleman has been misunderstood and that he is a much better person than he's been given credit for. The coach cited how beloved Coleman was by SU players and coaches and how many of his charitable acts have gone unnoticed. "This is a guy who spent $2 million of his own money to build a playground in his old, run-down Detroit neighborhood when the city couldn't come up with the money," Boeheim said. "And there are many other instances when he's went out of his way to help others down on their luck. The media has blown up the few things he did when he was immature and have overlooked the really good heart Derrick has. It's really too bad, because he really is a caring person, and that's not how he's been portrayed."

Billy Owens had taken on a much bigger role during his sophomore season, averaging 18.2 points per game. With Coleman and Thompson gone, Boeheim would ask Owens to carry even more of the load during the 1990–91 campaign. The junior was more than ready for the challenge of placing a basketball team on his broad shoulders the way he had done for four years in high school. Owens responded to Boeheim's request with one of the greatest individual seasons in SU hoops history, averaging 23.2 points and 11.6 rebounds per game while leading the Orangemen to a 26–4 regular-season record and the Big East title. Syracuse won its first 13 games, including a 77–74 upset of eighth-ranked Indiana in the Maui Classic in Hawaii, and wound up going 7–2 versus teams ranked in the Top 25 and climbing as high as No. 3 in the national polls. Although the team received solid contributions from center LeRon Ellis, guards Michael Edwards and Adrian Autry, and forward Dave Johnson, this clearly was Billy Owens' team. In fact, during their fast start, the Orangemen became known as "Billy and the Beaters." "I think people sometimes forget just how great an all-around player Billy Owens was," Boeheim said. "He was just spectacular his junior season. He did virtually everything that [future Syracuse star] Carmelo Anthony did during his freshman season, and he did so with a weaker supporting cast."

Unfortunately for Owens and his teammates, their spectacular regular season would be sullied by arguably the most disappointing postseason in program history. The Orangemen were knocked off by

Villanova 70–68 in the first round of the 1991 Big East tournament. The NCAA selection committee didn't put much stock in the loss, chalking it up to one of those things that happens in conference play, and installed Syracuse as the No. 2 seed in the East. That meant the Orangemen would face the 15th seeded Richmond Spiders in the first round at College Park, Maryland. Everyone expected SU to cruise into the second round, but Richmond had other ideas. For the first time in NCAA tournament history, a 15th seed knocked off a second seed, as the Spiders won 73–69 in a game that is still painfully known to Syracuse fans as "Arachnophobia." "That was the worst day of my life," Owens told *Syracuse Post-Standard* beat writer Mike Waters. "I was mad. I was mad at me. I was mad at the team. It really hurt me a lot." In retrospect, Boeheim said he believes the NCAA's ongoing investigation of the basketball program contributed to that monumental loss by sapping the team of its energy. "The circumstances that surrounded the game and the turmoil were really the reasons we lost, rather than Richmond outplaying us. Mentally, we were beat at the end of the day." Owens concurred, saying, "You could just tell on the court. You could see that game slipping away, and we didn't do anything. They were setting simple cross picks, and we were acting like we didn't know how to defend. I remember Boeheim screaming, 'We've got to fight through the picks,' and it didn't happen."

The NCAA infractions committee had decided to conduct its own investigation after the *Post-Standard* published its bombshell series by reporters Tom Foster and Todd Lighty on December 20 and 21, 1990. The stories detailed money gifts to players from boosters such as Bill Rapp Jr., a local car dealer and close friend of Boeheim's. It also alleged the changing of a player's grade so he would be eligible to play; unsavory dealings with a New York City "street agent" who steered players to SU; and player perks from local businesses, including free meals, clothing, legal help, and cut-rate use of cars by student athletes and their families. The stories also noted that such deals were in violation of NCAA rules and could result in players being declared ineligible and the suspension of entire teams from intercollegiate competition. Rapp and other boosters and alumni denied giving players money or free food and merchandise.

Clearly, the investigative series was not the present Boeheim had hoped to receive just five days before Christmas. "The NCAA has looked at everything we've done," he told Foster and Lighty. "They have talked to guys who have left here. And nothing was ever said. We try to do everything we can to see that nothing happens, because it is the right way to do things, No. 1, and because, No. 2, I want to coach here 30 or 40 more years."

In addition to instigating investigations by the university and the NCAA, the *Post-Standard's* series prompted national news organizations such as *Sports Illustrated*, *USA TODAY*, and *ESPN* to descend upon the Central New York city to report on the program that for years had been a source of civic pride and had bound a region stretching from Albany to Rochester. "Everyone who goes to that Dome to watch the basketball team feels ownership in that team," Syracuse Mayor Thomas Young told the *Washington Post*. "They feel they own it and are a part of it. And now they feel they have been hurt, too."

They also felt anger and a sense of betrayal toward their hometown newspaper. Phone calls and letters to the editor ran 50-to-1 against the paper, and more than 200 readers—including Boeheim—expressed their indignation by canceling their subscriptions. "To believe there would be no reaction would be naive," said *Post-Standard* executive editor Robert C. Atkinson. "It's disturbing to people that the local newspaper would not be totally supportive of the basketball program. In their eyes we have turned against the community. But we have a role here. We are not an arm of the university. We report the good and the bad." The "kill the messenger" response, though, didn't reach the proportions it did in Lexington, Kentucky, in 1985, when a series of stories in the *Lexington Herald-Leader* about the University of Kentucky's basketball program resulted in threats against the newspaper with deliverers being spat upon and an anti–*Herald-Leader* party being thrown by a booster at a local country club. Still, there was no question that many Syracusans—especially among the 28,000 SU basketball season-ticket holders—had little use for their morning paper. "Everybody thinks it's a bunch of crap," said Al Caza, who ran a barbershop across from City Hall. "The thing about Syracuse is that it's not the school's team; it's the city's team. When they screw around with the team, they're screwing around with the people."

Boeheim did his best to keep his focus on practices and games, but the probe clearly was weighing heavily on him. When he sat down for an interview with Bud Poliquin on February 16, 1991, the beleaguered coach spoke in a quiet voice that sounded, in the sports columnist's words, as if "it's coming from a distant radio station." Boeheim told him: "I've said it a million times already. I've never done anything as far as breaking NCAA rules with a kid. The coaches here have not done anything they shouldn't have done." Poliquin went on to write about the investigations' toll on the SU coach:

> Indeed there are snoops at the gates. Snoops from those running SU's in-house probe...and from the NCAA's investigative team...and from the media, from both his own community and abroad. And they have collected, with rope at the ready, to learn whether or not the king and his program are unclean.
>
> Clearly, all of this is very much bothering the 46-year-old coach of the Orangemen as has nothing else in his professional career. And, yeah, for good reason. After all, to suggest that the basketball program has cheated is to suggest that the man who runs it is either blind when blindness is convenient or, well, a cheater, himself.

Either way, it makes for a burdensome load, especially when hoisting that latter tag. You see, while Gaylord Perry rode the cheater's label with a sly smile all the way to baseball's Hall of Fame, college basketball coaches have been known to roll with it through doors and out onto curbs.

Not long after the disappointing finish to their 1990–91 season, Boeheim received some more bad news when Billy Owens announced he was forgoing his senior year to enter the NBA draft. The possibility that NCAA penalties might include banishment from the '91–92 NCAA tournament clearly was a factor in his decision. But Owens also had other reasons for turning pro. He was projected to be drafted third behind UNLV's Larry Johnson and Georgia Tech's Kenny Anderson. Had he waited until 1992, he likely wouldn't be drafted any higher because centers Shaquille O'Neal of LSU and Alonzo Mourning of Georgetown were slated to be chosen before him.

A month after that June's draft, Boeheim and Dick Vitale journeyed to Rochester, New York, to play a one-on-one basketball game for charity. The coach and the commentator had feuded briefly the previous season after Vitale said he believed Boeheim's job was in jeopardy because of the NCAA investigation. There were reports that Boeheim then contacted Vitale's bosses at ABC and ESPN and asked for them to reprimand the color analyst, but nothing happened beyond that and the two "kissed and made up," according to Vitale. The one-on-one game received national play in the media, and the two men good-naturedly traded verbal barbs after Boeheim's lopsided 15–3 win. "He's always accusing me of playing all easy games," the coach began. "Well, that was the easiest game I've ever played. We could go undefeated with opponents like that."

"You should be used to that, baby," Vitale howled in response. "Jimmy's used to playing those cupcakes in November and December.

He's just starting a little earlier this year." Afterward, Boeheim challenged Vitale to a free-throw shooting contest. Both men made eight of 10, but Boeheim won in a shoot-off. "Remember this," Vitale said. "I get the microphone last this year."

As it turned out, the NCAA did not complete its investigation until October 1992, so Syracuse remained eligible for postseason play in '91–92. With Owens gone, forward Dave Johnson assumed the leadership role, topping the team in scoring (19.8 points per game) and rebounding (seven rebounds per game). The Orangemen went 18–9 in the regular season and finished fifth in the Big East standings. They rallied, though, in the conference tournament, capturing the championship with a 56–54 upset against Georgetown in Madison Square Garden. The title earned them the 21st spot in the polls and an automatic NCAA tournament berth. But they didn't last long. After beating a pesky Princeton team in the first round, they were defeated by a favored University of Massachusetts squad 77–71 in overtime, finishing their season at 22–10.

On October 1, 1992, after nearly two years of controversy and uncertainty, the hammer came down on the Syracuse University basketball program. The NCAA infractions committee imposed a two-year probation on SU athletics. Men's basketball was singled out for the harshest punishment—including a ban from the 1993 NCAA tournament and the loss of one scholarship each in the 1993–94 and '94–95 school years. The 24-page report cited widespread violations in the basketball program from 1984–90, many of them booster related. David Swank, the chairman of the NCAA infractions committee, wrote in the report: "The basketball coach probably should have been aware these problems were occurring." In a news conference on campus that dark October day, SU Chancellor Kenneth Shaw called the findings "embarrassing because we take pride in running a clean program." But he also voiced strong support for Boeheim and athletics director Jake

Crouthamel. A haggard-but-relieved-looking Boeheim told reporters he accepted the NCAA's decision. He also said he was grateful that SU wasn't barred from playing on television, wasn't required to return any money from prior tournament winnings, and wasn't forced to fire anybody. Swank said those allowances were made because of the university's full cooperation throughout the investigation. Boeheim was disappointed that his four seniors—Mike Hopkins, Conrad McRae, Dave Siock, and Michael Edwards—wouldn't have the opportunity to play in the NCAA tournament because of the ban. "But this class has been to the last three tournaments, and they're going to have to accept it," he said. "There are a lot of kids, a majority of kids, who go to college and don't get to go to three NCAA tournaments."

The story received national play, and not all the commentaries were kind. *Sports Illustrated* described the punishment as a slap on the wrist and told its four million readers that Boeheim should have been fired. ESPN college basketball commentator Dick Vitale, though, felt the sanctions were just right and that the winningest coach in SU history deserved to keep his job. "The way to summarize it best—it's relief, baby, relief," he said. "It's got to be a very relieved moment for Jim Boeheim and his staff. They've been operating under such stress and pressure the last couple of years. Let's get on with it; that's got to be the philosophy. I certainly think they can sustain their program at the highest level. I think their program is bigger than this."

Boeheim knew the next few years would be crucial for the program and him. In the weeks after the NCAA announcement, he sat down for a series of wide-ranging and revealing interviews with *Post-Standard* sports columnist Sean Kirst. He told Kirst that his job was never in jeopardy, but he also said that, although he had no other plans, he wouldn't commit to coaching in Syracuse beyond the coming season. He also said he was sorry for the NCAA violations "we could have controlled," but contended many were beyond his immediate authority. And he addressed the issue of him being characterized as cold and aloof. "I'm just not an outgoing person," Boeheim said in a rare moment of public soul-bearing. "But when you're the basketball coach and you don't speak to everybody, then you're too big. You're too big for 'em. You think you're too important. But if I was just an ordinary guy, walking down the street, they wouldn't speak to me, either. They would just let me go."

Boeheim admitted to Kirst that he had attempted to thaw his chilly image. "I definitely tried to soften up a little bit," he said. "I don't think people can change tremendously. I think you change a little bit. Because I'm very introspective, I do try now to talk more to people so they don't think I'm snubbing them. I try to think about those things. I [went] to speak today, and as I was leaving, people would say hello and I'd say, 'hi,' just to make sure they know that. So, yeah, I think you change. [In the past] I didn't realize I might hurt somebody's feelings, because they expect more from me. I'm more sensitive to people's feelings, because if I don't say hello, [fans] take it like I don't care. It comes with the territory. If you don't want that, you have to do something that isn't quite so public. And I try to be better with the media, but I do take offense sometimes."

CHAPTER 10

A Major Change in Perception

WITH THE NCAA INVESTIGATION FINALLY BEHIND HIM, Jim Boeheim felt as if the weight of the world had been lifted from his shoulders. He looked forward to getting back to doing what he did best—coaching basketball. One of his biggest challenges, of course, would be keeping his team properly motivated throughout the 1992–93 season, now that it had been determined the Orangemen wouldn't be eligible for the NCAA tournament. Boeheim was confident his players would respond well because of a solid senior class, which included the super-competitive Mike Hopkins, and because of the expected contributions of sophomore guard Lawrence Moten and highly touted freshman forward John Wallace.

Moten would become another one of those great Boeheim recruiting coups from the Washington, D.C., area. Like Sherman Douglas before him, he wasn't widely recruited but would go on to become one of the greatest players in SU annals. The 6'5" Moten actually had developed a bigger rep as a high school football player, but his first love was basketball. Although Moten was not blessed with great speed or leaping ability, Boeheim liked his uncanny knack for finding different ways to score points and decided to offer him the last scholarship in a 1991 recruiting class that included Lucious Jackson, Anthony Harris, Glenn Sekunda, Lazarus Sims, and J.B. Reafsnyder.

Moten wasn't expected to see a great deal of playing time his freshman season, but when veteran Adrian Autry went down with a severely sprained ankle, Boeheim decided to replace him with his unheralded freshman. It was a risky move because Syracuse was going to play a powerful Florida State team that boasted future NBA players Sam Cassell and Doug Edwards. Moten proved equal to the task, scoring 18 points to lead SU to an 89–71 upset.

The superlative performance was a harbinger event, as Moten averaged 18.2 points per game that season to earn Big East freshman of the year honors. During the next three seasons, his silky-smooth, almost effortless style of play would become known as "Poetry in Moten," and he would go on to become the school's and Big East Conference's all-time leading scorer, with 2,334 points. The player who wore his socks knee-high—a basketball fashion style popular in the 1970s—also would be remembered for helping the Syracuse program weather the NCAA sanctions and remain a college basketball powerhouse. "He wouldn't win any races and he wasn't able to jump out of the building and his outside shot didn't have a great deal of trajectory, but Lawrence definitely had a nose for the basket and knew how to score," Boeheim said. "He was what I'd call an old-school player. He also was kind of a quiet assassin. You might not think he did much out there because he didn't look like he was expending a lot of energy. But then you'd look at the box score and see 25 points next to his name. He's another one of those guys who people tend to overlook when they talk about great Syracuse players. And that's a shame. I think it might be because he played during that period when we were coming off the probation."

The other player credited with tiding the Orangemen through their probationary period was Wallace. A 6'8" forward, Big John had guided his Greece Athena High School team to a New York state championship during a senior season that saw him named to the McDonald's, *Parade* magazine, and Converse All-America teams. Wallace had grown up in

Rochester, about 90 miles west of Syracuse, following the Orangemen, particularly his idol, Derrick Coleman. "I loved everything about the program," he said. "The fast-paced offense, the humongous crowds in the Carrier Dome, and the intensity of Big East play. When my high school coach [Don Brown] told me in the 10th grade that he had received a recruiting letter from Coach Boeheim, I was ecstatic."

Still, some wondered if the NCAA investigation and the threat of sanctions might test his loyalty. Kansas and Providence were among several schools that kept inquiring to see if he was still committed to the Orangemen. But their efforts to get him to change his mind were in vain. "I talked to coach about the possible penalties, and he was straight with me," Wallace recalled. "He told me that they probably were going to get hit with a one-year ban from the NCAA tournament, and I was fine with that because I was making a four-year decision, not a one-year decision."

Despite not having the carrot of a tournament bid to dangle in front of his players, the 1992–93 squad cobbled together a solid season, going 20–8 and making it all the way to the Big East championship game, where it was clobbered by Seton Hall by 33 points. The Orangemen opened the season with eight consecutive victories before losing to Boston College 94–93 in overtime, despite 20 points from Wallace. After that loss, Big John was distraught, shedding tears in the locker room. "I had lost just one game my senior year of high school, so I wasn't used to losing," he said. "In fact, I hated it. I guess I was kind of naive. I thought we were going to go undefeated. I didn't know any better." Wearing the same No. 44 jersey that Coleman had worn, Wallace finished his first season averaging 11.1 points and a team-leading 7.6 rebounds per game. Moten continued to outsmart people to the basket and averaged a team-high 17.9 points per contest. His heroics included a 10-foot jumper with 24 seconds to go to beat Providence, a 16-point second half to knock off Connecticut, 21 points in an upset of ninth-ranked Seton Hall, and a 26-point effort in a Big East tournament semifinal victory versus St. John's.

After the season ended, Boeheim received an offer to be one of the coaches playing themselves in a new Nick Nolte movie titled *Blue Chips*. The movie buff jumped at the opportunity and flew out to Los Angeles to film his cameo. The plot was about how a basketball coach from a fictitious university was feeling pressure to cheat by paying players in order to keep winning. Boeheim joined other real-life basketball luminaries, including Larry Bird, Shaquille O'Neal, Bobby Knight, Bob Cousy, and Rick Pitino. The movie would be released the following February. Four years later, Boeheim would play himself in another basketball flick—Spike Lee's *He Got Game*. "I'm kind of disappointed," the SU coach joked years later, "that I never received Oscar consideration for Best Supporting Actor."

Moten (21.5 points per game) and Wallace (15 points per game, 9 rebounds per game) continued to elevate their play during the 1993–94 season, as the Orangemen improved to 23–7, including 13–5 in conference play, and returned to the NCAAs. After being upset by Seton Hall in the opening round of the Big East tournament, SU went to the West Region in Ogden, Utah, where it knocked off Hawaii and Wisconsin–Green Bay to advance to the Sweet 16. Despite being heavy underdogs, the Orangemen took fifth-ranked Missouri to the limit before running out of gas and losing by 10 in overtime.

Because of a scheduling conflict with the football team, Syracuse was forced to begin its '94–95 season in Manley Field House instead of the Carrier Dome. The building that Georgetown coach John Thompson had pronounced "officially closed" after snapping SU's 57-game home court win-streak 15 years earlier was re-opened, but the results weren't good. For just the second time in Boeheim's 18 seasons, Syracuse dropped a season opener—111–104 in overtime to George Washington. After that defeat, the Orangemen strung together 14 straight victories, soaring to No. 6 in the national polls. Despite fielding a strong lineup that included Moten (19.6 points per game), Wallace (16.8 points per game, 8.2 rebounds per game), forward Lucious Jackson, guard Michael Lloyd, and the center tandem of Otis Hill and J.B. Reafsnyder, Syracuse stumbled down the stretch, losing six of its last nine games. For the second straight year, the Orangemen were one-and-done in the Big East tournament. They still managed to earn an NCAA bid and were sent to the Midwest Region in Austin, Texas. They beat a pesky Southern Illinois squad by four in the opener.

Their reward? A meeting against defending national champion Arkansas in Round 2. Moten had an unbelievable game, scoring 27 points against the Razorbacks' "40-minutes-of-hell" full-court, pressure defense. But it was a play near the end of regulation that would bring a premature end to SU's season and Moten's career. Rallying from a 12-point second-half deficit, the Orangemen took an 82–81 lead, and with just 4.3 seconds left, the Razorbacks attempted an inbounds. Jackson dived onto the floor to steal the pass. As an Arkansas player tried to wrest the ball from Jackson, Moten instinctively did what players do in those situations. He called a timeout so that SU would maintain possession. Unfortunately for him and his teammates, Syracuse didn't have any timeouts left, resulting in a technical foul. Arkansas converted one of two shots to send the game into an extra session and went on to nip the Orangemen 96–94. It was the third time in four years that Moten's season had ended with a loss in overtime in the NCAAs. His faux pas conjured memories of the championship game two years earlier, when Michigan's Chris Webber called a timeout he didn't have. What made Moten's mistake even more painful is the fact the possession arrow was in favor of the Orangemen when he signaled for a TO, meaning they would have retained the ball and been able to run out the clock in regulation.

Afterward, Boeheim consoled his senior captain, then staunchly defended him in the postgame news conference. "People forget that Lawrence had smartly used timeouts in those situations several times during the season—plays that helped us to win games," he said. "I think in the heat of the moment like that, your instincts take over. You forget the situation and just react. The other thing that people forget is that we aren't anywhere close to being in a position to win that game without Lawrence going off on the Razorbacks the way he did. Without Lawrence scoring like he did against that tenacious defense, we get run out of that gym."

Moten's college career was officially over, and it appeared that Wallace's might be, too. After a solid junior season in which he averaged 16.8 points and 8.2 rebounds, Big John decided to explore his NBA draft options. With Moten and two other starters graduating, Wallace figured maybe the timing was right. But after researching the draft and learning that he was projected as a late first-round, early second-round pick, he decided that another year of college seasoning would be beneficial. With Michael Lloyd gone, Lazarus Sims, the Syracuse high school product who rode the bench for three seasons, would finally get his chance to run the team. Few were more excited about that than Wallace, who had been good friends with the Z-Man since they met at an AAU tournament in the eighth grade. Joining Wallace in the front court would be senior center Otis Hill and promising sophomore forward Todd Burgan. Jason Cipolla, a hard-nosed junior college transfer from Queens, was slated to play shooting guard, while Marius Janulis, a Lithuanian native who had played his high school ball in Prattsburg, New York, would back him up and provide the Orangemen with another three-point threat. Reserve center J.B. Reafsnyder would complete Boeheim's seven-man rotation. "That may not have been the most talented team in my four years there, but it was the team where the pieces fit together best," Wallace said. "Most of the guys stayed in Syracuse that summer, and we played a lot of pickup basketball in our free time. I think that really helped us a lot. We developed a pretty tight bond."

SU began the season unranked but forced the pollsters to take notice with 11 consecutive victories, including a 79–70 upset of third-ranked Arizona on the road as Wallace had a monster game with 29 points and nine rebounds. The Orangemen didn't taste defeat until they lost 65–47 to top-ranked Massachusetts in the title game of the Rainbow Classic in Hawaii on December 30, 1995. Syracuse turned the ball over 24 times in that game and was limited to the lowest point total in Boeheim's 20 years as head coach. SU finished the regular season at 22–7 and won its first two games in the Big East tournament before being trounced by Connecticut by 18 points as Ray Allen scored 29.

Few expected much from the 13th-ranked Orangemen in the NCAA tournament, but Wallace could sense something special percolating after they crushed Montana State by 33 points and Drexel by 11 in the opening rounds of the West Regionals in Albuquerque, New Mexico. "I think everyone was starting to believe in themselves and in our team," he said. "Everyone was doing a great job fulfilling their respective roles."

The Sweet 16 matchup pitted them against the slightly favored Georgia Bulldogs at Denver's McNichols Sports Arena in a game that remains a Syracuse hoops classic. The fourth-seeded Orangemen wound up winning 83–81 in overtime, as Wallace made two of the most memorable plays in the program's history—one on a game-saving pass and one on a game-winning shot.

The Bulldogs were leading by two with 2.1 seconds remaining in regulation. In a strategic move that went against coaching convention, Boeheim instructed Wallace, his best player, to inbound the ball near halfcourt. Most coaches would have opted to have someone else pass the ball in and get it to Wallace for the final shot. But Wallace, who grew up playing football and dreaming of becoming the next Randall

Cunningham, had the best arm on the team (other than All-American quarterback Donovan McNabb, who also played basketball for two years before devoting himself full time to football). Wallace was to look for Sims, who already had drained two threes down the stretch to get SU back into the game. As it turned out, he was closely guarded by two defenders, so Wallace instead rifled the ball to Jason Cipolla, who sank a 12-footer at the buzzer to send the game into overtime. The instant Cipolla's shot swished through, the Syracuse players began whooping it up wildly in front of their bench. But Wallace, the senior leader, quickly restored order, reminding them that they still had a five-minute extra session to play. "I gave them a little history lesson about something they apparently had forgotten," Wallace said, smiling. "I reminded them about how we had lost in overtime in our last two trips to the NCAA tournament. I told them this game was far from over, and we needed to bust our butts in order to make sure we didn't repeat the history of last season and the season before that."

With about 10 seconds remaining in OT, Georgia took an 81–80 lead on a three-pointer. Wallace immediately grabbed the inbounds and began dribbling furiously upcourt. "I called for the ball right away, but I would have had an easier time getting a piece of meat from a hungry wolf," Sims said, chuckling. "John absolutely hated to lose, and he was determined that no one was going to stop him from making sure our season and our college careers didn't end there." Wallace pulled up at the top of the key and let fly with a shot that found nothing but net. The Bulldogs were unable to regroup in time to take a shot in the final seconds, and the horn sounded. Syracuse, a team that had begun the season unranked and finished fourth in the Big East, was going to the Elite Eight. "The funny thing is that just before John took that shot, I considered calling a timeout," Boeheim said. "I'm glad I didn't." Wallace was glad he didn't, too. "I just felt unstoppable on that play," he said after finishing with 30 points and 15 rebounds. "I was like, 'Give me the ball and get out of my way.'" After the buzzer, another celebration ensued—this time led rather than quashed by Wallace. He and his teammates began singing a rap song they had created. "When the 'Cuse is in the house, oh, my god, oh, my god," they sang loudly, lustily, and repeatedly as they bounded to the locker room.

Two days later, the 'Cuse not only would be in the house but in the Final Four after upsetting the fourth-ranked Kansas Jayhawks 60–57 in the West Finals. The victory had firmly established the Orangemen as the Cinderella team of the 1996 NCAA tournament—the underdog and overachiever fans nationwide were passionately backing. But, perhaps even more surprising than SU's victory was the dramatic change in the national perception of their underappreciated coach. Long portrayed by the media as a sarcastic sourpuss who knew how to recruit but not how to coach, particularly in big games, Jim Boeheim was now being feted by columnists coast-to-coast for maximizing the potential of a team many believed had no business making it this deep into the tournament. But the embracing of Boeheim went beyond his team's surprising tournament run. It also was a result of him willingly showing a side of himself—kinder, gentler, funnier—that the media hadn't always seen. His self-deprecating sense of humor was on display following the Kansas game for a national television audience to see when CBS' Al McGuire stuck a microphone in front of him and said: "Go ahead, whine about something." Boeheim, grinning broadly and playing right along, said, "Well, we missed those free throws at the end..."

In the postgame press conference, Boeheim was asked about the perception of him, particularly the sideline histrionics and blue language during games. "People don't like me," he said, calmly. "My image is bad. I know that. What people don't realize is that it is just an act, a role. It's like not liking Clint Eastwood because he shoots people in the movies. That's just an act. It's part of the role. I'm a pretty quiet, nice guy off the court. But on the court, you get up and you're emotional.

"Everybody says I'm tormented," he continued. "I'm not tormented. Everybody says I never smile. How many people smile when they're doing serious work? I'm working out there. I don't want to smile." Boeheim then told a story about realizing two weeks earlier how he forgot to book a hotel room for the Final Four, which most Division I basketball coaches normally attend. "It would have been a better story if I didn't get in [to a hotel], but I did," he joked. "You know, I've only done that twice, I swear to God, and that other time was in 1987 [when he lost to Indiana in the championship game]."

The only time he became agitated was when a reporter suggested that this game would be known as a Kansas loss rather than a Syracuse win. "If someone wants to think that Kansas lost because they missed shots, they know nothing about college basketball," he bristled. "We've held teams to 29.2 percent shooting from the three-point line all year. These kids gutted it out. They won the game. They won the game, and they deserve a tremendous amount of respect." When a reporter asked about him deflecting praise to his players, Boeheim answered: "I've never taken any credit, and I don't want to take any credit. This game is for the players. Too much is made about the coaches." That might be true, but there was no question Boeheim had done a masterful job with this group. When it came time for the players to be interviewed, they were quick to give their coach his due. And some did so, passionately. "You guys," Wallace said, glaring at a group of reporters, "always seem to say he can't coach and can't do this and, yet, here we go again [to the Final Four]." Jason Cipolla was less defiant but still intense. "Everybody says he doesn't win the big games," the junior shooting guard said. "Every year he wins 20, and he took a team this year that wasn't even supposed to win 20, one that was ranked 42nd in preseason, and did an unbelievable job. He won the big one tonight."

Indeed he had, and it was on to East Rutherford, New Jersey, and his second trip to the Final Four as a head coach.

One of the main story lines many reporters were hoping to pursue was a championship matchup between Syracuse and Kentucky, because it would pit Boeheim against his good friend and former assistant, Rick Pitino. Although powerful Kentucky was expected to reach the Final Two, the Orangemen entered their semifinal game against Mississippi State as slight underdogs. The Bulldogs were on a roll even more impressive than SU, having defeated three Top 5 teams—Kentucky, Connecticut, and Cincinnati—in the past month. The day before the game at Continental Airlines Arena in the New Jersey Meadowlands, Boeheim faced an even larger media throng than he had at the regionals, and his prickly image was again a hot topic. Asked how it felt to be criticized, he responded candidly. "It does bother me," he said. "I don't ignore it. I'm sensitive. I guess after a number of years, it doesn't bother you as much. If you hear it for a year or two, and then it gets to 10 or 12 or 15 years, it's harder for it to get through to you." He also admitted that he was "a hard guy to like. I do whine or whatever. I don't know if I do it more than others, but I do it." The next afternoon, his image as a coach was burnished when his Orangemen knocked off Mississippi State 77–69. Wallace paved the way with 21 points, Burgan added 19, and Sims had a marvelous day running the attack, with nine assists, zero turnovers, 11 points, and two steals. After falling behind 13–6 in the first four minutes, SU battled back to tie the game at 36 at the half. The Bulldogs had all sorts of problems with Syracuse's 2-3 zone and its traps and wound up turning the ball over 21 times. In a humorous moment with 1:56 to go and victory firmly in the Orangemen's grasp, Cipolla tumbled along press row. While getting up off one of the tables, he picked up a phone and shouted, "We're going to the championship game."

They were indeed, and members of the media got the matchup they were hoping for as Kentucky advanced as expected. Although his team was a heavy underdog against the second-ranked Wildcats, Boeheim seemed more relaxed than usual when he met reporters the day before the final game. He talked at length about his continuing friendship with Pitino and couldn't resist firing a few wisecracks at his former assistant. "Rick and I mostly talk about golf and the fact that he can get on Augusta [National] because of C.M. [Newton, Kentucky's athletics director], and I can't," Boeheim said, grinning. "The fact is I can play, and he can't. I don't really think it's fair." He also recounted the story about how he answered "Syracuse" when Pitino asked him where he would live if he could choose any place in the world. And, yes, he also addressed more questions about his personality. "Actually, I'm a whiner," he said, playfully correcting a reporter who asked him about being portrayed as a "complainer." "My image is something I have never been too concerned about. Somebody wrote that I'm judged by my temperament and not my triumphs. That's probably true. But I try not to analyze myself too much. I might not like what I see." He told the media throng that he hasn't watched the tape of his last championship game nine years earlier, in which Keith Smart sank a late jumper to propel Indiana to a one-point victory and break his heart. "It's too painful," he explained. Boeheim said he wasn't overly concerned about how others saw him at this point in his career, but there was one thing he wanted to change. "People don't have to say I'm a good coach," he said. "I would just be happy if people stopped calling me a bad coach. That would make me happy."

In his press conference, Pitino paid homage to the man who gave him his first big break in coaching. "If I had to pick one coach to lose to it would be Jim Boeheim," he told reporters. Pitino spent several minutes telling the hilarious story about how Boeheim literally took him away from his new bride on their wedding night to offer him the SU assistant coaching job. And Pitino also raised a few eyebrows when he mentioned his former boss' sense of humor. "Actually, Jim Boeheim is extremely funny," Pitino said. "If you go to a party with him—it's going to sound strange to you—but he's the life of the party. He has a great personality, great wit, great charm."

The Orangemen appeared to be as relaxed as their coach and were brimming with confidence heading into the game, undeterred that Kentucky featured a lineup of future NBA players, including Antoine Walker, Ron Mercer, Walter McCarty, and Tony Delk. SU's players, especially their lone superstar, John Wallace, clearly embraced the fact that most were betting against them. "We've been the underdog since the tournament started," he said. "That has no effect on us. We don't care about that. The other teams pull on their shorts the same as us. We don't care if people don't think we can win. As long as we think we can win—that's all that matters." On the morning of the April 1, 1996, championship game, nationally renowned basketball writer Dick "Hoops" Weiss gave Boeheim his due in a *New York Daily News* column headlined, "Famed Whine-Maker May Sip Champagne."

Wrote Weiss:

> *Syracuse coach Jim Boeheim deserves a little credit for what he's accomplished this season. He's made an amazing transition from a dumb coach with under-achieving players to a media darling who is part John Wooden, part Looie Carnesecca in one weekend after coaching the Clockwork Orange (29–8) into tonight's NCAA final against Kentucky (33–2) at the Meadowlands.*
>
> *Boeheim has brought out the best in a fourth-place Big East team since he discovered that 6'4" senior Lazarus Sims could be far more effective than Michael Lloyd was last year running an offense from point guard. And he has transformed Otis Hill into a force in the paint, allowing All-America forward John Wallace to flourish in a system that emphasizes individual freedom. The team has taken advantage of Wallace's newfound versatility and revived a musty 2-3 zone that mystified Mississippi State.*

Los Angeles Daily News columnist Michael Ventre wrote that he was actually pulling for the SU coach.

> *Boeheim has been at Syracuse for what seems like eons.... He is an institution there, which suggests that pet rocks and lava lamps are probably big sellers in Syracuse still. But what I want is for him to win Monday night. I think he would strike a blow for every mope, nudge, and schlub who ever laced on a pair of sneakers, only to discover that one end was way, way longer than the other. He is the anti-Pitino.*

That night, for 38 minutes, the less-talented but grittier Orangemen went toe to toe with Kentucky. Wallace was absolutely brilliant, scoring 29 points and hauling in 10 rebounds. But, in the end, talent triumphed over grit as the Wildcats prevailed 76–67. Syracuse shot 50 percent and held Kentucky to just 38 percent from the field but was done in by its 24 turnovers. The Orangemen's hopes for an upset died when Wallace picked up his fifth foul while scrapping for a loose ball with about two minutes to go and Syracuse trailing by three points. Before heading to the bench, Wallace gathered his teammates and gave them a pep talk. But without their leader and superstar, the Orangemen were no match for the Wildcats, who were able to seal the deal down the stretch. When the buzzer sounded, Hill, SU's brawny center, fell to his knees at one of the foul lines and began sobbing. Wallace pulled a towel over his head on the bench. "I still believe," he would say resolutely in an interview 14 years later, "that we would have found a way to win that game if I hadn't fouled out." In his postgame remarks, Boeheim gave Kentucky its due but also spoke glowingly about his team's effort. "They should be as proud as Kentucky is," he said. "They gave everything they had, and, that, as a coach, is all you can ask for."

After finishing his press conference and receiving a congratulatory phone call from President Bill Clinton, Boeheim went to the hotel occupied by Syracuse fans. They applauded the coach when he entered the ballroom. It was evident that, despite losing the big one, he finally had won over many of his critics. Boeheim had planned to make a brief appearance, then bolt to his hotel room. But the shy man who often had been portrayed as distant and antisocial changed his mind and stayed at the party until the wee hours of the morning, shaking hands, signing autographs, and accepting congratulations on what had been a truly remarkable season.

A month after the loss, Boeheim reflected on how the public's perception of him had undergone a facelift. He admitted that he had made a conscious effort to show his sense of humor more and let people see his softer side more. "It's definitely true. After 20 years I decided to be a little looser," he said. "I'm glad I did. I don't want that [whining] image. I whine somewhat but not as much as it's blown up." He said he finally began to understand why, in spite of being one of the five winningest active coaches, he was not receiving rave reviews. "When you're blunt, you become not only uncommunicative but a bad coach [in the eyes of critics]," he said. "If you lose, they think, 'Here's our opportunity. He can't coach.' If you're gruff or blunt or argumentative with the press, that should be one side. But when that side gets you into not being a good coach...I didn't think it was that way. I was naive. I might have been stubborn enough to go 20 years before I changed my approach."

Although the championship defeat wasn't as painful as the one he had suffered nine years earlier, the undertaker's son continued to be haunted by defeat. "I remember my last high school game I lost in Rochester," he said. "I remember '87. I'll remember those when I'm old. I hope to be old someday." As was the case following previous seasons, Boeheim spent a couple of weeks before deciding he would return as the SU coach for the 1996–97 campaign. "I've done that for 15 years," he said. "This one was a little easier."

He was ready for the challenges a new season would bring. For the fourth consecutive year, he would have to break in a new point guard, and he would have to find a way to fill the enormous void created by the graduation of John Wallace, who had finished his Syracuse career ranked third in scoring and second in rebounding before being chosen by the New York Knicks in the first round of the NBA draft. And Boeheim would have to deal with new expectations—a bar that probably would be set too high. "We'll probably be picked in the Top 20," he said, grinning, and invoking his trademark sarcasm. "Next year I'll be a bad coach, because we won't achieve what I'm picked to achieve."

CHAPTER 11

Finding True Love

A LITTLE MORE THAN A MONTH after his team lost to Missouri in overtime at the Sweet 16 in 1994, Jim Boeheim flew to Lexington to attend a Kentucky Derby party thrown by his longtime friend and former assistant, Rick Pitino. Boeheim and his wife, Elaine, had divorced a year earlier after an occasionally rocky, on-again, off-again 18-year marriage, and Jim was looking forward to getting away from it all, kicking back with close friends. Little did he know that his life was about to change dramatically—and for the better.

At the soiree, he was mesmerized by a tall, statuesque woman with long brunette hair named Juli Greene. He got up the gumption to approach Juli, a southern belle 20 years his junior, and the two hit it off immediately. They played backgammon, and she taught him the two-step. They spent hours giggling at each other's corny jokes. "They were like two teenagers in love," Pitino recalled. "It was a side of Jim that I had never seen before. Heck, I think it was a side of Jim *Jim* had never seen before." Boeheim was so enchanted with Juli that he postponed his flight for a few days so he could take her to dinner and the movies. (It was somehow fitting that the mortician's son would take her to a film titled *Tombstone*.) Upon returning to Syracuse, he discovered that he couldn't keep his mind off her, and she was experiencing the same longing for him. They found themselves conversing with each other by phone several times per day. Some of the conversations would last for hours.

On the surface, it seemed like the oddest of pairings. After all, he was much older and a northerner, a Yankee. Her parents, who reared her and her five older siblings in a small Kentucky town, would never, ever approve of this. But love works in mysterious and powerful ways, and Juli had a plan. "My family definitely was cold on the idea at first, but about a month after Jim and I met, I invited him back down to Kentucky for my sister's wedding," Juli recalled. "I was so nervous I was shaking because I didn't know how my family was going to react to Jim. Well, he comes down and charms all of them, and I never heard another bad thing from them. They say successful basketball coaches recruit not just the player but the whole family. Well, Jim showed us all why he is one heck of a recruiter."

Their relationship only grew stronger as time passed. About a year after they met, Juli decided to move to Syracuse and began work on her master's degree in SU's young children with disabilities program. "My reasons for coming were twofold," she said. "I wanted to continue my studies, but I also wanted to see what Syracuse was like and what Jim's life was like. I wanted to see if I would fit into all of this."

Growing up in the Bluegrass State, where University of Kentucky basketball is a state religion, Juli had no choice but to become smitten with the sport. She played hoops in the seventh and eighth grades but didn't pursue basketball in high school—a decision she regrets to this day. She was vaguely aware of Syracuse's rich hoops tradition, but it wasn't until she moved to central New York that she began to understand and appreciate Boeheim's role in the program's enormous success. She realized that she would be marrying not only a man but a basketball program, and that was fine with her. In time, she would become one of SU basketball's most ardent supporters.

She also would become close to Jim's daughter, Elizabeth Boeheim. For that, she can thank Jim's former wife, Elaine, who decided to share her daughter without rancor and accepted Juli without resentment.

Jim had met Elaine in the early 1970s at an oral surgeon's office, where she was working as an assistant. Boeheim was coaching under Roy Danforth at the time, and he would bring SU players there to have their teeth examined and cleaned. He eventually asked her out, and they wound up getting married in June 1976, just two months after he had been named Syracuse's new head basketball coach. His decision to get married took even his closest friends by surprise. "I think he kind of rushed into it," recalled Tony Santelli, who has known Boeheim since they were kids growing up in Lyons. "I really thought the timing was bad because I knew Jim was all basketball back then, and I really didn't think he was ready to devote himself to anybody or anything else. I felt badly for Elaine because Jim really didn't have room in his life for anything but basketball at that time."

By his own admission, Boeheim was not an easy person to live with during those years, when he was laying the foundation for his basketball coaching career. Things came easily for him in the beginning, as the Orangemen, fueled by the play of stars Roosevelt Bouie and Louie Orr, helped Boeheim record 100 wins in his first 117 games. But after several years of early exits from the NCAA tournament following scintillating regular-season records, the thin-skinned Boeheim began to feel the sting of criticism from the media and demanding Syracuse fans. Being a whale in a fishbowl was not easy on the coach or his wife. Boeheim would agonize over the losses and rarely savor the wins. He would bring his work and his pain home with him, often watching game films on a whirring projector deep into the night. There were times Elaine felt as if she didn't even exist. "He'd come home after two losses in a row and tell me, 'All right, curtail your spending. I'm going to be getting out of coaching,'" Elaine revealed in a 1996 interview with

Sports Illustrated basketball writer Jack McCallum. "Of course, he knew and I knew that he wouldn't be giving up coaching." The two wound up separating briefly in the early 1980s, then getting back together. In 1985, Elaine suggested they adopt a child. Jim strongly resisted at first before the couple adopted a baby girl. Elizabeth quickly became the apple of Boeheim's eye, a reminder that there was much more to life than just basketball. Boeheim became a devoted father, but his love for his wife never really blossomed, and the two divorced in 1993.

It was important to Elaine that Jim continue to be a big part of their daughter's life. Boeheim said he will be eternally grateful to his ex-wife as a result. "When you go through a divorce and you're in the public eye, it's very tough," Boeheim told McCallum. "But my ex-wife has been extraordinary. To enable me to see my daughter, to keep that most important part of my life intact, means more to me than I could ever describe. Elaine knew that everyone should have someone to love without reservation, and that's what Elizabeth is to me. I can never thank Elaine enough for allowing that."

And he could never thank her enough for also sharing Elizabeth with Juli, whom Elaine wound up befriending. "I can't think of anyone I'd rather have Elizabeth with," Elaine said. In fact, at the 1996 championship game, Elizabeth wound up sitting with Juli, just two rows in front of her mom.

Although Boeheim claimed that his kinder, gentler image was a result of him maturing and becoming more comfortable with his achievements, his closest friends weren't buying it. "I think," Santelli said, "Juli had a great deal to do with him changing during that time. Yes, it certainly helped that his team had that overachieving season in 1996 and was everybody's darling. But Jim finally started to curtail his whining and stopped constantly fighting battles he wasn't going to win against the media. And I think Juli's wonderful, optimistic personality began to rub off on him. He was clearly unhappy in his first marriage, and when you are unhappy in your marriage, that stuff carries over into other areas of your life. Jim had finally found true love and true happiness."

A few months after the loss to Kentucky in the title game, Boeheim showed up at the Civic Center in downtown Syracuse to film a television commercial. Just before the cameras started rolling, the coach was told that he would have to climb into SU's "Otto the Orange" mascot costume. A few years earlier, Boeheim probably would have had a snit and told the producers he had no intention of making a fool of himself. But the new Boeheim was game. "Jeez, I'm turning into Bill Frieder," he said, referring to the Arizona State coach who became known for his crazy marketing ploys.

Before the start of the 1996–97 season, Boeheim was faced with a recruiting dilemma regarding Jason Hart, a top-rated point guard from Los Angeles. Hart had signed a letter of intent with Syracuse before his senior year at Inglewood High School, but in the spring of '96 he asked to get out of the binding agreement so he could remain close to his older brother, Jadifi, who had undergone a kidney transplant. SU officials refused to grant him a release because they maintained Hart knew of his brother's condition when he signed up for the scholarship. There was heavy speculation in the Los Angeles area that the real reason Hart underwent a change of heart was that UCLA coach Jim Harrick suddenly had shown an interest in the guard after top Bruins recruit Olujimi Mann failed to qualify academically. The case went to the College Commissioners Association, and when it became apparent that the steering committee was going to rule in Syracuse's favor, Hart informed Boeheim and athletics director Jake Crouthamel that he would be accepting SU's scholarship after all.

Hart started right away, but unlike precocious SU point guards from the past, he struggled mightily during his rookie year of college ball. That it was going to be a long season for him and the Orangemen became apparent during the first game of the Great Alaska Shootout in Anchorage, as defending national champion Kentucky pounded SU by 34 points, the worst loss in Boeheim's coaching career. The Orangemen would stumble to a 3–3 start, another low-water mark for Boeheim teams, and drop out of the Top 20 for the rest of the season. The play of undersized center Otis Hill wound up being one of the few bright spots, as he topped the team in scoring (15.7 points per game) and finished second in rebounding (6.1 rebounds per game). A year after reaching the final game of the NCAAs, the Orangemen wouldn't even qualify for the tournament, winding up, instead, in the NIT, where they were bounced in the first round on their home court by Florida State. With a 19–13 final record, SU failed to reach the 20-win mark for only the second time in Boeheim's 21 seasons.

On October 10, 1997—a week before the start of basketball practices—Jim Boeheim married Juli Greene at Hendricks Chapel on the Syracuse campus. Elizabeth Boeheim, Jim's daughter, served as the maid of honor, and after a reception at nearby Lafayette Country Club, the couple headed to Bermuda for their honeymoon. The Orangemen began the season unranked, but they broke into the Top 25 for good after zooming to an 11–0 start. Hart clearly was feeling more comfortable with his supporting cast, which included senior forward Todd Burgan (17.6 points per game) and sophomore forward Ryan Blackwell (8.2 rebounds per game), a transfer from the University of Illinois who played his high school ball in nearby Rochester. But the biggest reason for SU's rapid start and improvement over the previous season was the rapid maturation of sophomore Etan Thomas. The muscular 6'9" center from Oklahoma had grown up a huge Georgetown fan and had dreamed of following in the large footsteps of Hoyas big men Patrick Ewing, Alonzo Mourning, and Dikembe Mutombo. But Georgetown never returned the phone calls of Thomas' high school coach. Boeheim, though, was very interested. He envisioned Thomas flourishing in time, but the coach realized that, as is the case with most big men, the development wouldn't happen overnight.

Thomas was very, very raw but still managed to average 5.7 points and 4.2 rebounds per game his freshman year while filling in for Hill, who missed the first seven games because of a suspension. Thomas loved blocking shots, and he wound up becoming SU's single-season and career record-holder in that category. But his attempts at swatting the ball away during his first season often resulted in him getting into foul trouble, as evidenced by his 58 fouls in just 408 minutes. After much work with assistant coach Bernie Fine, who handled the centers and forwards for Boeheim, Thomas evolved into a more intimidating, efficient force during his sophomore season. The dramatic improvement of his play was underscored when Thomas had 23 points, seven rebounds, and six blocks an 84–66 victory against Georgetown, the school that had spurned him. Thomas ended the season being voted the Big East's Most Improved Player.

An overtime victory against Georgetown in the final game of the '97–98 regular season in the Dome moved the Orangemen up two spots in the polls to 21st. SU won two games at the conference tournament before losing by five to Connecticut in the title game. The Orangemen needed a last-second three-pointer by Marius Janulis to avoid being upset by Iona in the opening round of the NCAAs, then dispensed with a scrappy New Mexico squad to advance to the Sweet 16. SU wound up playing Duke tough for 30 minutes before the Blue Devils pulled away for an 80–67 victory.

Less than a month after the season ended, Boeheim became a father at age 53 as Juli underwent an emergency C-section and gave birth to a baby boy who would be named James Arthur Boeheim III. Nineteen months later, they would become parents again, when Juli delivered twins—Jack and Jamie. "God bless him," joked Boeheim's lifelong friend, Tony Santelli. "I can't even imagine having kids at his age. But I think that's part of what has kept him young—having a young wife and young kids kind of rejuvenated him and changed him. There's nothing like young kids around to put things back into perspective."

Coaching also was keeping him young and energetic. He had been encouraged by the way his young team had played and was especially happy with the progress his young center had made. In an effort to become even stronger and more intimidating, Thomas spent the off-season lifting with members of the SU football team. He achieved his goal, reporting for the opening of practices in the fall of 1998 at a sculpted 256 pounds. The added bulk, without a loss in quickness, clearly helped him continue his ascent, as he averaged 12.3 points and 7.6 rebounds. Hart also continued to improve, taking on more of the scoring load while averaging a team-leading 13.9 points per game. Blackwell, SU's most fundamentally sound player, continued to be the team's top rebounder (7.8 rebounds per game). Paced by the efforts of that trio, the 20th-ranked Orangemen advanced to the semifinals of the Big East tournament but were no match for third-ranked Connecticut, losing by 19 in Madison Square Garden. They wound up losing their next game, too, 69–61 to Oklahoma State in the first round of the NCAAs, to finish at 21–12. It had been a feast-or-famine season for the Orangemen. Seventeen of their victories had been by 12 points or more; six of their losses were by 12 or more.

In the spring of 1999, news broke that the Washington Wizards were courting Boeheim. The thought of coaching in the NBA had always intrigued him, but he didn't allow the courtship to go very far. "I think I could have success at the NBA level because I'm an offensive-minded coach, and I know a thing or two about handling difficult players," he said. "But that time in my life has passed. I'm a college basketball coach. I've been a college basketball coach all my adult life. I'm sure that's what I'll end up being." And after spending 36 years at Syracuse, he still had no desire to be anyplace else. "Some people are just meant to be where they are, and that's it," he said. Then, with an impish grin, he added: "And people [read: critics] are just going to have to live with that."

With the return of their Big Three seniors, along with up-and-coming players such as Damone Brown, Tony Bland, and Preston Shumpert, expectations soared heading into the 1999–2000 campaign. The Orangemen didn't disappoint, as they won their first 19 games to climb to No. 4 in the polls. They would finish the regular season 24–4 as Thomas became one of the most dominating big men in the land, averaging 13.6 points, 9.3 rebounds, and 3.7 blocked shots per game.

Hart's play also would be key, as he drastically reduced his number of turnovers while handing out 6.5 assists per game. Following in the tradition of Pearl Washington, Sherman Douglas, and Eddie Moss had not been easy for the senior point guard. And his attempts to get out of his letter of intent had not endeared him to SU fans, many of whom had skewered Hart on the radio call-in shows. "He is the most heavily criticized player we've ever had, and that's a shame," Boeheim said. "I might understand it if he dogged it, but this kid gives it his all, all the time. All I know is we wouldn't be having anywhere near the success we're having without Jason Hart."

After being knocked out of the Big East tournament in their opening game against Georgetown, the 16th-ranked Orangemen headed to Cleveland, where they trounced Samford by 14, then nipped Kentucky by two. That set up a much-anticipated Sweet 16 meeting with second-ranked Michigan State, which would be playing what amounted to a home game in Auburn Hills, Michigan. SU hung for a while in the hostile environment but eventually ran out of gas against the more-talented Spartans, who pulled away to win by 17. Thomas would be drafted 12th overall that April by the Dallas Mavericks, making him the highest SU pick since Billy Owens was chosen No. 3

in 1991. Hart would eventually hook on with the Milwaukee Bucks and spend parts of nine seasons in the NBA with a variety of teams.

Since the beginning of Jim Boeheim's head coaching career he had been involved in local charitable causes, and he made sure his players and assistants were, too. Although he wound up being feted by organizations such as The Kidney Foundation, the Boys & Girls Club, Camp Good Days & Special Times, and the American Cancer Society, much of his community service work had been done behind the scenes, away from the limelight, which, as a private person, is what he preferred. There were numerous stories of him and his players showing up, gifts in hand, at the pediatric wards of local hospitals to spend time with children who were battling difficult illnesses. It was not uncommon for Boeheim to invite kids to practice so they could meet their heroes in person.

Of all his causes, none touched him more personally or became more important to him than the battle against cancer. It was easy to understand why. Boeheim's mother had died of leukemia at age 58 in 1976—not long after he became head coach—and his father had succumbed to prostate cancer at age 68 a decade later. Cancer also had claimed friend and highly respected Division I basketball official Pete Pavia, as well as two coaches he was particularly close to—Jim Valvano of North Carolina State and Jack Bruen of nearby Colgate University. Not long after Valvano's valiant struggle with cancer ended in death in 1993, Missouri coach Norm Stewart convinced the American Cancer Society and the National Association of Basketball Coaches to join fundraising forces, and Coaches vs. Cancer was born.

It started slowly but has since blossomed into a major organization, having raised more than $50 million since its inception. It really began to take off after Coaches vs. Cancer national director and former St. Bonaventure coach Jim Satalin convinced Boeheim to come on board. The Syracuse coach thought it was a perfect fit, and he and Juli began devising numerous creative ways to raise money—everything from golf tournaments to free-throw and three-point shooting contests at baskets set up behind the Carrier Dome curtain on game nights. "Jim went at it as fiercely as he went after victories on the court—only he realized this was a far more important thing he was doing than anything he could accomplish in basketball," Satalin said. "This was something personal, something that really hit home with him. By the end of the first year, he led all the coaches in the country in fundraising, easily by a 2-to-1 margin. And he kept raising the bar higher every year, while getting the word out and getting more of his peers involved. He really has been a great driving force behind the success of Coaches vs. Cancer."

In late-April 2000, Jim and Juli Boeheim took their fundraising efforts to yet another level when they staged their first Basket Ball gala at the Oncenter in downtown Syracuse. Nearly 700 people doled out big bucks to hobnob with ESPN announcers Mike Tirico and Bill Raftery, as well as SU players, including most of the current team and legends such as Pearl Washington, Roosevelt Bouie, and Leo Rautins. The dinner, which included a huge auction of sports memorabilia, raised more than $100,000. Boeheim was so overwhelmed by the community's response that he shed tears later that night. "Can you believe that?" he said to Juli after they returned to their suburban Syracuse home. "How can we ever top that? That was awesome." Juli knew exactly how he felt. "Jim was so moved, and at the same time it was humbling for him," she recounted later. "That night brought him to his knees. It really did."

Later that year, the cause would become even more personal to Boeheim. For several years, the coach had suffered from an enlarged prostate. He considered having surgery following the 2001–02 season, but just before practices officially began that October, his condition worsened to the point where he had to go to the bathroom every two hours during the night. Concerned that he might be suffering from something worse than an enlarged prostate, Juli convinced her stubborn husband that enough was enough and that he needed the surgery sooner rather than later. Boeheim agreed and found a stretch of the schedule where he would miss the fewest number of games. After the Orangemen opened the campaign with eight consecutive victories, the SU athletic department broke the shocking news. In a statement released to the media on December 3, 2001, Boeheim said: "I'm having surgery to address my prostate problem. My doctors anticipate a return to coaching within a couple of weeks. My health has always been a private matter, and I would hope people would respect those wishes." Boeheim added that his problem was 100 percent treatable. SU associate coach Bernie Fine, Boeheim's top assistant since the beginning of his head coaching career 25 years earlier, would direct the Orangemen in his absence.

After doing some research, Boeheim decided to have his surgery done by Dr. William Catalona, the same highly regarded St. Louis physician who had performed similar operations on thousands of men, including former New York Yankees manager Joe Torre. The night before the surgery at Barnes Jewish Hospital, Boeheim was understandably quiet. "It was scary," Juli recalled. "We just held each other." The toughest moment for the couple occurred the next morning when Boeheim was wheeled down the hallway to the operating room, and Juli couldn't join him on the elevator. "I love you," she said, tears in her eyes. "I love you, too," Boeheim said, tears in his eyes, as the door closed. The surgery to remove his cancerous prostate gland was successful.

The toughest part of the recovery for Boeheim wound up being his time away from his team. He tried to watch the games on television, but it was just too difficult. "It was very strange," he said. "It was like an out-of-body experience. I couldn't do it." Little by little his strength came back. Not long after the surgery he accompanied Juli on a trip to the toy store to buy Christmas gifts for the children. Pale and weak, he used the shopping cart as a walker. SU won the first game in his absence, crushing overmatched Hofstra by 26 points in the Dome, but dropped the next two in decisive fashion, by 14 points to North Carolina State and by 16 points to Georgia Tech. Although his wife wanted him to wait a little longer, Boeheim returned to the sidelines on December 20 and received a standing ovation from SU fans in the Dome as the Orangemen rebounded with an 80–68 victory against South Florida. In his postgame press conference, Boeheim thanked everyone for their support during this trying time for him and his family. He was asked if he was pushing it by being back just a dozen days after his surgery. "It was either come back early and coach," he joked, "or die from watching them play." He also thanked Juli, who had coached him through the most frightening moment of his life.

The experience clearly had changed him. In the weeks, months, and years that followed, Boeheim would pour his heart and soul into raising money and awareness. At every banquet he would make sure that, in addition to talking about basketball, he urged the men in the audience to undergo prostate examinations. And he would spend countless hours behind the scenes, talking on the phone and writing letters to friends and total strangers who had been diagnosed with cancer. One of Boeheim's acts of kindness came to light in a column by longtime college basketball writer Ken Davis in the November 2003 issue of *Basketball Times*. Davis had written Boeheim a letter congratulating him on winning the national championship earlier that year, and at the end he mentioned how his father-in-law, a huge Syracuse hoops fan, had been diagnosed with pancreatic cancer. Davis knew Boeheim would be extremely busy in the months following the biggest victory of his career, so he never expected the coach to contact his father-in-law. But in late June, an orange-and-blue note arrived in Bob Lenzen's mailbox in North Ft. Meyers, Florida. It read:

Bob,

    I'm so sorry to hear what a tough battle you are having with cancer. Having lost both of my parents to cancer, I know how tough this disease can be.

    Every time I hear about another relative of a friend of mine (imagine me calling a writer a friend!!!) with cancer it makes me do more to fight this disease.

    Hang in there and continue to wear the orange shirt.

Jim Boeheim

Lenzen was thrilled, and so was his son-in-law. "I would have understood if Boeheim hadn't written that note," Davis said. "But he did. Words cannot express the family's appreciation. Throughout the final weeks of Bob's life, that note gave him something to brag about. At a memorial service filled with laughter and tears, Boeheim's note was posted on a bulletin board along with other cards, poems, and letters Bob had received.

"My brother-in-law gave Bob's eulogy," Davis continued. "Near the end, he spoke about life in 'Bob's heaven.' In Bob's heaven, he said, Syracuse wins the national championship every year. In Bob's heaven, there's definitely no cancer. When that cure finally comes, there's a group of basketball coaches that deserve our thanks."

The victory against South Florida when Boeheim returned ignited a seven-game win streak that saw the Orangemen improve to 16–2 and climb to eighth in the polls. Despite the outstanding play of Preston Shumpert, a slick-shooting small forward who would lead the team in scoring (20.7 points per game) and rebounding (6.1 rebounds per game), Syracuse stumbled through the second half of the season, losing eight of its final 12 games, including its last three, to finish 20–10. One of those losses was to Georgetown on February 24, 2002, and spoiled a day in which the university officially named the Carrier Dome court after Boeheim.

The man who had been involved in 1,115 games either as a player or coach at his alma mater was moved by the gesture. "It's very humbling for a former walk-on to be able to hang in there this long and receive an honor like this," he said. "I've been very fortunate to have had a lot of good players and coaches and great fan support. They are the ones who made this possible. It's been quite a ride." When told that he had been around for 48 percent of the basketball games played by the 'Cuse in the program's storied 102-year history, Boeheim deadpanned: "All that means is that I'm getting old." Though 57 years old and just months removed from his cancer surgery, Boeheim said he felt even more energized and competitive than when he was as a young coach. "I have no idea when I'm going to retire," he said. "But I know I'm closer to the end than the beginning, so the games actually take on a greater significance. It's funny, but when I started, I said there's no way I'm coaching beyond 40. And then when I hit 40, I said there's no way I'll be doing this when I'm 50. Well, I'm closing in on that next milestone, and I'm not going to say 'No way' any more. When it stops being fun and meaning so much to me, I'll head to the golf course for good."

The poor finish coupled with a first-round elimination from the Big East tournament meant the Orangemen would miss the NCAAs for the first time in five years. They did receive a bid to the NIT, and after winning their first two contests in the Carrier Dome and a third game at Richmond, they went to the Final Four in New York, where they lost a semifinal game to South Carolina and a consolation game to Temple.

The season had not gone the way Boeheim had hoped. But he couldn't help but be excited about next year because he had recruited two of the nation's top high school players—a smiling, do-everything forward from Baltimore named Carmelo Anthony and a scrappy, dead-on shooter from Scranton, Pennsylvania, named Gerry McNamara. Together, this precocious duo would help Boeheim take the Orangemen to heights never visited before.

CHAPTER 12

Winning the Big One

SYRACUSE WAS NOWHERE TO BE FOUND in any of the 2002–03 preseason or early season Top 25 polls, and that was understandable. The Orangemen were returning just one senior (Kueth Duany) from a team that had stumbled into the NIT with eight losses in its final 12 regular-season games. Although Jim Boeheim had strengthened his squad dramatically with the addition of stellar recruits Carmelo Anthony and Gerry McNamara, the pundits believed it would be a difficult challenge playing three freshman and three sophomores in his eight-man rotation. So, it wasn't a huge surprise when Boeheim later revealed that even he hadn't voted for his own team in the coaches' polls early that season.

Yes, these Orangemen were green, but they also would prove to be precocious and skilled beyond their basketball years. This would be one of those rare seasons in which youth would not be wasted on the young and talent would trump experience.

Duany, who was fondly referred to as "Gramps" by his young, wise-cracking teammates, had a sense even before practices began that October that despite its inexperience, this team had the potential to be awfully good. Known for his ability to shut down the opposition's top scorer, Duany paired up against Anthony in a pickup game on campus that summer. The fabulous freshman from Baltimore did a number on SU's veteran defender. "Let's just say that I came away impressed with how developed his game was," Duany said. "I couldn't wait to see our opponents try to stop him." Duany also took notice of the grit and shooting skills of McNamara, the hard-nosed guard from Scranton, and Billy Edelin, the point guard who could do everything well except shoot from the outside. "The thing that struck me was not only how skilled they were, but how self-assured they were," Duany said. "I think Melo [Anthony], G-Mac [McNamara], and Billy were in so many pressure games in high school and AAU leagues that pressure didn't faze them. They arrived here with a big-game mentality. I had some doubts whether I'd be able to play at this level after my first few practices, but I never sensed any of those doubts from these guys. From Day 1, they showed no fear. They came in and immediately asserted themselves. We had lost some veteran players, there were some openings, and these guys didn't waste any time claiming the jobs. I had to keep reminding myself that they were only freshmen and sophomores. There were times when they played like seniors and times when they played like grad students."

Duany liked their infectious confidence and decided to build off it. So at the end of the team's first official practice, he gathered them all together, and at his urging, they shouted in unison, "Final Four," as they broke the huddle. Considering their best player had yet to play a college basketball game, it may have seemed a little brash and premature. But it wound up being a good omen.

Melo had created the type of buzz on campus not felt since the arrival of Pearl Washington two decades earlier. SU assistant Troy Weaver had caught Anthony's extraordinary act before other college coaches, and early during the 2001 season, he convinced his boss to do something he rarely did in-season—make a long recruiting trip. Melo was a junior at Towson (Maryland) Catholic High School at the time, and Boeheim agreed to travel with Weaver to see the young man play. "After five minutes," Weaver recalled, "Coach said, 'This is the best player in the country.'" From that point on, the Orangemen heavily recruited Anthony, and he accepted their scholarship offer shortly after transferring to national high school powerhouse Oak Hill Academy in Mouth of Wilson, Virginia, before his senior year.

"I committed early because I didn't want the stress of recruiting to take away from the enjoyment of my senior year," he said. "I had transferred to Oak Hill to get my academics in order and to play against the best competition possible. Syracuse seemed like the perfect place for me. I figured it didn't get much bigger than Syracuse when it comes to college hoops, so why wait?" The 6'8" forward with the incandescent, Magic Johnson smile and the versatile Magic Johnson game, wound up averaging 21.7 points and 7.4 rebounds per game for Oak Hill his senior season to earn McDonald's, *Parade*, and *USA TODAY* All-America honors. For a brief time, after all the accolades poured in, Anthony considered eschewing SU's scholarship offer to turn pro, but his mother was adamantly opposed to that idea. She wanted her son to experience college for at least one year. "In hindsight, I am so, so glad I listened to her because my time in Syracuse wound up being one of the greatest experiences of my life," he said.

McNamara also had no regrets choosing SU over Duke. The guard who led his Bishop Hannan High School team to one Pennsylvania state championship and two second-place finishes was captivated by the idea of joining Anthony in hopes of winning an NCAA championship just two hours north of his hometown. "I'll never forget that very subject being brought up when Coach Hop [Mike Hopkins] was taking me and my parents on a tour of the Carrier Dome," he recalled. "He said, 'Gerry, wouldn't it be great to have the opportunity to win the national championship in your own back yard?' He didn't mince his words. He was talking about them wanting to win a national championship. I liked that kind of thinking because I was a super-competitive person who was all about winning." And he certainly did a lot of that back in Scranton, guiding the Lancers to a 109–17 record while becoming the seventh-leading scorer in state history and the most heavily recruited basketball player ever out of northeastern Pennsylvania. "He had the weight of an entire program on his shoulders for four years in high school, so he's had to compete at a high level with a lot of pressure on him," Boeheim said during G-Mac's freshman season. "There's probably less pressure on him now than there has been in four years."

Boeheim clearly was as excited about Melo and McNamara as any freshmen he's ever recruited. But his optimism that this team might wind up being better than even he imagined also was fueled by the players he had returning. Duany was not only a solid defender but a dependable shooter and excellent leader and mentor. Sophomore forward Hakim Warrick would prove to be another of Boeheim's diamond-in-the-rough discoveries, making a quantum leap from his freshman season to earn Big East Conference Most Improved Player honors after averaging 14.8 points and 8.5 rebounds in 2002–03. Sophomore Josh Pace was one of those sparkplug guys off the bench who could do the dirty work and quickly fill up a stat sheet with points, rebounds, assists, and steals. Center was expected to be the team's Achilles heel, but the "McForth duo" of junior Jeremy McNeil and sophomore Craig Forth would combine for 7.1 points, 7.5 rebounds, and 141 blocks—not spectacular numbers but good enough to complement the sterling performances of their teammates. Boeheim knew he probably wouldn't get a definitive read on this team until the second half of the season because of its youth and Edelin's 12-game suspension at the outset for participating in a summer league not sanctioned by the NCAA.

Carmelo Anthony's first college points would come on a rim-rattling dunk early in a nationally televised game against Memphis in Madison Square Garden on November 14, 2002. Although SU wound up losing 70–63, both Melo and McNamara would provide a glimpse of the greatness to come. Anthony established a school freshman record for points in a game, with 27, and also hauled in 11 rebounds. McNamara's contribution of 14 points was less spectacular but still quite solid for a player making his first college start on a national stage. Interestingly, the SU locker room was so quiet after the game that you could hear a pin drop. Losing was something neither Anthony nor McNamara were accustomed to, so they took this defeat rather hard. But that wound up being a good thing. "It kind of forced us to refocus and realize that it wasn't going to come easy," McNamara said. "It made us hungrier, right out of the gate."

They wound up sating that hunger against their next 11 opponents as Anthony averaged 23.2 points. There were times when Boeheim couldn't help but marvel at Melo's man-against-boys performances. "You could be from another planet and not know a thing about basketball and see that he was far and away better than the other nine guys on the court," he raved. "Some stretches, he was unguardable."

SU's win streak was snapped by third-ranked Pitt on the road. But a more impressive streak would follow. On February 15, 2003, with nearly 2,000 Scrantonians among the 30,000 in the Dome, Melo kicked the ball out to McNamara, who sank a last-second, game-winning jumper against Notre Dame. That ignited a seven-game winning streak as the Orangemen closed the regular season with a 23–4 record and a No. 11 ranking. Three of the victories came on the road, at Michigan State, Georgetown, and Notre Dame. A total of 15 victories that season would come after they staged second-half comebacks, prompting many to refer to them as "Cardiac 'Cuse." "I think those wins on the road convinced people that this team had a chance to be extraordinary," Boeheim said. "Maybe these kids really were too young to realize that you aren't supposed to win three games in places like that or to come back from so many big deficits. There probably were five or six games that season we had no right winning because we had dug ourselves too big a hole. But somehow, someway, they found a way to come back."

After beating the Hoyas a third time, Connecticut bounced SU out of the Big East tournament in the semifinals. The NCAA Selection Committee, obviously impressed with the way the Orangemen finished the regular season, made them a third seed in the East, meaning their path to the Final Four would go through Boston and Albany, New York, each within comfortable driving distance for their fans. SU had little trouble disposing of Manhattan in the first round, but after falling behind Oklahoma State by 17 points in the first half of their second-round game in Beantown, it appeared that the Orangemen had finally dug a crater too big to climb out of. Boeheim, though, had a plan. He subbed with superior defenders McNeil, Pace, and Edelin and slapped on a full-court press. Pace and Edelin forced several turnovers, and on the occasions when the Cowboys were able to break the press, McNeil was there to compensate, blocking four shots that led to fast breaks. With blood trickling down his forehead from an errant elbow, McNamara sank a three early in the second half to give the Orangemen a lead they never relinquished as they won 68–56 to advance to the Sweet 16.

With Albany just a three-hour drive from Syracuse, it was not surprising that the 'Cuse would have a home-court advantage, as thousands of orange-clad fans turned the 15,000-seat Pepsi Arena into a mini–Carrier Dome. SU wound up beating Auburn 79–78 that Friday night in a game that wasn't as close as the score indicated. The Orangemen faltered a bit at the foul line and got lax on defense, as Auburn hit four threes in the final 90 seconds, including one at the buzzer. That set up a meeting with sixth-ranked Oklahoma from the Big 12, regarded that season as the nation's best basketball conference.

Minutes before boarding the bus for the NCAA East Region final, Boeheim was changing his baby son's diapers in his hotel room. Not exactly the way most coaches might prepare for the biggest game of the season but perhaps fitting, given the youthfulness of this SU team. Whether it was changing diapers or coaching Diaper Dandies, Boeheim was enjoying himself as much as he ever had. "I've never seen him happier," said Bernie Fine, his longtime sidekick. "He has a great relationship with his wife and his young children, and he's really enjoyed coaching this group of young men. I jokingly told him he better stop smiling so much because he's ruining his image as a grumpy old man." Boeheim seemed more relaxed than usual as he prepared for the tip-off against the slightly favored Sooners. "I think coach liked the way we were playing, the way everybody was contributing," Duany said. "I think he saw how confident we were. He knew we were focused. We were ready."

Ready, indeed. The Sooners looked totally flummoxed against SU's tenacious, matchup 2-3 zone. Oklahoma wound up making just 31 percent of its attempts from the field, and none of its shooters was more frigid than Hollis Price, the Big 12 player of the year who converted just 3 of 17. Point guard Quannas White made but 1 of 8 shots and committed five turnovers. The Sooners were 5-for-28 from beyond the three-point arc. The result was an easier-than-expected 63–47 victory and Boeheim's fourth ticket to the Final Four (three as a head coach and one as an assistant).

The story line was even more compelling because it would be staged at the New Orleans Superdome, the same building where Keith Smart and Indiana had handed him his most painful defeat 16 years earlier. The subject of his "Nightmare on Bourbon Street" was broached during his press conference following the Oklahoma victory. "I had a tremendous experience for five days, 39 minutes, and 56 seconds," he said, recounting the 1987 Final Four, which had been decided by Smart's jumper with four seconds remaining in the title game. "I'm gonna try to get that other four seconds in this time." Boeheim realized that you only get so many shots at a national championship. When the

'Cuse went to the Final Four in '75 and '96, the better team probably won. But in 1987 that may not have been the case. "It's been about once a decade for our program, so when you get an opportunity, you really have to go for it because there aren't any guarantees that you are going back any time soon," he said. "I thought we did all we could do in '75 and '96. I thought those teams went as far as they could go with it; they overachieved. But '87 is the one that you tend to play the 'what if' game with. When it comes down to one shot, you can't help but think you should have won it."

Boeheim would return to New Orleans with the distinction of being the coach with the most NCAA tournament victories (36) never to have won a national championship. He attempted to downplay the significance of capturing the one jewel missing from his coaching crown even before setting foot in the Bayou. "I'm happy to get there, and I'd like to win it," he said. "But a week after the season I'll be playing golf." No one—members of the media, his friends, or his players—were buying it. "Don't kid yourself," center Craig Forth said. "Coach Boeheim wants that national championship in the worst way." Forth spoke the truth, because in the deep recesses of Boeheim's hyper-competitive soul, he did want this missing piece of the puzzle in the worst way. It was time to head to New Orleans and see if the youngest team in his coaching career could help him return to the scene of his most painful basketball moment and exorcise a few ghosts.

On paper, the field of SU, Texas, Kansas, and Marquette seemed evenly matched. But the Orangemen appeared to have a couple of advantages. They were on what appeared to be a destined roll, and they had been playing great team basketball and hellacious defense. Interestingly, Melo's numbers in the tournament—17 points, 8.7 rebounds per game—had been down slightly from his regular-season stats, as opposing teams focused extra attention on him. That hadn't been a problem because this was a wonderfully balanced Orange squad with many weapons, so his teammates more than took up the slack. But before the semifinal against third-ranked Texas, Boeheim told Anthony this was his time to shine and that he needed to assert himself against the favored Longhorns and put SU on his shoulders. The All-American forward responded to his coach's charge with a vengeance, scoring 33 points on 12-for-19 shooting from the floor and hauling in 14 rebounds as the Orangemen won going away 95–84. Kansas defeated Marquette in the other semi, setting up a dream matchup not only between two storied programs but two legendary coaches.

Boeheim and his Jayhawks counterpart, Roy Williams, had been forced to bear the burden of being the two best coaches never to win it all. It was a monkey of King Kong–sized proportions that both were tired of lugging—a dubious distinction one of them finally would shed the night of April 7, 2003. Although the fourth-ranked Jayhawks were slight favorites, Boeheim had good vibes before tipoff. He believed his team was ready for the challenge, but he did have one concern. Late in the Texas game, Anthony had wrenched his back. Treatment before the championship game helped alleviate the tightness and pain, but there was a danger that it could flare up again. Based on Anthony's monster game against the Longhorns, Boeheim knew that Kansas would be devoting extra defenders to try to stop Melo. That meant others would have to step up. Gerry McNamara was only too happy to make the Jayhawks pay.

With Kansas sagging to defend him each time he touched the ball, Anthony, rather than force the issue against the double- and, sometimes, triple-teams, chucked the ball out to G-Mac. The ice-in-his-veins freshman guard was in one of those shooter's trances where the basket looked as big as the Bayou. He drained not one, not two, not three, not four, not five, but a record six first-half threes as the Orangemen sprinted to an 18-point lead and established a championship-game mark with 53 points before intermission. "It was just one of those inexplicable times when you feel as if everything you throw up is going to go in," McNamara said. "That I was in a zone in such a huge game made it all the more sweet."

Williams adjusted his defense in the second half, and G-Mac didn't score a single point the rest of the way. But the damage had already been done. Besides staking SU to a big lead, McNamara's outside efficiency had begun to open things up underneath for Melo, who wound up having another extraordinary game, just missing a triple-double, with 20 points, 10 rebounds, and seven assists. What made the performance even more remarkable is that Anthony played with a back so tight that by the second half he couldn't bend over to tie his shoes. Despite the limitations, he gutted it out for 37 minutes. "You spend a lifetime dreaming of playing on a stage like this," he explained afterward. "There was no way I was coming out of that game until the final buzzer sounded." SU also received solid performances from Kueth Duany, who hit 2 of 3 from beyond the arc for 11 points; 7' tall but vertically challenged center Craig Forth, who scored six points and blocked three shots; and bench catalysts Josh Pace and Billy Edelin, who teamed for 20 points, 10 rebounds, four assists, and six steals. The Orangemen needed every contribution they could find because, despite the huge first-half cushion, Kansas staged a furious comeback after intermission that put the game in doubt until the final seconds.

The last two minutes took 15 minutes of real time to play. It would seem like an eternity for Boeheim and every Syracuse player and fan as the Orangemen missed two layups, the front end of a one-and-one, and the first of two foul shots. They also breathed a sigh when Kirk Hinrich's potential game-tying three-pointer rimmed out.

Interestingly, it would be a player who had an off night offensively who would save the day with a moment that would replace Smart's jumper as the signature play in Syracuse basketball history. The Jayhawks had fouled Duany with 26 seconds remaining. He hit the first one to put the Orangemen up 81–78 but missed the second, and Kansas grabbed the rebound and worked the ball upcourt. "I was having flashbacks to '87 during the final seconds," Boeheim said. "We had just missed a few free throws—just like '87—and then I look to the corner, and I saw [Michael] Lee open, just like Smart was. It actually worked out for us because we had our centers out and we had put Hakim Warrick in at center. We didn't do it for defensive reasons but rather because I wanted to have our best ball handlers and shooters on the floor. If we had our centers in, it's doubtful one of them would have come out to contest Lee. But Hakim was thinking like a forward, so he went out there. It was an incredible play on his part. I still don't know how he got to that ball."

With 1.5 seconds remaining, Warrick came to the rescue by coming out of nowhere. The lithe, long-armed 6'9" sophomore forward had struggled mightily to that point, managing just six points and two rebounds in 31 minutes. But what he did with Lee's shot would atone for everything. As more than 65,000 spectators in the Superdome held their collective breath, Warrick extended his long left arm and rejected Lee's potential game-tying shot and the notion that history was about to repeat itself.

"Same building, same part of the court, similar situation," Boeheim said later. "If that had gone in…"

The Jayhawks then inbounded the ball, and Hinrich chucked up a prayer shot that Duany plucked out of the air as the final horn sounded. An emotionally drained Boeheim breathed a huge sigh of relief as his players and assistants piled joyously on each other at center court. The coach walked over and shook hands with his counterpart. He knew exactly how Williams was feeling because he had experienced that same devastating, oh-so-close moment himself on this very same floor. While congratulating him, Boeheim pulled Williams close and uttered words of encouragement similar to the ones that Indiana's Bob Knight had offered the SU coach 16 years earlier. "I said what Coach Knight told me...that I would be back," Boeheim recounted later. "[Knight] didn't tell me it would be that long, but he told me I would be back here. I told Roy that I firmly believe he will win a championship."

After shaking hands with the Kansas players and hugging several of his players and assistants, Boeheim kissed Juli and their four-year-old, James Arthur Boeheim III, who was wearing a tiny Carmelo Anthony jersey, a pair of blue Mardi Gras beads, and a coast-to-coast smile. Someone placed a black NCAA championship baseball cap on Boeheim's head, and one of his players excitedly handed him a copy of the *Syracuse Post-Standard* with the instant headline "CHAMPS." Boeheim was numbed by it all. He kept staring at the scoreboard high above him as if to make sure this really had just happened, that this wasn't all a dream.

His emotions finally got the better of him when his daughter, Elizabeth, joined him and Juli and Jim Jr. on the court and buried her head in his chest. "You did it, Dad," she said, her sobs muffled by his sports coat. As he squeezed Elizabeth, a tear rolled down his cheek. "Yes, we did," he said, removing his glasses to wipe his eyes. "Yes, we did."

At long last, he had taken the program he had loved since arriving as a skinny walk-on 41 years earlier to the top of the basketball mountain. No longer would he have to answer the skeptics who said he couldn't win the big one. No longer would he be subjected to comparisons with the Buffalo Bills, Susan Lucci, or Adlai Stevenson. The albatross of so many near-misses and failed expectations had finally been removed. James Arthur Boeheim Jr., the son of a Lyons mortician, the kid who had been smitten with hoops since he was knee-high to a ball rack, had won it all. And he had done so with a bunch of green Orangemen who had refused to act their age, who had refused to listen to the pundits who said you can't possibly capture a championship with a lineup as inexperienced as this. His road to the Final Four and the national championship had seen him beat higher-seeded teams and a string of highly respected coaches that had included Eddie Sutton, Kelvin Sampson, Rick Barnes, and Williams. So, on this night at least, the most famous SU alum was no longer Dick Clark or Peter Falk or Stephen Crane or Jim Brown or Ted Koppel or Bob Costas. It was James Arthur Boeheim Jr., the walk-on who never left, the Orangeman who had remained true to his school.

Before the trophy presentations and the ascent up the ladders to cut down the nets, Boeheim's longtime coaching rival and good friend, John Thompson, stopped by and hugged him so hard the SU coach's glasses nearly fell off. "They won this game because of you," Big John bellowed. "I got some great kids," Boeheim responded. "They got themselves a great coach," Thompson replied. A few moments later, Thompson reminisced about all those great matchups between Georgetown and Syracuse and between him and Boeheim. "We called each other SOBs more often than you can count," he said, laughing.

Amid the hoopla, someone handed Boeheim a cell phone. On the other end of the line was Orange basketball legend Derrick Coleman calling to congratulate his old coach. "You're off the hook, Derrick," Boeheim joked, referring to D.C.'s missed free throws in the late going of the '87 title game that would have made Keith Smart's jumper meaningless.

As the legendary coach walked out with his players to receive the championship trophy, the tens of thousands of fans who remained in the Superdome began chanting lustily and in unison: "Boeheim! Boeheim! Boeheim!" "It was a surreal experience," he said later, "like a fantastic dream."

In the postgame press conference, Boeheim was in a playful mood with reporters, his self-deprecating sense of humor on full display. "I don't feel any smarter [tonight]," he joked. "Maybe tomorrow." He went on to say he was extremely happy for his players and the SU fans, particularly the ones who had traveled in large numbers to Boston, Albany, and New Orleans during the NCAAs. He reminisced about his time at SU as a player. "I got a scholarship because a guy got thrown out of school my second year," he deadpanned. "And I was smart. I roomed with Dave Bing, and he liked me." He said how, after the disappointment of the '87 national title game in the Superdome that "maybe this building owed us one." And he recounted how Sherman Douglas, one of the stars on that runner-up team, had been back to campus a month earlier to have his jersey retired and deliver a pep talk to the current squad. "Sherman told our team that day, 'I think you can get to New Orleans, and when you do, finish the job,'" Boeheim said. "Well, we finished the job."

After the interviews were finished, the man *Sports Illustrated* labeled "coaching's favorite curmudgeon" decided to let his thinning hair down. Joined by family and friends, they headed to the French Quarter. Before they knew it, they were leading a procession of hundreds of adoring, orange-clad Syracuse fans, Pied-Piper style, down Bourbon Street. Stranger after stranger stopped Boeheim to shake his hand and thank him for leading SU to the national championship. "I think that was the greatest part," he said, "seeing the impact it had on our alumni and fans." Before calling it a night in the wee hours of that Tuesday morning, a fan presented Juli with a garish, orange velour cowboy hat. Her wild and crazy husband decided he would wear it while carrying the championship trophy off the plane. The thousands who had gathered at the Syracuse airport for the team's return roared with laughter. Boeheim would break out the hat at several team functions that followed, and it eventually was placed in a Manley Field House display case devoted to the championship season.

Just five days after knocking off the Jayhawks, more than 25,000 fans congregated in the Carrier Dome to say thanks amid an atmosphere that resembled a high-energy rock concert. As Boeheim emerged from a cloud of smoke holding aloft the national championship trophy, one couldn't help but think of one of his musical heroes, Bruce Springsteen, whom the coach first watched rock the Dome back in 1985. But unlike the Boss' famous rock 'n' roll lyrics, glory days clearly had not passed Boeheim by. The face of Syracuse basketball wore that goofy cowboy hat and a smile radiant enough to light up the arena. And a region that had taken its share of hits for its rugged winters and stagnant economy was smiling right along with the man who had guided SU basketball to 653 victories, 22 NCAA tournaments, three Final Fours, and one national title in 27 years. "This team has elevated the spirit of the community and made us proud," said Syracuse Mayor Matt Driscoll, who presented each team member with a key to the city following a parade through downtown. "They captivated all our hearts and won the hearts of the entire nation. We have this whole year to brag to anyone who will listen that we have the No. 1 team in the nation." School spirit also was soaring. "This is honestly the coolest thing I've ever lived through," biochemistry major Tiffany Roy told the *Utica Observer-Dispatch* the day after the victory against Kansas. "Last night and today were worth every snowy day, every cloud in the sky, every dollar we've paid to go here."

Even the news of Carmelo Anthony's decision to declare himself eligible for the NBA draft at a teary-eyed press conference just 17 days after the national championship game couldn't put a damper on the glow people were feeling. Melo had captivated fans with his effervescent personality and sublime game. But he was projected to go in the top three picks, which meant he would make millions and be able to remove his mother and siblings from the rough Baltimore neighborhood where he was raised. Still, it was not an easy decision, because he had enjoyed immensely everything about college. "I was still uncertain until about 15 minutes before the press conference started," he recalled. "I loved Syracuse University. I loved my teammates and Coach Boeheim. But like coach told me, you've accomplished in one year everything a college player could hope to accomplish. But no matter how long I play this game, nothing will ever top that feeling of winning the national championship. That was as good as it can ever get." In that one season with the 'Cuse, Anthony had averaged 22 points and 10 rebounds per game, was named first-team All-American, national freshman of the year and Most Outstanding Player of the Final Four. The Denver Nuggets wound up drafting him with the third overall pick two months later, and he would go on to become a perennial NBA All-Star and win an Olympic gold medal at the Summer Games in Beijing in 2008, with Boeheim as one of the USA's assistant coaches.

Boeheim had joked with reporters before the national championship game that win or lose, he would be working on his golf game within a matter of days. He clearly had no idea how wonderfully chaotic things become for the coach who wins it all. There would be scant time to work on his chipping and putting. In the three months that followed, he would learn what life is like in the fast-break lane. His hectic schedule would include ringing the bell at the New York Stock Exchange, throwing out the first pitch at a Syracuse Chiefs minor-league baseball game, trading verbal barbs with David Letterman on television, dancing and singing on stage with the Temptations, being honored by his hometown of Lyons, answering more mail than Santa, giving more speeches than a politician during campaign season, and visiting the White House with his team to be feted by President George W. Bush.

"It is so much bigger than I ever could have anticipated," he said while catching his breath at his Manley Field House office late that summer. "It's almost like having a baby. You think you know what it might be like, but until it happens, you have no idea about the magnitude of it all." Boeheim admitted to mornings when he woke up and had to remind himself that he wasn't dreaming, that this really did happen. It was a nice change from 1987 when he awakened, wishing he had been dreaming and that the loss to Indiana had not occurred. This happy ending clearly had exorcised the ghosts of Keith Smart for him and anybody who rooted for the Orangemen. "I can't tell you the number of times I've been out speaking when someone will come up to me and say, 'Thanks, Coach. I don't have to hear about that damn Keith Smart anymore.'"

Everywhere the Boeheims went that year, they felt the love. "I was in the grocery store and a woman came up to me and started crying tears of joy and telling me to thank my husband and all the players," Juli recalled. "You should see some of the letters Jim has received. This accomplishment really unleashed a lot of emotions in people." Although he had told reporters before the title game in New Orleans that he didn't need a national championship to validate his career, capturing one enabled him to get the last laugh on his detractors. Just 12 years earlier, he was labeled "the worst coach in the NCAA tournament" by respected sportswriter and author John Feinstein in a cover story for the *National Sports Daily*. That paper became defunct, as did Feinstein's observation. "I actually saw some people holding up a copy of that issue in New Orleans," Boeheim said, grinning. "John and I have buried the hatchet, but I had to razz him about it after winning the national championship. I told him, 'That story didn't do much for your credibility as a basketball expert. I guess I'm not quite as bad a coach as you thought.'"

One of the additional benefits of the national championship was that it increased Boeheim's power as a fundraiser. A few weeks after the title game, he and Juli staged their annual Basket Ball gala and raised more than $300,000 for Coaches vs. Cancer. The Temptations performed at the black-tie affair, and Boeheim, a huge fan of Motown music since his college days, joined the group on stage for his own rendition of "My Girl." Instead of singing the words "my girl" he sang "my wife" and pointed to Juli in the crowd.

Of all the appearances, though, none appeared to move him more than being honored by his hometown on May 25, 2003. A fire engine led Boeheim and his family on a parade through town that ended at the steps of the Wayne County courthouse, just around the corner from the Williams Street funeral home where Jim had grown up. "I'd rather be here than the White House," Boeheim told a cheering crowd of nearly 400 who had gathered despite a steady rain. "This is the best." During the ceremony, Lyons Mayor John Cinelli and village trustee Jack Bailey presented the coach with a plaque and the key to the village. "We know we can't compete with the Dome or Letterman or ringing the bell on Wall Street, but we're honored," Cinelli said after the presentation. "I think it means a lot to the village of Lyons. It's a chance for us to shine. He's a great man. He deserves whatever appreciation he receives."

After they were done, town justice Jimmy Blandino gave the famous native son a replica of an orange sign that would grace the main roads coming into Lyons. It read: "Welcome to Lyons, N.Y. Hometown to Legendary Coach Jim Boeheim of the Syracuse University NCAA National Champions, 2003." "I owe my success to my parents and [high school basketball coach] Dick Blackwell," Boeheim said. "For 40 years I've watched high school basketball across the country, and I've never seen a better coach." Blackwell, who had suffered a serious stroke that left him paralyzed, couldn't make the ceremony, but five of Boeheim's teammates from his high school days were there. After about 45 minutes of speeches and presentations, the coach spent more than a half hour inside the village fire hall, signing everything from copies of *Sports Illustrated* to church bulletins. "I've been living in Syracuse for 40 years," he told one of the autograph seekers. "But when people ask me where I'm from, I always say Lyons, New York."

CHAPTER 13

A Call from the Hall

THERE WERE RUMORS following his national championship season
that Jim Boeheim was contemplating retirement. After all, what more
was there for the winningest coach in Syracuse basketball history to
accomplish, now that he had finally won the big one? He was financially
set for life, he had a young family he could spend more time with,
and the timing seemed right. But the rumors were more off target
than an air ball. Despite a whirlwind offseason that included public
appearances nearly every day of the week, Boeheim felt energized by
the time practices began in mid-October 2003. "I haven't lost any of
my desire to coach," he said. "If anything, the excitement of winning
the title and everything that happened as a result of it has only made
me hungrier. I'm really looking forward to getting back to it."

Despite the loss of superstar Carmelo Anthony to the NBA and
solid performer Kueth Duany to graduation, Boeheim liked the team
he had returning and believed the Orangemen had a chance of going
far again in the NCAAs. Unlike the previous season, Syracuse would
not begin the year off anybody's radar screen. The Top 25 voters,
obviously impressed by the return of seasoned players such as Hakim
Warrick and Gerry McNamara, installed the Orangemen as the nation's
seventh-ranked team in the preseason poll. They wouldn't hold that
position very long, though, as Charlotte came to town and stunned

them 96–92 in the season opener at the Carrier Dome. That wake-up call ignited a 13-game win streak, but the Orangemen hit a rut in the middle of the Big East schedule in late January and early February, losing four of five games to drop out of the Top 25. They rebounded to win their last five to finish the regular season at 21–6. That final flourish was enough in the minds of the NCAA Selection Committee to earn them a berth in the tournament despite a one-and-done showing at the Big East Tourney in New York.

SU was shipped out to Denver, where it beat Brigham Young 80–75 in the first round, thanks to a magnificent performance by McNamara, who scored a career-high 43 points—28 of them in the first half alone. "That was as good a performance as I've ever seen in college basketball," Boeheim said. "Gerry was in another world." The win set up a meeting between SU and Maryland, and between Boeheim and his golfing buddy Gary Williams. The Orangemen wound up edging the Terps by two, but their hopes of defending their national title would end five days later in Phoenix when Alabama beat them by nine in the Sweet 16. Although disappointed by the way the season ended, Boeheim was encouraged by the continued improvement of Warrick, who led SU in scoring (19.8 points per game) and rebounding (8.6 rebounds per game) and appeared primed for a superb senior season.

SU opened the 2004–05 campaign by winning 20 of its first 21 games—its only loss coming against fifth-ranked Oklahoma State at the Jimmy V. Classic at Madison Square Garden. But as had been the case throughout much of Boeheim's tenure, the fast start was followed by a stumbling finish that saw the Orange men lose five of their last nine and three of their last five to complete the regular season at 24–6. They did, however, redeem themselves by beating Rutgers, Connecticut, and West Virginia to win their first Big East Tournament title in 13 years. That earned them a fourth seed and a first-round game in Worcester, Massachusetts. Despite being heavy favorites, their season came to a premature end with a 60–57 overtime loss to 13th-seeded Vermont. Boeheim was perturbed with the way the season abruptly ended, and he felt especially badly for Warrick, the senior who had again paced SU in scoring (21.4 points per game) and rebounding (8.6 rebounds per game). But the coach's anger didn't last long, because at the Final Four he received some great news that would further validate his basketball coaching credentials.

On April 4, 2005, Boeheim learned that he would be inducted into the Naismith Memorial Basketball Hall of Fame that September. "It's incredible," he said. "The national championship—you think there's nothing better—but this is it. I think this is something that goes beyond that, and I didn't think anything could possibly go beyond that. It's really hard to describe. You don't even think about getting into the Basketball Hall of Fame. When you're a coach, you might think about winning the league and you might think about going to the [NCAA] tournament and doing well in the tournament. You may even think that someday you might win the national championship. But to think about the Hall of Fame—it's almost something that is beyond reach."

What made it even more special was that Boeheim would be going in with his longtime coaching counterpart and friend, Jim Calhoun of Connecticut. The two veteran Big East coaches had been joined at the hip for some time. They had won back-to-back national championships—SU in 2003 and UConn in 2004—and recorded their 700th victories in the same week during the recently completed season. More important, when Calhoun was diagnosed with prostate cancer, one of the first people to call and offer advice was Boeheim. "He put it into perspective and told me exactly what happened to him," Calhoun recalled. "Jim took me through the scenario of what would happen. Jim has been in my life more than I realize. We're the two old-timers in the league, but we're also two good friends."

A month after the announcement, Jim and Juli staged their sixth annual Basket Ball gala and raised another $340,000 for Coaches vs. Cancer. ESPN analyst Jay Bilas served as the master of ceremonies and wound up roasting Boeheim with several zingers that had the 700 attendees at the Turning Stone Resort and Casino in Verona, New York, roaring with laughter. Among Bilas' barbs:

- "It's always a pleasure to be here with Jim Boeheim. And it serves the dual purpose for me of fulfilling the community-service portion of my sentence."

- "Jim Boeheim grew up with an inferiority complex. It turned out, that was just good judgment."

- "I asked Hakim Warrick: 'Does Jim Boeheim ever smile?' And he said: 'I don't know. I only played here four years.'"

Boeheim took the good-natured ribbing in stride. He was more than willing to be the butt of jokes if it meant raising money to battle the disease that had taken both of his parents and several of his close coaching friends. Since immersing himself in the cause nearly a decade earlier, he had become the top fundraiser among his peers, adding more than $3 million to the Coaches vs. Cancer coffers. "You know, $3 million sounds like a lot, and it is," he said. "But when you consider how much we need to raise to knock out cancer, it's not much at all."

That September, Boeheim, Juli, and their three kids journeyed to Springfield, Massachusetts, for Jim's induction into the Naismith Memorial Basketball Hall of Fame. It was a weekend none of them would ever forget. Like the night of the national championship victory, there was a surreal, almost dreamlike feel to the event for Boeheim, who still was having problems grasping that he was indeed about to join basketball's most exclusive club—a club featuring many of the players and coaches he grew up following as a kid in Lyons.

A few hours before the ceremonies, he and the other inductees were presented with navy blue blazers featuring an orange Hall of Fame patch on the breast pockets. The distinguished-looking garb was a far cry from Boeheim's wardrobe of the 1970s, when he modeled on game day some of the ugliest plaid sport coats known to man. "This is the best one for sure," he said during the presentation. "It even fits perfectly. It has permanently banished all of the bad sport coats."

The bad sport coats, like the questions about his place in hoops history, had officially been placed in mothballs. With 703 victories, a national championship, and membership in a club featuring the likes of Wilt the Stilt, the Wizard of Westwood, and Dr. J, Boeheim's legacy was now secure. "It's really kind of the final statement, although there are, hopefully, a lot more games to play," he said. "Once you're in the Hall of Fame there really isn't a lot to talk about after that. You just don't have to answer as many questions about coaching or anything. I just put my jacket on and point to this [gesturing to the Hall of Fame patch]. I think it's the final answer to all the questions, really."

Fifteen of his former players had made the trip to Springfield, including Pearl Washington, Derrick Coleman, Hakim Warrick, Roosevelt Bouie, and John Wallace. They couldn't have been more proud of the man who had shaped their basketball careers and lives. "I'm probably one of Coach Boeheim's biggest supporters," said Wallace, who had just returned from playing professional basketball in Italy after several seasons in the NBA. "I'll always be grateful to him for showing faith in me from the start. When I was a freshman, he let me make mistakes that freshmen make. He wasn't constantly looking over your shoulder. As long as you were doing things beneficial to the team, he was cool with that. He didn't over-coach." Boeheim was touched that his former players had showed up to share in his special moment. "There really is no coach in the Hall of Fame who didn't have great players," he said. "I've really been very fortunate to have had a lot of great players who put me on their shoulders."

Dave Bing, Boeheim's close friend and former teammate, served as the coach's presenter that night. During his speech, Boeheim thanked Bing for taking him under his wing when they were SU freshmen. He also praised his late parents; his former wife, Elaine, and current wife, Juli; his high school coach, Dick Blackwell, and his college coach, Fred Lewis; his assistant coaches through the years—especially Bernie Fine—and his players. "As far as I'm concerned, most of the people in the Hall are on a different level from me," he said, obviously humbled by the honor. "Those are people I grew up following and admiring. I don't have the credentials of most of them. They are legends." But Bing, who had been inducted more than a decade earlier, disagreed. He believed his friend's credentials matched up favorably with the coaches enshrined. "Jim Boeheim *is* Syracuse University basketball," Bing said. "The players come and go, but the one constant these past three decades has been Jim Boeheim."

A few days after returning from his unforgettable weekend in Springfield, Boeheim headed out on the road again to recruit. At age 60 and with 29 years in the business, he showed no signs of slowing down. The 2005–06 Orange would field a young lineup, with senior guard Gerry McNamara the only returning starter. Boeheim was hoping for big things from highly touted underclassmen Eric Devendorf, Terrence Roberts, and Darryl Watkins. In an exhibition game against the College of Saint Rose five days before the season opener, the Hall of Fame coach experienced something he never had before at SU: He was ejected from a game. As a Carrier Dome crowd of 6,635 looked on, Boeheim expressed his displeasure in R-rated fashion to officials Pat Driscoll and Mike Kitts about the way the game was being called, with about 30 seconds remaining in the half. Driscoll nailed him with a technical foul, and Boeheim thought that was the end of it. But as he returned to the bench he was informed that Kitts had given him the heave-ho. "I've never even been close to getting thrown out of a game, that's how farcical this is," Boeheim said. "Never even close. Ever. In any game. Of any kind. Not even close." For the first time in well over 1,000 games as a player, assistant coach, and head coach, he had been sent to the showers early. "History was made, I guess," he said. "There's good history and bad history, and that was bad history. But that's the way it is."

SU opened with three wins before dropping back-to-back games to Florida and Bucknell. The Orange men responded with 12 straight victories after that to climb back into the Top 20, but they would struggle badly down the stretch, losing four straight and nine of their last 13 to finish the regular season at 19–11. If they wanted to earn a spot in the NCAAs they probably would need to do something that never had been done before—win four games in four days to capture the Big East Tournament.

The Orange men arrived at Madison Square Garden as the ninth seed. Given their poor play in the second half of the season, most figured SU would get bounced early and wind up in the NIT. What the pundits didn't count on was McNamara turning in the greatest series of performances in Big East Tournament history. His heroics began on the first night when he drilled a three-pointer at the end to beat Cincinnati by a point.

But G-Mac's clutch shot wound up being overshadowed by his coach's profanity-laced, impassioned defense of him in the postgame press conference. An anonymous survey of 15 Big East Conference assistant coaches conducted by the *Syracuse Post-Standard* drew Boeheim's ire because McNamara was the top vote-getter in the category of "most overrated player." "I have to laugh a little bit when our own paper is calling him…overrated," the coach began. "They actually listened to a couple of assistant coaches who I guarantee you will never be head coaches if they think Gerry McNamara is overrated.

"Without Gerry McNamara, we would have won 10 [bleeping] games this year," Boeheim continued, his neck veins bulging, his face growing redder with each word. "Okay? Not 10. The other guys just aren't ready. They needed him. Without him there, not 10. We wouldn't be here to even have a chance to play this game. And everybody's talking to me and writing about Gerry McNamara being overrated? That's the most [bleep] thing I've seen in 30 years—and especially if it comes from people in our papers.

"But they've quoted somebody else, an anonymous assistant coach. Let the assistant coach come up to me and say, 'Gerry McNamara's overrated.' I'd like to see one of those guys come up to me and say that. He's been double-teamed every game this year, and the coaches voted him first-team all-conference. The head coaches don't know [bleep], I guess."

To his credit, McNamara remained relatively calm when asked if the "overrated" stories bothered him. He said he preferred to let his play speak for him, and over the next three days, it would speak volumes. The following day against a Connecticut team that was ranked No. 1 in the nation, G-Mac hit a three to send the game into overtime and handed out 13 assists as Syracuse upset the Huskies 86–84. In the semifinals against Georgetown, McNamara managed just two points in the first half as the Hoyas took a 15-point lead into the locker room. But G-Mac came alive after intermission, scoring 15 points. During the final 52 seconds, he drained a three to cut the deficit to one point, assisted on Eric Devendorf's go-ahead basket, and forced a turnover with 1.5 seconds remaining to seal a 58–57 win. McNamara completed his Garden Party with 17 points and five assists in a 65–61 victory against Pitt in the championship game. As he held aloft the Dave Gavitt Most Outstanding Player Award following that game, thunderous chants of "Gerry! Gerry! Gerry!" rocked the arena. Boeheim, who had apologized for his outburst, smiled like a proud father from the bench as he watched the celebration. McNamara had proven his detractors wrong—with unforgettable actions rather than profane words.

Sadly, the G-Mac era would come to an abrupt end a week later in a 66–58 loss to Texas A&M in the first round of the NCAAs in Jacksonville, Florida. McNamara had severely strained his groin during the Big East Tournament and attempted to gut it out against A&M, but it was no use. The injury stifled his quickness, and he became just a shell of his former self, finishing with but two points. McNamara had played in 135 games for Syracuse, starting every one, and had endured a spate of injuries that included sprained ankles, torn rotator cuffs, and a groin injury so bad as a sophomore that it caused damage to his pelvic bone. "He's a warrior," Boeheim said. "If it was any other player, I wouldn't have played him after the first two minutes, but with Gerry you just keep thinking he's going to get it going." He never did. And so a brilliant career came to a disappointing ending. McNamara finished as the school's fourth all-time leading scorer, with 2,099 points. Only Jason Hart had more steals than G-Mac's 258, and only Sherman Douglas had more assists than his 648. He did wind up as the school's all-time leader in three-pointers and free throw percentage (89 percent). But the things he'll be most remembered for are his record six treys in the first half of the 2003 national championship game and his clutch performances at the Big East Tournament.

"His legacy is pretty clear-cut to anybody that follows the game of basketball," Boeheim said. "He gives you everything he's got from Day 1. He was an integral part of us winning the national championship. It wasn't just the Kansas game. It was the Oklahoma State game and every other game we played in the tournament and leading up to the tournament that got us the national championship. And winning the Big East Tournament last year and winning it this year and winning the regular-season championship in four years—that's a pretty good legacy.

"He's won 103 games, and every defense we played this year and really most of last year was geared to trying to stop him," the coach continued. "He still made first-team all-conference both years despite that kind of defensive pressure. I don't think there's been many players that have had a comparable-type career to this kid. He's a special player. He's a one-of-a-kind kid."

McNamara's value would be further realized the following season as Syracuse struggled to a 16–8 start with turnover-prone junior Josh Wright at point guard. After a sloppy performance by Wright in a 67–60 loss at Connecticut on February 5, 2007, Boeheim decided to shuffle his lineup, switching sophomore Eric Devendorf to point guard and putting Andy Rautins at shooting guard. The moves worked, as the Orange men cut down on their turnovers, and Rautins displayed a deft touch from beyond the arc. The result was five wins in their final six games and a 10–6 record in the highly competitive Big East. After beating Connecticut in the first round and losing to Notre Dame in the second round of the conference tournament, Boeheim figured his 22–10 squad had done enough to earn an NCAA bid, but the Selection Committee thought otherwise. For the first time in history a Big East team that had won 10 conference games was excluded from the Big Dance. SU accepted a bid to the NIT, winning two games at home before losing on the road to Clemson in the quarterfinals.

Although Syracuse had lost leading scorer Demetris Nichols (18.9 points per game) and leading rebounder Terrence Roberts (8.1 rebounds per game) to graduation, Boeheim felt good about the team he would field for the 2007–08 season. He expected forward Paul Harris, who had made the Big East's all-rookie team the year before, to improve markedly in his sophomore season, and he was looking forward to welcoming highly regarded recruits Donte Greene and Jonny Flynn. Greene had been the Maryland Gatorade Player of the Year, while Flynn had been named New York state's "Mr. Basketball" after a superb senior season for Niagara Falls High School. All three would come through for Boeheim that season, as Greene led the team in scoring (17.7 points per game); Flynn averaged 15.7 points and 5.3 assists; and Harris contributed 14.5 points, 8.2 rebounds, 3.3 assists, and 1.7 steals per game. But their contributions weren't enough to offset season-ending knee injuries to both Rautins and Devendorf. Once again, SU found itself NIT-bound, and once again it would win two games before being eliminated in the quarterfinals, this time by Massachusetts, which beat Syracuse for a second time that season.

Boeheim wouldn't spend much time dwelling on the disappointing finish because a new, exciting challenge awaited him that off-season—a challenge that would take him halfway around the world and fulfill a lifetime dream. Two years earlier, Duke coach Mike Krzyzewski asked him to become an assistant on the U.S. Olympic men's basketball team, and Boeheim, who had been involved with USA Basketball programs since 1982, jumped at the opportunity. He had been enthralled with the Olympics since seeing the movies *Jim Thorpe—All-American* and *The Bob Mathias Story* as a young, impressionable boy growing up in the early 1950s. "To me, both of those movies were pretty compelling stuff," he said. "Then, over the years, I watched it all. The running. The speed skating. The field events. The skiing. Summer. Winter. I live and die with the Olympics. Always have. If you ask me, it's the greatest show on earth."

The idea of representing his country at the Olympics had always been a goal. To have it finally come true that summer in Beijing blew his mind. "I've been watching the Olympics my whole life, and when I do, I can't tell you how hard I pull for the Americans. Whether it's a boxing match or track and field or swimming, it doesn't matter. I'm pulling as hard as I've ever pulled for Syracuse University or any of the athletes we've ever had. Basketball has been my whole life, in terms of my working life. And this is the biggest thing. The NCAA championship is unbelievable, but it's a university thing, an individual thing. This is your country. I don't think people out there understand how huge this is to the players and to the coaches. I guarantee you that this is as important, to me, as anything I've ever done."

Coach K had asked him to join his staff because Boeheim had coached seven USA development teams in the past 26 years and because of his knowledge of the zone, which was a big part of international play. Krzyzewski also would be assisted by two NBA coaches—Mike D'Antoni of the Phoenix Suns and Nate McMillan of the Portland Trail Blazers. The three assistants had a total of 1,294 victories—771 by Boeheim—in 46 seasons.

Boeheim also was looking forward to the experience because it would reunite him with his former star player Carmelo Anthony of the Denver Nuggets and give him the opportunity to work with other NBA superstars, such as LeBron James and Kobe Bryant. Anthony was looking forward to the reunion, too. "We talk all the time about the national championship in '03," Melo said, smiling, "and how I got that monkey off his back." The trip to Beijing would be even more special because his wife, Juli, his sister, Barbara, and his four children would be accompanying him.

After playing a few exhibition games in China that July, Boeheim could joke that he "now knows what it must have felt like to travel with the Beatles." Such was the mania surrounding Bryant, James, and the other stars on the Olympic basketball team. The 1.4 billion people there couldn't tell you who Brett Favre or Derek Jeter were, but they followed the NBA fervently because of the exploits of their own Yao Ming with the Houston Rockets. "They love the NBA, and they know the players like the backs of their hands," Boeheim marveled when the team finally arrived in Beijing. "And they like Kobe and LeBron so much, I don't know if China is necessarily going to have a home-crowd advantage when we play them." The Chinese love of basketball apparently didn't extend to the U.S. college game. They didn't appear to know much about Boeheim, and that suited him just fine. "I'm enjoying my anonymity," he joked. "I'm definitely not in Syracuse anymore."

Boeheim said he and the players were focused on reclaiming the Olympic gold medal the U.S. had failed to win in 2004. They had been dubbed the "Redeem Team," a takeoff on the U.S. basketball "Dream Teams" of the 1990s that were undisputed world champions. Boeheim had watched on television as the dream turned into a nightmare at the Athens Games four years earlier. He wanted in the worst way to be a part of a basketball redemption, but he realized that the road to the gold wasn't going to be easy. The world no longer was a pushover. "Our players understand how good these teams are and how difficult this is going to be," he said. "So, none of us has any illusions. No country is going to dominate international basketball anymore, the way we once did." His players were still adjusting to the differences between the NBA game, which emphasizes more one-on-one play and is less physical, and the foreign game, which places a premium on outside shooting and team play. "In the NBA," he explained, "you might have two guys per team who can really shoot it, so if you screw up and not cover somebody, it won't necessarily hurt you. But most of these foreign teams put five guys on the floor who can shoot it. And if you fail to cover one of them, you are going to get burned."

Although it was an intense experience, with long days and practices, Boeheim and his family still managed to take in the sights—none of which was more impressive than the Great Wall of China. "He kept wondering how in the world they built that thing and how the people even got up there in the mountains to build it," recalled Juli Boeheim. "With him it was just, 'How...how...how?' He understood the commitment it took, and he realized the pain and suffering of the people who built it. Jim loves history, and that Wall is just a huge piece of history. So, he was very much moved by that. He was in awe, frankly, and he just took it all in. Like I said, he's a historian."

The "historian" would help the U.S. team make history over the next three weeks. The Americans mowed through China, Angola, Greece, defending world champion Spain, and Germany by an average of 32 points per game to advance to the medal round, where their dominance continued. In the semifinals, Anthony scored 21 points as the United States cruised past Angola 101–81; then, on August 24, 2008, the Redeem Team reclaimed the Olympic gold medal by defeating Spain 118–107. Only athletes receive medals at the Olympics. But after the Redeem Teamers received theirs and stood at attention for the national anthem, they came down off the stand and draped their medals around their four coaches, so they could have their photos taken wearing the gold. "One of the greatest moments of my life," said Boeheim.

CHAPTER 14

Adding to His Legacy

THE 2008 SUMMER OLYMPICS had been an exhilarating and educational experience for Jim Boeheim. The legendary coach had learned some new drills and plays while working with Mike Krzyzewski, Mike D'Antoni, and Nate McMillan in Beijing, and he couldn't wait to implement them when Syracuse practices resumed in mid-October. The big news in the off-season involved the departure of Donte Greene. The man who broke Gerry McNamara's single-season mark for threes decided to declare early for the NBA draft and wound up being chosen 28th overall by the Minnesota Timberwolves, who immediately traded him to the Houston Rockets, who immediately traded him to the Sacramento Kings. Though he was very talented, many viewed Greene's departure as addition by subtraction, because he was prone to shoot too much and his lackadaisical defense led to many easy buckets. With the return of Andy Rautins and Eric Devendorf from knee injuries and with the addition of much-heralded recruits Kris Joseph and Mookie Jones, SU figured to be ready to snap its two-year NCAA tournament drought during the 2008–09 campaign.

Boeheim's confidence was brimming because of his faith in Jonny Flynn. The precocious point guard wouldn't disappoint during his remarkable sophomore season. With Greene gone, Flynn assumed the go-to role and wound up leading the team in scoring (17.4 points per game) and assists (6.7 per game) as the Orange went 23–8 and reached the Sweet 16. But what really set Flynn apart was his remarkable endurance. There was one stretch during the season when he played every minute of every game for several games in a row—his only blows coming during timeouts and intermissions. Flynn averaged 37.3 minutes per contest, all the more remarkable considering his heavy ball-handling and decision-making responsibilities at the point.

Although the Orange men's season would conclude with a frigid shooting performance in which they missed their first 11 shots from beyond the arc in an 84–71 loss to All-American Blake Griffin and his Oklahoma Sooners teammates, that campaign will forever be remembered for what occurred a week earlier in the Big East Tournament quarterfinals at Madison Square Garden. In a game that tipped off during the evening of March 12, 2009, and concluded at 1:25 AM the following morning, SU defeated Connecticut 127–117 in six overtimes. Interestingly, what would become the second longest game in college basketball history appeared to be over in regulation when Devendorf swished a jumper at the buzzer after taking an improbable length-of-the-court pass from Paul Harris. Immediately after sinking the shot, Devendorf leaped onto the scorer's table and began celebrating. But the three officials said they needed to check the courtside monitors to see if the ball left his hand before the horn sounded. After a few minutes reviewing the tapes, they determined that it hadn't, and the basket was waved off, sending the game into overtime.

By the fourth extra session, the 6'7" Joseph had to jump center for SU because post players Arinze Onuaku, Rick Jackson, and Kristof Onganaet had fouled out. When Devendorf fouled out in the fifth overtime, Boeheim had no choice but to insert walk-on Justin Thomas.

At the end of the fifth OT, Flynn, who already had played 62 minutes, looked at his teammates in the huddle, and said: "If we can win one tip we'll win the game." With Connecticut's 7'3" center Hasheem Thabeet fouled out, Syracuse finally won an opening jump, and Andy Rautins drained an outside shot that gave the Orange their first lead since regulation. It would be a lead they wouldn't relinquish, making a prophet of Flynn and ending college basketball's version of *War and Peace*.

Flynn's reputation as a marathon man only grew that night—and morning—as he played 67 of a possible 70 minutes, scoring 34 points, including 26 during the overtimes. Harris finished with 29 points and 22 rebounds. "If you're a basketball fan, at some point you have to look around during that game and say, 'There's never been anything quite like this before,'" marveled Boeheim in his postgame news conference. "During the fourth overtime, I looked at the guys on the scorer's table and said, 'What in the world are we a part of right now?' I mean, we're down in five different overtimes and come back every time. How incredible is that?" When it was mentioned that the longest game in college basketball history—a 1981 matchup between Bradley and Cincinnati—went seven overtimes, Boeheim astutely pointed out, "Yeah, but that was before the shot clock. Those guys were holding the ball. I would make the case this is something none of us have ever seen or are likely to ever see again."

About 90 minutes after the classic clash, Joyce Hergenhan, a lifelong Syracuse fan, donor, and member of the SU board of trustees, walked into a Manhattan deli with Boeheim and some other school officials. A group of UConn fans approached them. "They thanked him for giving them the opportunity to watch the greatest game they had ever seen," recalled Hergenhan. "It was a wonderful moment in sports." One of the Big Apple tabloids summed up the game later that morning with a headline blaring "Six in the City," a clever takeoff on the popular *Sex in the City* television series and movies. By the following week, orange T-shirts with that headline were being sold on the SU campus.

Just in case Boeheim, his players, or Orange fans didn't get their fill of basketball from that game, Syracuse played another overtime period while beating West Virginia 74–69 later that day in the semifinals. That set up a championship matchup with Louisville. The Orange led at halftime, then understandably ran out of gas after intermission, as the Cardinals captured the tournament title 76–66. Flynn, who had played a mind-boggling 181 of a possible 195 minutes in four days, was named the tournament's most outstanding player. Devendorf, who set a tournament record with 84 points, also earned a spot on the all-tourney team.

Boeheim's off-season would be joyfully hectic as usual, and the highlight occurred on September 24, 2010, when Carmelo Anthony returned to campus. The anchor of SU's 2003 national championship was back in town for a ribbon-cutting ceremony to officially open the new Carmelo K. Anthony Basketball Center next door to Manley Field House and the school's athletic offices. Although Melo had played just one season before leaving for the riches of the NBA, it was clear that his year at SU had made an indelible impression on him. As an expression of gratitude, Anthony donated $3 million to build a state-of-the-art center that featured two NCAA-regulation basketball courts, locker rooms for the men's and women's teams, coach's offices, study halls, and training rooms. "I would never in a million years think I would be sitting here today six or seven years after winning a national championship, doing the ribbon cutting for my building," Anthony told the media and benefactors before snipping the orange ribbon with a pair of scissors. After the ceremony, the Denver Nuggets all-star forward was taken inside the building, where he officially christened the men's court by sinking a free throw. "Carmelo is one of the most generous, giving people you're ever going to meet," Boeheim said, reflecting on that day. "He's done so much to help people wherever he's been—whether it was his hometown of Baltimore or Denver or Syracuse. He has a huge, huge heart."

Interestingly, none of Syracuse's top three players would return for the 2009–10 season. Following his sensational sophomore campaign, Flynn entered the NBA draft and was chosen sixth overall by the

Minnesota Timberwolves. Devendorf and Harris also opted to turn pro but were ignored by the NBA and wound up seeking minor-league deals, here and abroad. That was a lot of experience to lose from a Sweet 16 team, but Boeheim wasn't fretting. He believed his squad was much better than his Big East counterparts anticipated. They had selected Syracuse to finish sixth in the conference in the coaches' annual preseason poll. And Boeheim also felt he knew his players' potential better than the Associated Press voters who had left his Orange men out of the Top 25.

The coach had spent the previous season watching Iowa State transfer Wesley Johnson light it up in practice. At times, the sleek small forward had been unstoppable. Although Boeheim had kept saying this young man had a chance to be not only the Big East Player of the Year but maybe even the national player of the year, not enough people listened to him. With Johnson now eligible after sitting out a season following his transfer and with the dramatic strides Andy Rautins had made as a player and a leader while logging time with the Canadian national team, Boeheim was sure he had a solid foundation upon which to build.

Although his team wasn't deep, he liked his seven-man rotation. Brawny senior center Arinze Onuaku was a rock in the middle. Junior forward Rick Jackson was a beast on the boards. Sophomore guard Scoop Jardine had matured physically, mentally, and emotionally while rehabbing from a stress fracture in his shin that sidelined him the previous season. Jardine and highly touted freshman Brandon Triche from nearby Jamesville-DeWitt would provide a dependable, complementary tandem at the point. Sophomore forward Kris Joseph was ready to become a solid contributor off the bench. And Rautins was a money-in-the-bank outside shooter who would prevent teams from sagging extra defenders near the basket. "I liked our balance a lot," Boeheim said. "The pieces fit together really well. They are an unselfish group, and they play great team basketball."

Before the 2009–10 season tipped off, the Orange would receive quite a jolt, as crosstown LeMoyne College, a Division II school, upset them 82–79 on a three-pointer at the buzzer in an exhibition in front of about 5,000 fans in the Carrier Dome. Although the game didn't count, it was embarrassing nonetheless, and served as a loud wakeup call for the SU players, who were forced to view the result ad nauseum for the next several days on ESPN's *SportsCenter*.

Five days later, on November 9, the real schedule began, and the Orange took nothing for granted this time, crushing overmatched University of Albany by 32 points to give Boeheim his 800th win. As usual, the coach downplayed the milestone, saying he was focusing on his next victory, not his previous 800.

Over the next several weeks, college basketball fans across America would see why the coach had been so high on Johnson and this team, as SU dispensed with No. 6 North Carolina 87–71 and No. 10 Florida 85–73 in nationally televised games en route to a 13–0 record. In the victory against the Tar Heels, the Orange wrested control with an incredible 22–1 run at the start of the second half. Johnson lived up to Boeheim's advance billing in that game with 25 points and eight rebounds—a trend he would continue for much of the season. Syracuse didn't suffer its first defeat until January 2, losing to Pitt by 10. That loss was promptly followed by an 11-game win streak.

On January 25, the Orange men shook off a horrible start in which they fell behind 14–0 and stormed back to clobber Georgetown 73–56 on the road as Joseph played the role of catalyst with 15 points off the bench. A week later, an NCAA on-campus record, orange-clad crowd of 34,616 watched Boeheim's boys beat Villanova 95–77, a victory that improved their record to 27–2 and moved them to the top of the AP poll for the first time since the 1989–90 season.

Despite losing their regular-season finale to Louisville and their Big East Tournament quarterfinal game to Georgetown, the Orange men were installed as the No. 1 seed in the NCAA West Region. Unfortunately for them, they were forced to enter the tournament at less than full strength because during the loss to the Hoyas at Madison Square Garden, Onuaku tore his quadriceps muscle. The 'Cuse was able to get by Vermont and Gonzaga in the opening rounds at HSBC Arena in Buffalo, but the big center's absence coupled with a poor performance by Jackson, who had been moved from forward to center, contributed to their loss to Butler at the Sweet 16 in Salt Lake City. The Bulldogs would advance to the Final Four in Indianapolis and take Duke to the limit before losing in the national championship game.

While it had been one of the most enjoyable runs in Boeheim's 34 seasons at Syracuse—a run that earned him Naismith, *Sporting News*, Associated Press, and NABC national coach of the year awards—he couldn't help but be haunted by thoughts of what might have happened had Onuaku been healthy, especially given how close Butler had come to upsetting Duke. "You only get so many shots at the title," the coach said. "And the way that team was playing, I really would have liked our chances. But we'll never know. The timing of him getting hurt couldn't have been worse."

Boeheim clearly had put the painful ending of that season behind him by the time his team took the floor for practices at the Anthony Center the following October. He was in a jovial mood because more than a dozen of his former players and his one-time teammate and roommate, Dave Bing, had returned to take part in a ceremony in which Boeheim would receive one of his coach of the year awards at a halftime ceremony during an NBA exhibition game being played in the Carrier Dome. "Wouldn't have missed it for the world," said John Wallace, the star of the 1996 SU team that made it to the national championship game. "I feel as if I'm a part of an extended family, and that family is Syracuse basketball. The great thing is that it doesn't matter if you are an All-American or a walk-on, if you wore that Syracuse jersey for any length of time you're always a part of this family, always an Orangeman. Coach Boeheim makes it that way."

Even players who transferred from SU or who had problems with the law have been welcomed back with open arms. "A lot of people talk about their programs being like family, but they don't really treat everybody like family," Boeheim said. "I've heard coaches talk about players and say things like, 'He did this, so I'm not going to help him.' That's not the way I try to work. These players are like your kids. Your children might do something you dislike or disapprove of, but you don't disown them. I've had 10 guys who left the program come back and tell me years later that they made a mistake, that they should have stayed. We're happy to see them come back. We try to help them if we can." Matt Roe is a perfect example of a player who transferred whom Boeheim later helped. When Roe applied to be a color analyst on SU basketball broadcasts, his former coach gave him a rousing recommendation. "There was no reason for me to hold a grudge," Boeheim said. "Sometimes young people make decisions they regret, like transferring instead of sticking it out. But that shouldn't tar them for life. Heck, I know I made some foolish choices when I was their age."

Talent would not be an issue during the 2010–11 season, as a solid nucleus of experienced players—Jackson, Joseph, Jardine, and Triche—would be joined by a much ballyhooed quartet of newcomers, led by center Fab Melo. The 7-footer from Brazil had played only one year of high school basketball in the United States, but the rawness of his game didn't stop him from being named a McDonald's All-America and the Big East Freshman of the Year in a preseason vote of the league's coaches. As it turned out, Fab was rarely fabulous, hamstrung much of the season by a lack of stamina and experience and an overabundance of fouls. Still, neither his struggles nor the growing pains encountered by fellow freshman center Baye Moussa Keita were enough to stop the Orange from rolling to the second-best start in school history.

Thanks, in large part, to Jackson's play underneath, Syracuse won its first 18 games. Motivated by his poor showing in the loss to Butler in the 2010 NCAAs, Jackson shed 25 pounds in the off-season. Less proved to be more as the 6'9" senior led the Big East in rebounding and double-doubles while earning conference Defensive Player of the Year honors. Although the 18–0 start impressed the pollsters, who ranked the Orange men as high as No. 3 by mid-January, Boeheim repeatedly cautioned reporters that he didn't believe SU was necessarily as good as its record indicated. After an early season close call against an opponent with far less talent, Boeheim groused that this was the most overrated team he had ever coached.

His concerns about the inconsistent play of his veterans, especially redshirt junior point guard Scoop Jardine, were justified during a mid-season swoon that saw SU drop four straight for only the second time in Boeheim's illustrious career. On February 14, the Orange stopped a two-game losing streak with a 63–52 victory over West Virginia in the Dome. But, in his postgame press conference, rather than highlight how the up-and-down Triche had asserted himself or how it felt good to steady the ship after a stretch that included six losses in eight games, Boeheim said there was too much focus on the doom-and-gloom surrounding SU's recent performances.

"When we lose a couple, we're not playing right," he began. "People think the season's over. The season's over when we play 18 games in the league. We have four more games left by that count. People start talking about the end of the world around here when it starts raining. It rains a lot here. I think we need to keep perspective a little bit."

The coach then ripped members of the Syracuse media, including two *Post-Standard* beat reporters. Boeheim clearly was irked by a recent story and graphic that pointed out he had lost six straight games against Rick Pitino's Louisville Cardinals.

"There are some coaches in the Hall of Fame that I've beat 80 percent of the time," Boeheim said, clutching the podium, his anger growing with each word. "And you are going to look at a couple of coaches that beat me? I've coached against Rick Pitino when he was at Providence five times and once at Kentucky where we were 6–0 against them. One of his teams went to the Final Four; we beat them three times. So now we're all of a sudden going to put in the paper that I've lost six straight to Rick Pitino? Why don't we put in that I beat him six straight?"

A reporter then asked Boeheim if he felt he had been treated unfairly by the local media.

"I don't think it's fair to take a snapshot," he said. "You write, what, 100 articles a year for the paper? One-hundred-fifty? Two hundred? Someone looks at six or seven of them and says, 'This is bad.' Is that a good judgment of your career? No, I don't think so. I don't think that's how you judge people or coaches or players. I don't think that's what you do. But that's the way it's done around here. Doesn't mean I'm going to like it. Doesn't mean I'm going to stand up here and let it go. Because when I let things like that go, it will be time for me to leave."

Asked if he took criticism personally, Boeheim didn't hesitate. "You want to talk about personal?" he said. "Yeah, it's personal. When people write and say things about me, it's personal to me. Always will be."

The coach went on to quiz reporters about his record against various other coaches. Snippets of the uncomfortable news conference were replayed by media outlets beyond central New York in the days that followed, and several national columnists and commentators criticized Boeheim for his "Valentine's Day" media massacre.

It may have been coincidence, but after his outburst, Syracuse won its final five games of the regular season to earn one of four double-byes in the Big East Tournament. The Orange men won their first game at the Garden 79–73 against St. John's, and in an interview afterward with ESPNNewYork.com, an exhausted Boeheim raised some eyebrows when asked about retirement. "It's definitely getting closer and closer," he said in a voice barely audible. "I can see it. I can see the end. I'm getting close; I really feel that way. I'm not making any calls at this stage of the season, but this league has gotten awfully tough. It's a real grind out there."

As the dean of Big East coaches, Boeheim already had logged nine seasons before his friend and counterpart Jim Calhoun had taken over the Connecticut program in 1986. He had been around long enough to have coached against John Thompson and Patrick Ewing at Georgetown in the mid-'80s and their sons a generation later. He had far outlasted the legendary coaches who had once been his contemporaries—the Thompsons, the Looie Carneseccas, the Rollie Massiminos. "Yeah, I'm proud of it," Boeheim said, when that was pointed out. "It's not easy to outlast people. I've outlasted them, and I've outlasted several of my critics, so that's a good thing."

The next night, he couldn't outlast Calhoun as eventual national champion Connecticut eliminated Syracuse in the Big East semifinals. Based on their 26–7 record and strong regular-season finish, the Orange men received a third seed in the East. They won their opener against Larry Bird's alma mater, Indiana State, but were bounced in the second round by Big East foe Marquette, which also had beaten them in Milwaukee in the regular season. SU played hard but sloppily much of the night, turning the ball over 18 times and committing six offensive fouls. Despite their many errors, the Orange men still had a chance to win in the final minute but were done in by a blown call by the officiating crew. With the score knotted at 59 and 51 seconds to play, Jardine was called for an over-and-back violation on an inbounds from Dion Waiters. The call gave Marquette possession and 25 seconds later, Darius Johnson-Odom nailed a three-pointer to give the

Golden Eagles the lead. Syracuse was unable to convert on its ensuing possession and wound up losing 66–62.

A few days later, NCAA officiating coordinator John Adams said the crew had erred and that Jardine should have been allowed to catch the ball in the backcourt. When notified of the mistake, Boeheim took the high road. "We all make mistakes," he said. "We didn't lose that game because of an official's mistake. We lost it because of all the mistakes we made."

In the weeks following the season-ending loss, Boeheim regained his energy and enthusiasm. He no longer sounded like a coach on the verge of retirement. "I was just talking in general when the subject was brought up at the Big East Tournament," he said. "I said that retirement is in the back of my mind. That doesn't necessarily mean in a year or two. But it also doesn't mean I'm going to be around here 10 years from now, because I'm not."

Boeheim had reason to look forward to the 2011–12 season because most of the players were expected to return. He said he was hoping to see veterans Jardine, Joseph, and Triche develop into take-charge guys, and he expected freshmen C.J. Fair, Melo, and Keita to become bigger contributors as sophomores, as they matured and attempted to fill the void left by Rick Jackson's graduation. The coach also had just landed another Top 10 recruiting class, headed by shot-blocking center Rakeem Christmas, so the roster would be stocked with top-shelf talent for several years to come.

In late April, Boeheim announced that assistant coach Rob Murphy was leaving to take the head coaching job at Eastern Michigan University. Though saddened to lose such a valued assistant, Boeheim had lobbied hard for Murphy to become a head coach because he believed he was ready for the opportunity after five productive years working with the forwards at Syracuse. Murphy was the latest in a long line of former Boeheim players or assistants to become head coaches in college. Other members of that impressive coaching tree include Rick Pitino (Louisville), Louis Orr (Bowling Green), Wayne Morgan (Iowa State), and Stephen Thompson (California State–Los Angeles). The vacancy on SU's staff didn't last long, as Boeheim brought in former Orange point guard and Virginia Tech assistant Adrian Autry to replace Murphy. Autry, 39, had led SU in assists four straight years in the early 1990s and played professionally for 11 seasons in Turkey, Germany, Italy, France, and Poland before embarking on a successful AAU coaching career. The addition of Autry meant the entire SU staff would be composed of former Orangemen—Boeheim (Class of 1966); Bernie Fine ('67); Mike Hopkins ('93); Autry ('94); Lazarus Sims ('96); and graduate assistant Gerry McNamara (2006).

The remainder of Boeheim's offseason would be busy, as usual— devoted to raising money for the Jim and Juli Boeheim Foundation and Coaches vs. Cancer, working with Mike Krzyzewski on the U.S. basketball team's defense of its gold medal at the 2012 Olympics in London, collaborating with former player Carmelo Anthony on the construction of new basketball courts in inner-city Syracuse, recruiting future Orange men, running his various basketball camps, and watching his sons' and daughter's youth-league baseball and basketball games.

"They play virtually every night, and I really enjoy that," he said. "It's funny that they would choose to play the same two team sports I loved as a kid. When I watch them, it does take me back a bit to when I was their age."

Although time and loved ones have mellowed Boeheim some, it was clear from his occasionally prickly press conferences and sideline theatrics during the 2010–11 season that the passion to coach—and to win—still burned fiercely as he approached his 67th birthday on November 17. Although he publicly downplayed the milestones every step of the way, Boeheim, the hoops history student, couldn't help but know how close he was to surpassing some of the game's greatest coaching legends.

If he goes on to achieve his average season output of 24 wins in 2011–12, Boeheim would leap-frog Kentucky's Adolph Rupp (876) and North Carolina's Dean Smith (879) into third place on the all-time coaching victory list.

By doing so, he also would become the coach with the most victories ever at a single school. Toss in wins accumulated as a player and an assistant, and the numbers become staggering. Heading into the 2011–12 season, Boeheim had been a part of 1,047 of the 1,810 wins by the Syracuse program in its 112-year history.

"I'm definitely proud of what we've been able to do here, but I don't dwell on it," he said from his campus office in the spring of 2011. "There isn't time to because there's so much to think about and worry about on this job. You need to look forward, not backward, in this position if you want to keep having success."

Boeheim said he is as enthused about coaching as he's ever been because he realizes "there is a limited amount of time left in my career. When you are much closer to the end than the beginning, you tend to take even less for granted and become even more focused with the job at hand because you hear the clock ticking."

When the final buzzer does sound on one of the most extraordinary college coaching careers of all time, Boeheim expects to become even more involved in the foundation he and his wife started a few years ago to help improve the lives of children in the Syracuse area. In other words, he has no intention of leaving the snowy, cloudy "paradise" he has called home since arriving as a skinny, bespectacled 18-year-old nearly a half-century ago. And he'll remain true to his school, while rooting for his hand-picked successor, Mike Hopkins, to continue the winning tradition.

"My favorite color," Boeheim said, chuckling, "will continue to be orange."

Statistics, Records, and Miscellany from Jim Boeheim's Career

Year-by-Year Coaching Record

Year	Overall W–L	Pct.	Big East W–L	Pct.	Postseason
1976–77	26–4	.867			NCAA "Sweet 16"
1977–78	22–6	.786			NCAA
1978–79	26–4	.867			NCAA "Sweet 16"
1979–80	26–4	.867	5–1	.833	NCAA "Sweet 16"
1980–81	22–12	.647	6–8	.429	NIT Finals
1981–82	16–13	.552	7–7	.500	NIT
1982–83	21–10	.677	9–7	.563	NCAA
1983–84	23–9	.719	12–4	.750	NCAA "Sweet 16"
1984–85	22–9	.710	9–7	.563	NCAA
1985–86	26–6	.813	14–2	.875	NCAA
1986–87	31–7	.816	12–4	.750	NCAA Finals
1987–88	26–9	.743	11–5	.688	NCAA
1988–89	30–8	.789	10–6	.625	NCAA "Elite Eight"
1989–90	26–7	.788	12–4	.750	NCAA "Sweet 16"
1990–91	26–6	.813	12–4	.750	NCAA
1991–92	22–10	.688	10–8	.556	NCAA
1992–93	20–9	.690	10–8	.556	

	Overall		Big East		Postseason
Year	W–L	Pct.	W–L	Pct.	
1993–94	23–7	.767	13–5	.722	NCAA "Sweet 16"
1994–95	20–10	.667	12–6	.667	NCAA
1995–96	29–9	.763	12–6	.667	NCAA Finals
1996–97	19–13	.594	9–9	.500	NIT
1997–98	26–9	.743	12–6	.667	NCAA "Sweet 16"
1998–99	21–12	.636	10–8	.556	NCAA
1999–00	26–6	.813	13–3	.813	NCAA "Sweet 16"
2000–01	25–9	.735	10–6	.625	NCAA
2001–02	23–13	.639	9–7	.563	NIT Semifinals
2002–03	30–5	.857	13–3	.813	NCAA Champions
2003–04	23–8	.742	11–5	.688	NCAA "Sweet 16"
2004–05	27–7	.794	11–5	.688	NCAA
2005–06	23–12	.657	7–9	.438	NCAA
2006–07	24–11	.686	10–6	.625	NIT
2007–08	21–14	.600	9–9	.500	NIT
2008–09	28–10	.737	11–7	.611	NCAA "Sweet 16"
2009–10	30–5	.857	15–3	.833	NCAA "Sweet 16"
2010–11	27–8	.771	12–6	.667	NCAA
35 years	856–301	.740	338–184	.648	28 NCAAs, 6 NITs

Numbers and Achievements of Note

- First all-time among NCAA Division I basketball coaches with 33 20-win seasons

- First all-time in Big East victories (338)

- Fifth all-time in Division I basketball coaching victories. Needs 21 wins to supplant Kentucky's Adolph Rupp (876) for fourth place; 24 to surpass North Carolina's Dean Smith (879) for third place, and 47 to move past Bob Knight (902), who's two victories ahead of Duke's Mike Krzyzewski, who's still active

- Third all-time Division I victories at one school, trailing only Smith and Rupp

- 1,047–394 record as a player (52–24), full-time assistant (139–65), and head coach at SU

- Zero losing seasons

- Three NCAA Final Four appearances as head coach (2003, 1996, 1987) and one as an assistant (1975)

- Nine Big East regular-season titles

- Five Big East tournament titles

- Four-time Big East Coach of the Year

- Nine consensus All-Americans

- Coached 16 first-round NBA draft picks

- Coached 24 players who have gone on to play in the NBA

- Naismith, Associated Press, NABC, and *Sporting News* Coach of the Year (2010)

- Inducted into the Naismith Memorial Basketball Hall of Fame (2005)

Playing Career (High School, College, Pro)

Lyons High School

Year	PPG
1959–60	8.3
1960–61	19.3
1961–62	24.7*
3 seasons	17.8

*Led Wayne County Finger Lakes League in scoring; named MVP of
Section V Tournament

Syracuse University

Year	G	FG	FGA	PCT.	FT	FTA	PCT.	ASST	REB	PTS	PPG	RPG	APG
1963–64	25	50	105	47.6	31	38	81.6	NA	41	131	5.2	1.6	NA
1964–65	23	91	194	46.9	23	39	59.0	NA	58	205	8.9	2.5	NA
1965–66	28	179	317	56.5	51	74	68.9	88	78	409	14.6	2.8	3.1
3 seasons	76	320	616	51.9	105	151	69.5	NA	177	745	9.8	2.3	NA

Scranton (Eastern Professional Basketball League)

Year	G	FG	3-PT.	FT	FTA	PCT.	ASST	REB	PTS	PPG	RPG	APG
1966–67	27	116	8	68	82	.829	129	105	308	11.4	3.9	4.7
1967–68	32	266	8	127	170	.747	128	149	667	20.8	4.7	4.0
1968–69	27	234	11	154	190	.811	123	103	633	23.4	3.8	4.5
1969–70	24	159	2	86	109	.789	90	64	406	16.9	2.7	3.8
1970–71	15	85	1	38	48	.792	63	38	209	13.9	2.5	4.2
1971–72	11	38	1	8	14	.571	30	16	85	7.7	1.5	2.7
6 seasons	136	898	31	481	613	.785	563	475	2,308	17.0	3.2	4.4

Boeheim's Hall of Fame Induction Speech, September 9, 2005, Springfield, Massachusetts

"THANK YOU. This is a tremendous night, and to have Dave Bing up here is very special to me. When I was that walk-on at Syracuse who couldn't really play that well, Dave was there, and he always kind of looked out for me, as a good roommate should. He kind of got me through those years when I really couldn't play to where I could just play a little bit. When you played with Dave Bing you didn't have to be very good because two or three guys on the other team were guarding him.

"The guys up there on that video, I'd like to thank them all, especially P.J. [Carlesimo]. Without P.J., I'd be another two years getting into the Hall of Fame.

"This is about thank yous. It's about thanking my parents, who started me on this road, who were always there to support me. My high school coach, who was just an unbelievable coach. He disciplined every player on the team—he taught me there was only one way to play basketball. I learned that at an early age, and it carried over. I was very fortunate to have Dick Blackwell for my high school coach.

"My college coach, Fred Lewis, taught me all about recruiting, how you do it. Fred's philosophy was very simple. He knew Dave was interested in one other school, and he figured, 'Well, that's good. Now it's just that school and us.' He showed me how to get out and get great players. To talk Dave Bing into coming to Syracuse—after all, at that time, Syracuse had lost 32 straight games—the guy knew how to recruit.

"I'd like to thank all the people along the way. My first wife, Elaine, and my daughter, Elizabeth. Elaine is still a good friend of mine. She's actually a better friend of my wife, Juli. Although that might sound unusual, it's true, and it's what's made everything about my career special. My daughter, Elizabeth, is in Paris right now, and I'm thankful for her. She really was the first person to change Jim Boeheim. When you go 42 years with no children, you really don't understand what life's about. My daughter, Elizabeth, changed my life.

"Then Juli came along and decided to triple my life, in terms of Jimmy and Jack and Jamie. I believe that we won the national championship and we've had such great success, and I really believe I owe it to my family, my wife, who've been there for me and who've made it possible for me to just coach basketball. Everybody who's in this business understands that you don't do this, you don't get up here unless your wife is there every day for you. I'm just blessed to have a wife like Juli Greene Boeheim. Thank you, honey.

"I'm up here because of guys like Scotty Hicks and Rick Callahan, Tim Welch, Ralph Willard, Timmy O'Toole. Guys like Mike Hopkins, Rob Murphy, Troy Weaver, Wayne Morgan, Brendan Malone, Rick Pitino, and especially, Bernie Fine. Bernie's been with me 29 years, and if you know Bernie and if you know me, you know there's no one who could put up with either one of us except each other. Those guys have done the work and made me look good. You're not up here as a coach unless you've had great assistant coaches, and I've had that.

"I've had players who are just an unbelievable group of players. So many of them are here tonight. To start with, Louis Orr and Roosevelt Bouie and Pearl Washington and then Sherman Douglas and Rony Seikaly. Derrick Coleman. The nicest things he's ever said about me and the only nice things he's ever said about me, I think, were up there on that wall. Then Billy Owens and, of course, John Wallace and Lazarus Sims, who got us to our second Final Four in 1996.

"The guys, Jason Hart, who's here, Allen Griffin, who's here. Then I think that guy Carmelo had something to do with me being up here, too. And a little guard named Gerry McNamara. Those guys—that's why I'm here. We've had some great players at Syracuse, and they are the guys who have gotten me here.

"People always ask me what it means to be in the Basketball Hall of Fame. When you start out at five years old and all you want to do is play basketball and then, when you can't play anymore, you want to coach the game of basketball, it's almost impossible. I've been thinking for seven or eight months—how do you describe it? To me, the only way I can describe it is to say the names like John Wooden, Adolph Rupp, Hank Iba, Red Auerbach, John Thompson, Morgan Wooten, Bill Russell, Oscar Robertson, Jerry West, Larry Bird, Dave Bing. When you join those people, when you're able to get into that building, and you thought the only way you were going to be able to get in was to buy a ticket at that door, you can't describe what it means. Everybody in this room understands the game of basketball, some a lot better than others, although I know there are a lot of good coaches out here who don't even coach for a living. But to be with those names, to be in this building, is an unbelievable feeling for me.

"I've never been so grateful for any award. I'd like to thank each of the committee members personally, if I knew who they were, but I will thank them publicly. To be here with Hubie Brown, and to be here with Sue [Gunter] and Hortentia [Marcari] and Jim Calhoun. The only thing I can find wrong with the Hall of Fame is that it's a little too close to Connecticut. But Jim and I go back—we've had a lot of battles, and we're going to have a lot more, I hope, in the future. We're both pretty healthy, and we've been through a lot. A lot of the same things.

"I overheard him talking; he's going to see this kid we're recruiting on Monday. I just called the kid, and I want you to know, Jimmy, I'm going in Sunday. I told the kid, 'I really like ya; Jim just likes ya a little bit.' I know I'm way over the time limit, but, again, I'd like to thank everybody who has made it possible, particularly and mostly, my assistant coaches and my players. When I didn't know much about the game of basketball they carried me, and they've continued to carry me to this day and I hope for a long time. I'm just privileged to be in this building, and to actually have my picture up there is something beyond anything I could ever imagine.

"Thank you very much."

About the Author

A NATIVE OF ROME, NEW YORK, and a magna cum laude graduate of Syracuse University, Scott Pitoniak has been writing about people and the games they play for nearly four decades. He spent 35 years in the newspaper business, mostly as a sports columnist and feature writer, and has written 14 books and hundreds of magazine articles. Along the way, he has received more than 100 national and regional journalism honors and has covered the Olympics, Super Bowls, World Series, NCAA basketball tournaments, the Stanley Cup playoffs, and major golf tournaments.

His work, which often deals with the human side of sports, has been cited in *The Best American Sportswriting* anthology. Scott was inducted into Rochester's Frontier Field Walk of Fame in 1999, SU's Newhouse School of Public Communications Hall of Fame in 2000, and the Rome Sports Hall of Fame in 2009. He also was selected as a torchbearer for the 2002 Winter Olympic Games.

Scott currently writes columns for his website (ScottPitoniak. com), *Buffalo Bills Digest*, and rochesterhomepage.net, and does on-air work for Rochester's CBS and Fox television affiliates. He is a regular contributor to *Central New York Sports Magazine*, published by the *Syracuse Post-Standard*, and co-hosts a weekly sports radio show.

Scott is passionate about giving back to his community. Through the years, he has mentored scores of students, taught journalism at the college level, and been heavily involved in charities and community service organizations. He is past president of the Rochester Press-Radio Club, which has donated hundreds of thousands of dollars to local children's charities.

His most cherished moments are spent with his wife—the former Beth Adams—his children, Amy and Christopher, and their energetic family cat, Sassy.

Published Works
of Scott Pitoniak

Pitoniak, Scott. *The Official Buffalo Bills Trivia Book*. New York: St. Martin's Press, 1989.

———. *The Official Buffalo Bills Trivia Book II*. New York: St. Martin's Press, 1992.

Mandelaro, Jim, and Scott Pitoniak. *Silver Seasons: The Story of the Rochester Red Wings*. Syracuse, NY: Syracuse University Press, 1996.

Pitoniak, Scott. *Playing Write Field: Selected Works of Scott Pitoniak*. Rochester, NY: Cass Publications, 1997.

———. *Baseball in Rochester*. Mount Pleasant, SC: Arcadia Publishing, 2003.

———. *Syracuse University Football*. Mount Pleasant, SC: Arcadia Publishing, 2003.

Maiorana, Sal, and Scott Pitoniak. *Slices of Orange: Great Games and Performers in Syracuse University Sports History*. Syracuse, NY: Syracuse University Press, 2005.

Tasker, Steve, and Scott Pitoniak. *Tales from the Buffalo Bills Sidelines*. Champaign, IL: Sports Publishing LLC, 2006.

Pitoniak, Scott. *The Good, The Bad & The Ugly: Heart-Pounding, Jaw-Dropping, and Gut-Wrenching Moments from Buffalo Bills History.* Chicago: Triumph Books, 2007.

———. *Memories of Yankee Stadium.* Chicago: Triumph Books, 2008.

———. *Buffalo Bills Football Vault: The First 50 Years.* Atlanta: Whitman Publishing, 2010.

———. *Jewel of the Sports World: The Hickok Belt Story.* Rochester, NY: RIT Press, 2010.

Mandelaro, Jim and Scott Pitoniak. *Silver Seasons and a New Frontier: The Story of the Rochester Red Wings.* Syracuse, NY: Syracuse University Press: 2010.

Index